# SOCIAL CLASS AND CHANGING FAMILIES
## IN AN UNEQUAL AMERICA

# SOCIAL CLASS AND CHANGING FAMILIES IN AN UNEQUAL AMERICA

*Edited by Marcia J. Carlson and Paula England*

STANFORD UNIVERSITY PRESS

STANFORD, CALIFORNIA

Stanford University Press
Stanford, California

Printed in the United States of America on acid-free,
archival-quality paper

Library of Congress Cataloging-in-Publication Data

Social class and changing families in an unequal America /
edited by Marcia J. Carlson and Paula England.
    pages cm
Includes bibliographical references and index.
 ISBN 978-0-8047-7088-0 (cloth : alk. paper) —
 ISBN 978-0-8047-7089-7 (pbk. : alk. paper)
1. Families—United States. 2. Social classes—United
States. 3. Equality—United States. I. Carlson, Marcia J.,
editor of compilation. II. England, Paula, 1949- editor of
compilation.
 HQ536.S665 2011
 306.850973—dc22
                                        2010050158

Typeset by Bruce Lundquist in 10/13 Sabon

*To Frank F. Furstenberg*

*Scholar, teacher, and wonderful human being*

# CONTENTS

FIGURES AND TABLES

*Marcia (Marcy) J. Carlson* is Associate Professor of Sociology at the University of Wisconsin-Madison. Her primary research interests center on the links between family contexts and the well-being of children and parents, with a current focus on unmarried fathers. Her recent work has been published in *Demography* and *Journal of Marriage and Family*.

*Andrew J. Cherlin* is Professor of Sociology and Public Policy at Johns Hopkins University. His recent articles include "The Deinstitutionalization of American Marriage" in the *Journal of Marriage and Family* and "Family Instability and Child Well-Being" in the *American Sociological Review*. He is the author of *The Marriage-Go-Round: The State of Marriage and the Family in America Today*.

*Amanda Cox* is a doctoral student in Sociology of Education at the Stanford University School of Education. Her interests are social class and the reproduction of inequality, with a focus on elite education. She has conducted ethnographic research on the role of cultural capital in an educational program designed to help low- and moderate-income students of color gain access to elite educational institutions.

*Kathryn Edin* is Professor of Public Policy at Harvard University. Current research interests include disadvantaged youth and the transition to adulthood, the tradeoffs parents consider as they make residential choices, how housing—broadly conceived—influences the well-being of young children, the growing class gap in civic engagement, and the meaning of fatherhood among disadvantaged urban men.

*Paula England* is Professor of Sociology at New York University. Her recent research focuses on class differences in early, unintended pregnancy and births. She is also studying dating, "hooking up," and relationships among college students. She is the author (with George Farkas) of *Households, Employment, and Gender*.

*Frank F. Furstenberg, Jr.*, is Professor of Sociology at the University of Pennsylvania where he is also a member of the Population Studies Center. His most recent book is *Destinies of the Disadvantaged: The Politics of Teenage Childbearing*. He has served as the Chair of the MacArthur Network on Adult Transitions and is a co-editor of *On the Frontier of Adulthood*.

*Annette Lareau* is the Stanley I. Sheerr Professor in the Department of Sociology at the University of Pennsylvania. She is the author of *Unequal Childhoods* and *Home Advantage*. She also edited *Social Class: How Does It Work* (with Dalton Conley) and *Educational Research on Trial* (with Pamela Barnhouse Walters and Sherri Ranis). In 2011, the University of California Press will publish a second edition of *Unequal Childhoods*; it includes 100 new pages describing the results of follow-up interviews completed a decade after the original study.

*Elizabeth Aura McClintock* is a PhD candidate in Sociology at Stanford University. She studies gender and romantic relationships. Her recent articles have been published in *Journal of Marriage and Family* and in *Population and Development Review*.

*Sara McLanahan* is the William S. Tod Professor of Sociology and Public Affairs at Princeton University, where she also serves as founding director of the Center for Research on Child Wellbeing, and editor-in-chief of the Future of Children. Her research interests include the effects of family structure and relationship transitions on child well-being, social policies relating to children and families, and poverty and inequality. She is a principal investigator of the Fragile Families and Child Wellbeing Study, and her books include *Fathers under Fire: The Revolution in Child Support Enforcement*, *Social Policies for Children*, and *Growing Up with a Single Parent*.

*S. Philip Morgan* is Professor of Sociology and Norb R. Schaeffer Professor of International Studies at Duke University. He is former president of the Population Association of America and former editor of the journal *Demography*. He has chaired the Sociology Departments at the University of Pennsylvania (1993–96) and Duke University (2002-08). Beginning in July of 2008, Morgan assumed the directorship of Duke's Social Science Research Institute. Morgan's work focuses on family and fertility change (over time) and diversity (across groups). Much of his work has focused on the United States but he has collaborated on projects focusing on other countries, both developed and developing.

*Timothy J. Nelson* is Lecturer in Social Policy at Harvard's Kennedy School of Government. He is the author of *Every Time I Feel the Spirit*, an ethnography of an African American congregation, and the co-author with Kathryn Edin of a forthcoming book tentatively called *Fragile Fathers*, based on interviews with low-income, noncustodial fathers in Philadelphia and Camden, N.J.

*Joanna Miranda Reed* received her PhD in Sociology from Northwestern University in 2008. She is now a Lecturer in Sociology at the University of California, Berkeley, and a Postdoctoral Research Fellow at Stanford University.

*Emily Fitzgibbons Shafer* is currently a Robert Wood Johnson Health and Society Scholar at Harvard University. She received her PhD in Sociology from Stanford University in 2010. Her research interests include gender, family, and health.

*Timothy (Tim) M. Smeeding* is the Arts and Sciences Distinguished Professor of Public Affairs and Economics at the University of Wisconsin-Madison and Director of the Institute for Research on Poverty. Smeeding's recent publications include the *Oxford Handbook of Economic Inequality*, co-edited with Brian Nolan and Weimer Salverda and *The American Welfare State: Laggard or Leader?*, with Irv Garfinkel and Lee Rainwater. His recent research has been on public policy, economic mobility, and poverty in low-income families.

# SOCIAL CLASS AND CHANGING FAMILIES IN AN UNEQUAL AMERICA

# Social Class and Family Patterns in the United States

*Marcia J. Carlson and Paula England*

The latter half of the twentieth century witnessed dramatic changes that increased the diversity and complexity of U.S. families. The longstanding link between marriage and childbearing weakened. Today, adults are likely to spend time living with more than one partner in marital and/or cohabiting unions, and children often experience several changes in which adults live with them. More and more children spend years living apart from one of their biological parents—typically the father. Over the last quarter of the twentieth century, we also saw a tremendous increase in U.S. economic inequality, whether measured with respect to wage rates, earnings, or family incomes (Gottschalk and Danziger 2005). Inequality rose in the 1980s, slowed somewhat in the 1990s during the economic expansion, then continued to rise as we entered the twenty-first century. Recent cross-national comparisons show that the United States has by far the highest level of family income inequality among all industrialized OECD countries; in 2000, a high-income American (at the ninetieth percentile of the income distribution) had roughly five and one-half times the family income of a low-income American (at the tenth percentile), even after adjusting for taxes, transfers, and family size (Brandolini and Smeeding 2006).

Family patterns have not only changed; they have also become more unequal by education and other measures of social class. Highly educated individuals are now more likely to marry (Goldstein and Kenney 2001); less-educated couples have always been more likely to divorce; but the gap between the two has grown (S. Martin 2006). Being born to unmarried parents is also tied to social class: while there has been very little increase in nonmarital childbearing among highly educated women since 1970, there has been a substantial increase among women in the bottom two-thirds of the distribution (Ellwood and Jencks 2004). Mothers giving birth outside

We sincerely appreciate the thoughtful comments of two anonymous reviewers about this and all chapters in the volume.

of marriage typically have a high school education or less, whereas mothers giving birth within marriage typically have at least some college education. In turn, there are growing gaps in the experiences of children by their parents' socioeconomic status (McLanahan 2004), and such differences in family structure appear to be important factors in increasing American inequality over the past forty years, both within and across generations (M. Martin 2006; McLanahan 2004; McLanahan and Percheski 2008).

This book is focused on changing family life in the context of growing socioeconomic inequality in the United States. Each chapter highlights a unique aspect of family behavior with a particular connection to socioeconomic (sometimes called class) inequality. Some chapters explore contrasts between those with low and high socioeconomic status (often measured by education), while other chapters focus on what's happening within one particular socioeconomic group. It is important to note that while race/ethnicity and class are certainly correlated, we focus here on family patterns that vary by socioeconomic status—a topic that has received less explicit attention in past research. Our view is that in the changing America of the past half-century, social class has become an increasingly important locus of differentiation in the life course with respect to union formation and dissolution, fertility, and parenting behaviors. While race differences likely compound (and interact with) class differences, there appears to be increasing similarity within class (especially educational groups)—regardless of race—in how individuals experience family life in the United States. It is this topic on which the volume is focused. Before briefly summarizing each chapter, we first provide a brief review of key areas of change in families that have occurred over the past half-century, and we highlight patterns that suggest growing differentials by socioeconomic status.

## MARRIAGE, DIVORCE, REMARRIAGE, AND STEPFAMILIES

At the core of changes in family life over the past half-century are shifts in the nature of union formation and marital behavior. Marriage has become less central to the life course both because Americans are marrying later (with a small percentage not marrying at all) and divorcing more often (Cherlin 2009). The freedom to leave unhappy relationships might be counted as a victory for adults, but the same cannot be said for children. Although problems of causal inference plague this literature, the best evidence suggests that, on average, children fare best when they grow up living with both of their biological parents, assuming that the parental relationship is not too conflictual (McLanahan and Sandefur 1994; Sigle-Rushton and McLanahan 2004).

While divorce marks the end of an existing nuclear family unit, as Furstenberg and Cherlin noted (1991), from a child's perspective, marital dissolution also typically marks the beginning of a series of family changes. One parent (typically the father) moves out of the household, resulting in significantly reduced father-child interaction (Furstenberg, Morgan, and Allison 1987; Seltzer 1991), and in time, it is likely that one or both parents will remarry or cohabit with a new partner. Stepfamily life is complicated by the lack of clear norms about how the stepparent should relate to the child (Cherlin 1978), and not surprisingly, since stepparents come into a child's life later, they often do not care as deeply about the child, even when they have the best of intentions. Perhaps this is why McLanahan and Sandefur (1994) found that children whose mothers divorce and remarry do no better than those whose mothers divorce and are stably single, suggesting that the costs and benefits from stepfathers just about cancel each other out, on average. Of course, this literature too, like that on the effects of divorce itself, is beset with questions of whether effects of remarriage on children are causal or due to the selectivity of individuals who will divorce and remarry (Castro-Martin and Bumpass 1989; Furstenberg and Spanier 1984). At the least, changing marital partners has important effects on children's kinship networks (Furstenberg 1990). Indeed, even the elderly seem to have fewer kinship ties if they divorced earlier in the life cycle, because new step-kin do not fully replace the contacts lost (Wachter 1997).

Another change across cohorts is that unmarried cohabitation has arisen as a precursor to—or possible substitute for—legal marriage, such that today over 60 percent of marriages are preceded by cohabitation, and nearly half of all women have cohabited at some point by their late thirties (Bumpass and Lu 2000; Smock 2000). Cohabitation is common both before marriage and after divorce (Bumpass, Raley, and Sweet 1995). Further, many cohabiting households include children born to the couple while they are living together or that are the product of one partner's prior relationship (Kennedy and Bumpass 2008).

## NONMARITAL AND TEEN CHILDBEARING

Concurrent with the changes in marriage practices has been a sharp increase in childbearing outside of marriage. In 1940, only 4 percent of all births occurred outside of marriage, while in 2009 (the latest year for which data are available), fully 41 percent of all births occurred outside of marriage (Hamilton, Martin, and Ventura 2010; Ventura and Bachrach 2000). While "traditional" family formation in the United States has typically followed a linear course—first dating, then marriage, then childbearing—the rise in nonmarital childbearing (along with concomitant changes in union formation) has yielded a range of complex and diverse family arrangements, which are strongly differentiated by socioeconomic status (Mincy and Pouncy 1999).

Today, it is common for intercourse and conception to occur outside marriage. The vast majority of unmarried women are sexually active: 77 percent of women age 20 to 29 in 1995 reported engaging in sex during the previous year (Ventura and Bachrach 2000). Also, most pregnancies among unmarried women are unintended, and most unintended pregnancies are not voluntarily terminated: 78 percent of pregnancies among never-married women in 1994 were unintended (Henshaw 1998), and four of every ten pregnancies among unmarried women in 1995 ended in abortion (Ventura and Bachrach 2000). Further, while in the 1950s and 1960s, 52 to 60 percent of first births conceived before marriage were resolved by a "shotgun" marriage before the birth, this was the case for only 23 percent of premaritally conceived first births in the period 1990–94 (Bachu 1999).

These facts about sexual activity and pregnancy resolution portend that the nonmarital birth rate is not likely to attenuate at any time in the near future. Although much of the recent increase in nonmarital childbearing can be attributed to births to cohabiting couples (Bumpass and Lu 2000; Smock 2000), this does not mean that children born into these couples come into a stable union; such unions are highly unstable, much more so in the United States than in other nations (Andersson 2003; Kiernan 1999; Osborne and McLanahan 2007). Indeed, despite positive attitudes toward and expectations about marriage expressed at the time of a nonmarital birth, only a minority of unmarried couples (including cohabitors) will subsequently marry—17 percent by five years after the child's birth (Carlson and McLanahan 2010; Carlson, McLanahan, and England 2004). As Sara McLahanan's chapter in this volume shows, among those cohabiting at the nonmarital birth of a child, 48 percent broke up within five years, 26 percent got married, and 26 percent continued to cohabit.

Teen childbearing has been a particular cause for social concern because of the greater economic disadvantage among—and welfare use by—teenage mothers. Nonmarital birth rates for teenagers (age 15 to 19) rose steadily between 1940 and 1994 but declined after that (Ventura and Bachrach 2000), except for a brief upturn over the past several years in births among older unmarried teens (age 18–19) (Ventura 2009). Unmarried birth rates fell among teens of all races after 1994, dropping the most for black teenagers (Ventura and Bachrach 2000). Overall, teen births as a proportion of all unmarried births declined from 50 percent in 1970 to 23 percent in 2007, primarily due to declines in nonmarital birth rates among teens and increases in birth rates for unmarried adult women (Ventura 2009). Still, births to teens are much more likely to occur outside of marriage than births to older women; 94 percent of births to 15–17-year-olds, and 84 percent of births to 18–19-year-olds, occurred outside of marriage, compared to 62 percent of births to women in their early twenties and 34 percent to women in their late twenties (Hamilton, Martin, and Ventura 2010). Moreover, births to unmarried teens account for about half of all *first* nonmarital births (Moore 1995). Many women who have a teen nonmarital birth go on to have a second nonmarital birth (often by a different partner). Thus teen childbearing remains an important aspect of nonmarital childbearing and family formation among unmarried parents.

Teen childbearing has been linked to a higher risk of negative outcomes for children, including socio-behavioral and cognitive problems in early/middle childhood, as well as delinquency, dropping out of high school, and early childbearing in adolescence and early adulthood (Brown and Eisenberg 1995; Geronimus and Korenman 1992; Hoffman, Foster, and Furstenberg 1993; Haveman, Wolfe and Peterson 1997; Klepinger, Lundberg, and Plotnick 1995, 1999; Levine, Pollack, and Comfort 2001; Moore, Morrison and Greene 1997; Maynard 1997). Further, there is a greater likelihood of divorce if/when teen mothers marry (Furstenberg, Brooks-Gunn, and Morgan 1987). At the same time, Furstenberg observed a cohort of teen mothers in Baltimore for several decades and found that estimates of the "consequences" of teen childbearing have been exaggerated because they do not account for preexisting characteristics correlated with both teen motherhood and disadvantageous outcomes—especially low socioeconomic status and opportunities (Furstenberg 2003). These findings are consonant with a growing body of econometric studies that adjust for unobserved differences (e.g., using sibling or community-level fixed effects) and find that estimates of the effects of having a teen birth are diminished—though in many cases not eliminated (Fletcher and Wolfe 2008; Geronimus and Korenman 1992; Hoffman, Foster, and Furstenberg 1993; Rosenzweig and Wolpin 1995).

MULTI-PARTNERED FERTILITY

At the intersection of the trends in marriage and fertility is the reality that a non-trivial and rising fraction of adults have (or will have) biological children by more than one partner, a pattern sometimes referred to as "multi-partnered fertility" (and abbreviated as MPF) (Furstenberg and King 1999). Several recent studies have found that a sizable fraction of individuals in various specific demographic groups have children by more than one partner, including low-income teenage mothers in Baltimore (Furstenberg and King 1999), a national sample of adult men (Guzzo and Furstenberg 2007a), adolescent and early adult women (Guzzo and Furstenberg 2007b), unwed parents in large U.S. cities (Carlson and Furstenberg 2006; Mincy 2002), and mothers receiving welfare in the Midwest (Jayakody and Seefeldt 2006; Meyer, Cancian, and Cook 2005).

Multi-partnered fertility is more likely to occur among unmarried and low-SES (socioeconomic status) parents. For example, estimates from a recent birth cohort study of urban parents suggest that for three-fifths of unmarried couples who had a child together in the late 1990s, either the mother or the father (or both) already had a previous child by another partner at the time of their common child's birth; the same was true for less than a quarter of married couples (Carlson and Furstenberg 2006); also, MPF is more common among racial/ethnic minorities and men who have a history of incarceration. In a representative sample of American men, 16 percent of men age 35–44 had children by two or more partners, and successive cohorts appear to be transitioning to multi-partnered fertility at even higher rates, suggesting that the overall prevalence is rising (Guzzo and Furstenberg 2007a).

Multi-partnered fertility has important implications for children's well-being because it affects the organization of family life and kinship networks. When parents are called upon to provide resources to children in more than one household—or to children of different biological relatedness within the same household—the resulting complexities may compromise the quantity or quality of parental investment that children receive. This is because when parents (typically fathers) live apart from their children, they contribute fewer financial resources than when they live with them (Weiss and Willis 1985), and there are higher transaction costs of arranging to spend time with children. Also, evolutionary theory suggests that biological parents will invest more in children than unrelated social parents because the former have an evolutionary interest in ensuring the success of these children (Emlen 1997). Further, as described in the stepfamily literature, the divergent biological ties to children resulting from multi-partnered fertility (with repartnering) obfuscate parental roles and weaken the social capital within the family unit (Furstenberg and Cherlin 1991). Given that multi-partnered fertility occurs disproportionately among low-income and minority subgroups, this phenomenon may also contribute to social and economic inequality over time, or exacerbate the negative effects of growing up in economically disadvantaged families (Duncan and Brooks-Gunn 1997).

## FATHER INVOLVEMENT AND THE ROLE OF MEN IN FAMILY LIFE

Although the father's role in family life has historically been defined by financial contributions (i.e., "breadwinning"), fathers today are involved in childrearing in numerous ways. Contemporary fathering may include providing economic support; nurturing and caregiving; engaging in leisure and play activities; providing the child's mother with financial, emotional, or practical support; providing moral guidance and discipline; ensuring the safety of the child; connecting the child to his extended family; and linking the child to community members and resources (Cabrera et al. 2000; Lamb 2004; Marsiglio et al. 2000; Marsiglio and Day 1997; Palkovitz 2002; Pleck and Masciadrelli 2004). Although the "new" father role has often been discussed with respect to higher-SES fathers, ethnographic studies report that many unwed and low-income fathers describe their roles in terms similar to those used by married and middle-class fathers, even though they face much greater economic constraints (Furstenberg, Sherwood, and Sullivan 1992; Jarrett, Roy, and Burton 2002; Waller 2002).

Yet the reality is that low-income fathers are much more likely to live apart from their children and thus to be less involved than their higher-income counterparts. This dichotomy in fathering by SES, which Furstenberg observed and identified as the "good dad-bad dad complex," emerged from the decline in the gendered division of household labor (Furstenberg 1988); as men who live with their children's mother were freed from the expectation that they would be the primary breadwinner, they also became free to participate in family life more fully—and many did. But at the same time, marriage became more optional and detached from childbearing, giving men more freedom to eschew family responsibilities entirely, and women more freedom to shut men out by leaving relationships. Thus, as fatherhood has become a more voluntary role, only the most committed and financially stable men choose to embrace it.

As noted earlier, research suggests that children who live apart from their biological fathers do not fare as well on a range of outcomes as children who grow up with both biological parents (McLanahan and Sandefur 1994). Children in single-parent families are often deprived of two types of resources from their fathers—economic (money) and relational (time) (Thomson, Hanson, and McLanahan 1994). The economic circumstances can be most easily quantified: female-headed families with related children under age 18 have a significantly higher poverty rate (39 percent in 2009) than married-couple families with children (8 percent in 2009) (DeNavas-Walt, Proctor, and Smith 2010), and living in extreme poverty has adverse effects on child development and well-being (Duncan and Brooks-Gunn 1997; Duncan, Kalil, and Ziol-Guest 2008). Yet it is important to recognize that the correlations of family structure with economic well-being are not necessarily (or entirely) causal, though recent evidence suggests that there is some causal effect of marriage on family income (Sawhill and Thomas 2005). Children in single-parent families also receive less parental attention and emotional support from their fathers. Nonresident fathers see their children less often than resident fathers, and lack of interaction decreases the likelihood that a father and child will develop a close relationship (Seltzer 1991; Shapiro and Lambert 1999).

While the benefits of nonresident fathers' economic contributions have been demonstrated by research (Amato and Gilbreth 1999; Argys et al. 1988; Knox and Bane 1994), the benefits of their relational involvement when living apart from their children are less clear. In fact, studies of the frequency of contact between nonresidential fathers and their children do *not* demonstrate that greater father-child interaction has beneficial effects for children and adolescents (Crockett, Eggebeen, and Hawkins 1993; Furstenberg, Morgan, and Allison 1987; Hawkins and Eggebeen, 1991; King 1994a, 1994b). This lack of effects of father-child contact exists regardless of the child's race, gender, mother's education, or marital status at birth (King 1994b). Several researchers have suggested that the *quality* of the father-child relationship may be more important than the quantity (Crockett et al. 1993; King, 1994b; Simons et al. 1994; Amato and Rivera 1999; Harris, Furstenberg, and Marmer, 1998; Harris and Marmer, 1996). In sum, low-SES children (who are likely to live apart from their fathers) typically get fewer resources—both money and time—from their biological fathers than their high-SES counterparts (who are likely to live with their fathers).

## LENGTHENING AND DIVERGENCE IN THE TRANSITION TO ADULTHOOD

Along with the major changes in family demography and roles noted above, new and diverging patterns have emerged with respect to the timing and nature of how youth enter adulthood. While those coming of age in the middle of the twentieth century typically left home in their late teens to go to college—or get a job or enter the military (men) or get married (women)—today's youth experience an extended period of becoming an adult that is less guided by a normative sequence of events. As Furstenberg and colleagues have written, "the timing and sequencing of traditional markers of adulthood—leaving home, finishing school, starting work, getting married, and having children—are less predictable and more prolonged, diverse, and disordered" (Furstenberg, Rumbaut, and Settersten 2005, p. 5).

The patterns by which individuals enter adulthood are profoundly shaped by socioeconomic status—the focus of Annette Lareau and Amanda Cox's chapter in this volume. Those raised in high-SES families typically first leave home to enter a four-year college, and upon graduation will likely get a job, get an apartment, and begin to establish a career before "settling down" to get married and have children. Parental transfers along the way help pay tuition and connect youth to a career job, thereby leaving such graduates with limited college debt and connected to a high-paying job.

By contrast, those from low-SES backgrounds may or may not finish high school, and if they do finish and go on to college, they are more likely to incur significant debt and to combine work and college-going, thereby prolonging the amount of time they take to earn a degree (Turner 2006; Dickert-Conlin and Rubenstein 2006). Further, those who do not graduate from high school (or those who do not obtain a college degree within six years of high school graduation) are more likely to have children before marriage. Those without a college degree (and sometimes even without a high school diploma) face a dismal labor market with limited job prospects and often have no clear plan for leaving the parental home or assuming the other characteristics of adulthood, such as getting a career job or a place of their own. Indeed, early parenting without a partner makes it even harder to progress up the SES ladder today than twenty years ago. Trying to complete education, pay bills, and find a job and a partner along the way—with a child to raise—is much harder under conditions of a lengthening time to adulthood and poor labor market prospects for the inexperienced and undereducated.

## GROWING DIVERSITY IN FAMILY LIFE

Taken together, these changing patterns suggest growing diversity in the experience of family life. They raise concerns about growing social and economic stratification. Of course, the family has long been a mechanism by which advantage—and disadvantage—is transferred across generations. Higher-SES families have for many decades (if not longer) had lower fertility, higher income, and more cognitive and network advantages to pass on to children, and had lower divorce rates. What has changed is the magnitude of the SES differences in income and family structure: SES differences in income are greater today because earnings inequality has risen, along with women's employment and educational homogamy in marriage (Schwartz and Mare 2005). More poor children have always grown up without their fathers owing to higher rates of divorce and death, but today that is compounded by higher levels of, and widening SES differentials, in nonmarital births, combined with the fact that unmarried parents often break up within a few years of the child's birth. These differences by SES in the resources that children receive is of concern in its own right in a society that values equality of opportunity. At the same time, they raise questions about the future of the next generation at the low end of the socioeconomic spectrum, to the extent that childhood disadvantage creates barriers to individual human capital development and long-term economic self-sufficiency. The chapters in this volume highlight different aspects of how class inequality is linked to family patterns, and in some cases, how these patterns are changing in the context of an increasingly unequal America.

Paula England, Elizabeth McClintock, and Emily Shafer point out socio-economic differences in a wide range of behaviors that lead less-advantaged individuals to have not only more children, but also earlier births and more unplanned births. In analyses controlling for race, they classify a young adult's SES level in terms of his or her mother's education—whether she completed less than high school, finished high school and/or attended some college, or was a college graduate. Those whose mothers are less educated have their first experience of sexual intercourse slightly earlier (about half a year), are less likely to consistently use contraception, and are more likely to conceive early, more likely to have unplanned pregnancies, and less likely to abort if they get pregnant. Given all these factors, those from lower-SES backgrounds start childbearing earlier and have more unplanned births. Many of their births are outside of marriage.

The authors point out that past literature has focused intently on the class gradient in nonmarital births, attributing it largely to the difficulties less-educated men have in finding stable and well-paying jobs, which lead the men and their partners to consider themselves unready for marriage. While not disputing the relevance of how available marriage seems, England and her coauthors claim that other class-linked behavioral constellations are prob-ably more important. They delineate three explanations of class differences in sexual initiation and consistent use of birth control. Economists argue that the opportunity costs of having a child are greater for women with better job prospects, and this gives them greater incentives to abstain, use contraception consistently, and use abortion as a backup. A second possibility is that so-cial roles, such as "student" or "professional," discourage early childbearing through mechanisms other than economic incentives—such as the expecta-tions of peers and the formation of an identity consistent with one's role. For example, a college student may see becoming a mother as wildly inconsistent with the life stage she is in, quite apart from how it would affect her career prospects. A third possibility is a class gradient in the ability to self-regulate and the belief in one's own efficacy; young women need both of these to help them abstain from unprotected sex or undergo the hassles of using contracep-tion consistently, and growing up poor may make it harder to develop either.

S. Philip Morgan also focuses on group differences in fertility patterns—especially how many children people have and how early they have them. He uses the "theory of conjunctural action" (TCA) to organize his account of differences. Incorporating insights from several disciplines, TCA sees both structure (material circumstances) and culture as affecting behavior. Behav-ior flows, in part, from the material circumstances that groups face, which also affect the particular situations, called "conjunctures," they experience. TCA also stresses the importance of cultural schemas, which often affect how members of groups will construe the meaning of a particular situation.

Applying this to fertility patterns, he argues that some differences, such as those between Hispanic and other immigrants, are transitional and fade across generations after arrival in the United States, owing to increasingly similar schemas and situations.

By contrast, other differences, such as fertility differences by education or socioeconomic status, appear to be more stable. Although fertility has fallen, there remains a tendency for the less-educated to end up with larger families than the better-educated. The difference in average number of children by the end of the childbearing age between the least- and most-educated averages approximately one child—a substantial difference when average family size is fewer than two children. Morgan posits that a cultural schema in favor of two children is in force across social classes, a point also made by England, McClintock, and Shafer in this volume. Consistent with this, he shows that the number of children wanted by young women in different educational groups is almost identical. Yet, both the life circumstances and the construals of the meaning of pregnancy are very different by SES. Though class differences in fertility could change if group differences in circumstances changed enough, in fact, total fertility differences have not changed much.

In contrast, Morgan shows that other group differences in fertility have changed. For example, Catholics used to have higher average fertility, but this is no longer true. Today, *how* religious one is, rather than one's denomination, predicts family size. In another example of dynamism, Morgan argues that anti-abortion activism has probably increased the prevalence of construing the decision to take an unplanned, unwanted pregnancy to term as the moral thing to do. Changing schema and construals have valorized taking unintended pregnancies to term in many groups. This may be part of why abortion rates have declined in recent years, while the percentage of births classified as unwanted went up. Of course, the unavailability of public funding for abortion is a relevant material factor as well.

Many SES differences are monotonic—increasing or decreasing consistently with each gradation of education, income, or occupational status. Most of the differences discussed in the chapters by England and her coauthors and by Morgan are of this type. In contrast, Andrew Cherlin focuses in his chapter on nonmonotonic differences. He provides evidence that the family patterns of those with moderate education—a high school degree (or a GED) and perhaps some college, but no four-year college degree—are distinctive. In particular, they go through more co-residential partners than either those with more or less education. If we count either a cohabitation or a marriage as one union (i.e., a cohabiting couple who later marry counts as one union, not two), the moderately educated have had unions with more partners by middle age than either those above or below them in educational attainment.

And interestingly, whites are more apt than either blacks or Hispanics to have lived with more cohabitational or marital partners by middle age. In a proximate sense, what explains why both the least- and most-educated have fewer partners than this middle group is that the least-educated marry less, while the most-educated cohabit less. But why is this? Cherlin argues that the moderately educated still believe in the viability of marriage for themselves more than the poor do, but they face increasingly difficult economic circumstances that lead them to choose cohabitations that they hope will turn into marriages, and sometimes to even have children in these unions. Discussions of economic change in America emphasize the hollowing out of the middle of good paying, often unionized and blue-collar jobs that (especially white) men with high school degrees used to work in. The sons of the men who held those jobs are likely to be closer to the poor in job prospects today, and this has made many couples hold off on marriage, and it has broken up some existing marriages. Of course, the poor are even less likely to believe that their economic circumstances warrant marriage, and their marriages have even higher rates of breakup. But the combination of degenerating marriageability, especially given the higher "bar" for marriage imposed today (Gibson-Davis, Edin, and McLanahan 2005)—but still intact optimism about their ultimate marriageability—has led the moderately educated to experience an unusually high number of co-residential partnerships.

The next two chapters describe aspects of nonmarital childbearing in the United States. The chapter by Kathryn Edin, Timothy Nelson, and Joanna Reed focuses on low-income fathers and their roles as partners and parents after a nonmarital birth. Using data from two qualitative studies of urban unwed fathers, they discuss how few pregnancies are planned, the often ambiguous nature of the couple relationship, and the short tenure of most couples' relationship (less than one year) at the time that a pregnancy occurs. Yet fathers are typically enthusiastic about the news of an impending birth, and the relationship often "steps up" in seriousness after a conception is announced. Driven by their desire to be involved with their children, men endeavor to invest in the couple relationship and share the responsibilities of childrearing. It is typical for unmarried parents to grow closer and move in together with the news of a pregnancy. However, problems of infidelity, sexual jealousy, and gender mistrust are common and often lead to repeated breakups. Further, women's expectation of men's economic contributions—in the face of men's limited economic capacities—creates conflict between them, disappointment on the part of mothers, and disinvestment on the part of men. Thus, while propelled by early optimism after a conception, relationships among low-income fathers and their partners ultimately prove to be tenuous, while men's desire to remain involved with their children—though often not realized—persists.

Sara McLanahan turns our attention to children in the context of non-marital childbearing. She summarizes what has been learned to date from the Fragile Families and Child Wellbeing Study, a unique data resource that she developed, with Irv Garfinkel, in order to better understand the nature and consequences of U.S. nonmarital childbearing at the end of the twentieth century. McLanahan describes the characteristics and capabilities of unmarried parents (as compared to married parents) around the time of a new baby's birth, finding that, relative to married parents, unmarried parents are significantly more disadvantaged with respect to age, education, earnings, physical health, and mental health. While most unmarried parents are in a romantic relationship at the time of their baby's birth and express "high hopes" for marriage, by five years, only one-third of unwed couples are still together (married or not). McLanahan presents evidence describing the relational instability that typically ensues after the dissolution of a union—and its consequences for parents and children. A number of low-income unmarried parents break up only to repartner, have another child in a complex family, and then break up again, and possibly repeat the cycle. Whereas earlier writing on family structure focused on questions of whether children were disadvantaged by spending years in a single-mother rather than a two-parent family (e.g. McLanahan and Sandefur 1994), in this chapter McLanahan suggests that it is the long-term pattern of instability (and the associated complexity) that may have adverse effects, and that, by contrast, a stable single-mother family may sometimes be more favorable. She presents evidence suggesting that there are notable adverse consequences of family instability for fathers' earnings and for mothers' income (largely because mothers lose access to sharing the father's earnings), mental health, parental stress, and time spent with children, as well as for children's cognitive and social-behavioral development. While she acknowledges that there may be unobserved factors correlated with both family structure or stability and the outcomes, she suggests (with a number of robustness checks) that the evidence is consistent with a causal interpretation. Ultimately, McLanahan concludes that children born to unmarried parents are disadvantaged compared to their counterparts born to married parents—both because of the parents' lower initial economic resources and social capital, and because of the instability and complexity that typically ensues, which further diminishes parental resources and family relationships.

In the next chapter, Annette Lareau and Amanda Cox explore how parents of different social classes foresee and help solve the problems their children have during the transition to adulthood. Drawing on in-depth follow-up interviews of the twelve youth followed in Lareau's landmark book, *Unequal Childhoods*, on differences in parental childrearing styles by socioeconomic status (Lareau 2003), Lareau and Cox examine the resources that parents bring to bear in helping older youth enter adulthood. They find that working-class parents provide material resources (e.g., car insurance payments) to their young adult children, but that they view those children (as the youth view themselves) as "grown." By contrast, the parents of middle-class youth play a more active role in their daily lives and continue to intervene to help them address problems and navigate choices, especially concerning college entry and completion. A particular emphasis of their chapter is that middle-class parents have more of the cultural knowledge necessary to help their children interact with institutions—such as gaining access to college-prep courses in high school and navigating the college admission process. Lareau and Cox argue that these class differences in parents' cultural resources serve to exacerbate inequality in the life chances of youth from different classes, especially in getting a college education.

The tax and transfer system, charged with supporting families in diverse circumstances, is the topic of Timothy Smeeding and Marcia Carlson's chapter. The authors review public policies in three major areas—those designed to increase economic resources, those designed to strengthen family relationships, and those aimed at preventing the formation of unstable families in the first place. Within each area, they describe particular challenges, mismatches, and conundrums related to contemporary family patterns, and they suggest policy revisions and alternatives that hold promise for strengthening families and reducing poverty even amidst complex family dynamics. For example, during the George W. Bush administration, a new initiative was developed to encourage couples with children to marry (the Healthy Marriage Initiative). Given the high prevalence of union instability and multi-partnered fertility among unmarried parents, a marriage between the parents of a given focal child will likely create a stepfamily—as opposed to a traditional nuclear family—and may not last very long. Hence, Smeeding and Carlson suggest that in addition to policies that secure economic resources for children, relationship education programs could focus on strengthening the co-parenting relationship among parents of biological children, regardless of the trajectory of the couple's own romantic relationship.

In the final chapter, Frank Furstenberg provides a thoughtful and incisive overview of the unprecedented change in the American family that has occurred over the past half-century, a time that also spans his career to date as a family scholar. He describes entering graduate school in the 1950s when structural functionalism was the dominant theoretical model about family life, and the data, methodological tools, and computing power available today were as yet unimagined. In 1965 he began what would become a famous and lifelong study of teenage mothers in Baltimore, which he later recognized as a "harbinger of things to come" for the retreat from marriage throughout the United States. In this chapter, Furstenberg documents the "'unpackaging' of elements of the family and kinship system" as part of a process of family change that has been ongoing for centuries—not just since the so-called traditional family of the 1950s, which he identifies as a "social fiction . . . about the recent past." With the de-linking of sex and marriage, and of marriage and parenthood, and the growing diversity in the transition to adulthood, family formation has become more flexible and adaptable to changes over the life course and at the same time less uniform and stable, with potential adverse implications for the well-being of children. Consonant with the broader focus of this volume, Furstenberg notes the growing divergence in family formation and childrearing patterns by socioeconomic status and the important role of educational and economic opportunities in shaping family life. He anticipates several areas of likely change in the future, particularly as related to gender, sexual and contraceptive practices, marriage, parenting, the intergenerational flow of resources, and the intersection of work and home. He concludes by noting that "Nothing that has happened during the past half-century has undermined the importance of the family, despite our apprehensions to the contrary." We concur with his optimism and hope that this volume will add to our understanding about how family life continues to change and evolve in the context of social and economic change.

REFERENCES

Amato, Paul R., and Joan G. Gilbreth. 1999. "Nonresident Fathers and Children's Well-Being: A Meta-Analysis." *Journal of Marriage and the Family* 61: 557–73.

Amato, Paul R. and Fernando Rivera. 1999. "Paternal Involvement and Children's Behavior Problems." *Journal of Marriage and the Family* 61: 375–84.

Andersson, Gunnar. 2003. "Dissolution of Unions in Europe: A Comparative Overview." Working paper #2003-004. Rostock, Germany: Max Planck Institute for Demographic Research.

Argys, Laura M., H. Elizabeth Peters, Jeanne Brooks-Gunn, and J. R. Smith. 1988. "The Impact of Child Support on Cognitive Outcomes of Young Children." *Demography* 35: 159–73.

Bachu, Amara. 1999. "Trends in Premarital Childbearing, 1930 to 1994." In *Current Population Reports*, P23-197. Washington, DC: U.S. Census Bureau.

Brandolini, Andrea, and Timothy Smeeding. 2006. "Patterns of Economic Inequality in Western Democracies: Some Facts on Levels and Trends." *PS: Political Science & Politics* 39: 21–26.

Bumpass, Larry, and Hsien-Hen Lu. 2000. "Trends in Cohabitation and Implications for Children's Family Contexts in the United States." *Population Studies* 54: 29–41.

Bumpass, Larry L., R. Kelly Raley, and James A. Sweet. 1995. "The Changing Character of Stepfamilies: Implications of Cohabitation and Nonmarital Childbearing." *Demography* 32: 425–36.

Cabrera, Natasha J., Catherine S. Tamis-LeMonda, Robert H. Bradley, Sandra L. Hofferth, and Michael E. Lamb. 2000. "Fatherhood in the Twenty-First Century." *Child Development* 71: 127–36.

Carlson, Marcia J., and Frank F. Furstenberg, Jr. 2006. "The Prevalence and Correlates of Multipartnered Fertility among Urban U.S. Parents." *Journal of Marriage and Family* 68: 718–32.

Carlson, Marcia J., and Sara S. McLanahan. 2010. "Fathers in Fragile Families." In *The Role of the Father in Child Development*, 5th ed., edited by Michael E. Lamb, pp. 241–69. New York: Wiley & Sons.

Carlson, Marcia, Sara McLanahan, and Paula England. 2004. "Union Formation in Fragile Families." *Demography* 41: 237–62.

Castro-Martin, Teresa, and Larry L. Bumpass. 1989. "Recent Trends in Marital Disruption." *Demography* 26: 37–51.

Cherlin, Andrew. 1978. "Remarriage as an Incomplete Institution." *American Journal of Sociology* 84: 634–50.

———. 2009. *The Marriage-Go-Round: The State of Marriage and the Family in America Today*. New York: Random House.

Crockett, Lisa J., David J. Eggebeen, and Alan J. Hawkins. 1993. "Father's Presence and Young Children's Behavioral and Cognitive Adjustment." *Journal of Family Issues* 14: 355–77.

DeNavas-Walt, Carmen, Bernadette D. Proctor, and Jessica C. Smith. 2010. U.S. Census Bureau, Current Population Reports, P60-238, *Income Poverty, and Health Insurance Coverage in the United States: 2009*, U.S. Government Printing Office, Washington, DC.

Duncan, Greg J., and Jeanne Brooks-Gunn. 1997. "The Consequences of Growing Up Poor." New York: Russell Sage Foundation.

Duncan, Greg J., Ariel Kalil, and Kathleen M. Ziol-Guest. 2008. "Economic Costs of Early Childhood Poverty." Issue Paper #4. Washington, DC: Partnership for America's Economic Success. http://www.browncountyunitedway.org /files /Poverty%20Website/Costs_of_childhood_poverty.pdf.

Ellwood, David T., and Christopher Jencks. 2004. "The Uneven Spread of Single-Parent Families: What Do We Know?" In *Social Inequality*, edited by K. M. Neckerman, pp. 3–78. New York: Russell Sage Foundation.

Emlen, Stephen L. 1997. "The Evolutionary Study of Human Family Systems." *Social Science Information* 36: 563–89.

Fletcher, Jason M., and Barbara L. Wolfe. 2008. "Education and Labor Market Consequences of Teenage Childbearing: Evidence Using the Timing of Pregnancy Outcomes and Community Fixed Effects." Working Paper #13847. Cambridge, MA: National Bureau of Economic Research.

Furstenberg, Frank F., Jr. 1988. "Good Dads—Bad Dads: Two Faces of Fatherhood." In *The Changing American Family and Public Policy*, edited by A. J. Cherlin, pp. 193–209. Washington, DC: Urban Institute.

———. 1990. "Divorce and the American Family." *Annual Review of Sociology* 16: 379–403.

———. 2003. "Teenage Childbearing as a Public Issue and Private Concern." *Annual Review of Sociology* 29: 23–39.

Furstenberg, Frank F., and Andrew Cherlin. 1991. *Divided Families: What Happens to Children When Parents Part.* Cambridge, MA: Harvard University Press.

Furstenberg, Frank, F., Jr. and Rosalind Berkowitz King. 1999. "Multipartnered Fertility Sequences: Documenting an Alternative Family Form." Earlier version presented at the 1998 annual meetings of the Population Association of America, Chicago, IL.

Furstenberg, Frank F., Jr. and Graham B. Spanier. 1984. "The Risk of Dissolution in Remarriage: An Examination of Cherlin's Hypothesis of Incomplete Institutionalization." *Family Relations* 33: 433–41.

Furstenberg, Frank F., Jr., J. Brooks-Gunn, and S. Philip Morgan. 1987. *Adolescent Mothers in Later Life.* Cambridge, UK: Cambridge University Press.

Furstenberg, Frank F., Jr., S. Philip Morgan, and Paul D. Allison. 1987. "Paternal Participation and Children's Well-being after Marital Dissolution." *American Sociological Review* 52: 695–701.

Furstenberg, Frank F., Jr., Ruben G. Rumbaut, and Richard A. Settersten, Jr. 2005. "On the Frontier of Adulthood: Emerging Themes and New Directions." In *On the Frontier of Adulthood: Theory, Research, and Public Policy*, edited by R. A. Settersten, Jr., F. F. Furstenberg, Jr., and R. G. Rumbaut, pp. 3–25. Chicago: University of Chicago Press.

Furstenberg, Frank F., Jr., Kay E. Sherwood, and Mercer L. Sullivan. 1992. *Caring and Paying: What Fathers and Mothers Say about Child Support.* New York: MDRC.

Geronimus, Arline T., and Sanders Korenman. 1992. "The Socioeconomic Consequences of Teen Childbearing Reconsidered." *Quarterly Journal of Economics* 107: 1187–1214.

Gibson-Davis, Christina, Kathryn Edin, and Sara McLanahan. 2005. "High Hopes but Even Higher Expectations: The Retreat from Marriage among Low-Income Couples." *Journal of Marriage and Family* 67: 1301–1312.

Goldstein, Joshua R., and Catherine T. Kenney. 2001. "Marriage Delayed or Marriage Forgone? New Cohort Forecasts of First Marriage for U.S. Women." *American Sociological Review* 66: 506–19.

Gottschalk, Peter, and Sheldon Danziger. 2005. "Inequality of Wage Rates, Earnings and Family Incomes in the United States: 1972–2002." *Review of Income and Wealth* 51: 231–54.

Guzzo, Karen Benjamin, and Frank F. Furstenberg, Jr. 2007a. "Multipartnered Fertility among American Men." *Demography* 44: 583–601.

———. 2007b. "Multipartnered Fertility among Young Women with a Nonmarital First Birth: Prevalence and Risk Factors." *Perspectives on Sexual and Reproductive Health* 39: 29–38.

Hamilton, Brady E., Joyce A. Martin, and Stephanie J. Ventura. 2010. *Births: Preliminary Data for 2009, National Vital Statistics Reports*, vol. 59, no. 3. Hyattsville, MD: National Center for Health Statistics.

Harris, Kathleen Mullan, Frank F. Furstenberg, Jr., and Jeremy K. Marmer. 1998. "Paternal Involvement with Adolescents in Intact Families: The Influence of Fathers over the Life Course." *Demography* 35: 201–16.

Harris, Kathleen Mullan and Jeremy K. Marmer. 1996. "Poverty, Paternal Involvement, and Adolescent Well-Being." *Journal of Family Issues* 17: 614–40.

Hawkins, Alan J., and David J. Eggebeen. 1991. "Are Fathers Fungible? Patterns of Coresident Adult Men in Maritally Disrupted Families and Young Children's Well-Being." *Journal of Marriage and the Family* 53: 958–72.

Henshaw, Stanley K. 1998. "Unintended Pregnancy in the United States." *Family Planning Perspectives* 30: 24–46.

Hoffman, Saul D., E. Michael Foster, and Frank F. Furstenberg, Jr. 1993. "Reevaluating the Costs of Teenage Childbearing: Response to Geronimus and Korenman." *Demography* 30: 291–96.

Jarrett, Robin L., Kevin M. Roy, and Linda M. Burton. 2002. "Fathers in the 'Hood': Insights from Qualitative Research on Low-Income African American Men." In *Handbook of Father Involvement: Multidisciplinary Perspectives*, edited by C. Tamis-LeMonda and N. Cabrera, pp. 211–48. Mahwah, NJ: Erlbaum.

Jayakody, Rukmalie, and Kristin S. Seefeldt. 2006. "Complex Families, Multiple Partner Fertility, and Families across Households: Implications for Marriage Promotion Efforts." Paper presented at the IRP Working Conference on Multiple-Partner Fertility, September 14–15, 2006, Madison, WI.

Kennedy, Sheela, and Larry Bumpass. 2008. "Cohabitation and Children's Living Arrangements: New Estimates from the United States." *Demographic Research* 19: 1663–92.

Kiernan, Kathleen. 1999. "Cohabitation in Western Europe." *Population Trends* 96: 25–32.

King, Valarie. 1994a. "Nonresident Father Involvement and Child Well-Being: Can Dads Make a Difference?" *Journal of Family Issues* 15: 78–96.

———. 1994b. "Variation in the Consequences of Nonresident Father Involvement for Children's Well-Being." *Journal of Marriage and the Family* 56: 963–72.

Knox, Virginia, and Mary Jo Bane. 1994. "Child Support and Schooling." In *Child Support and Child Wellbeing*, edited by I. Garfinkel, S. S. McLanahan, and P. K. Robins, pp. 285–310. Washington, DC: Urban Institute Press.

Lamb, Michael E. 2004. "The Role of the Father in Child Development." New York: John Wiley & Sons.

Lareau, Annette. 2003. *Unequal Childhoods: Class, Race, and Family Life*. Berkeley: University of California Press.

Marsiglio, William, and Randal Day. 1997. "Social Fatherhood and Paternal Involvement: Conceptual, Data, and Policymaking Issues." Presented at the NICHD-sponsored Conference on Fathering and Male Fertility: Improving Data and Research.

Marsiglio, William, Paul Amato, Randal D. Day, and Michael E. Lamb. 2000. "Scholarship on Fatherhood in the 1990s and beyond." *Journal of Marriage and the Family* 62: 1173–1191.

Martin, Molly A. 2006. "Family Structure and Income Inequality in Families with Children, 1976 to 2000." *Demography* 43: 421–45.

Martin, Steven P. 2006. "Trends in Marital Dissolution by Women's Education in the United States." *Demographic Research* 15: 537–60.

McLanahan, Sara. 2004. "Diverging Destinies: How Children Are Faring under the Second Demographic Transition." *Demography* 41: 607–27.

McLanahan, Sara, and Christine Percheski. 2008. "Family Structure and the Reproduction of Inequalities." *Annual Review of Sociology* 34: 257–76.

McLanahan, Sara, and Gary Sandefur. 1994. *Growing Up with a Single Parent: What Hurts? What Helps?* Cambridge, MA: Harvard University Press.

Meyer, Daniel R., Maria Cancian, and Steven T. Cook. 2005. "Multiple-Partner Fertility: Incidence and Implications for Child Support Policy." *Social Service Review* 79: 577–601.

Mincy, Ronald B. 2002. "Who Should Marry Whom? Multiple Partner Fertility among New Parents." Working paper #2002-03-FF. Center for Research on Child Wellbeing, Princeton University.

Mincy, Ronald B., and Hillard Pouncy. 1999. "There Must Be Fifty Ways to Start a Family: Public Policy and the Fragile Families of Low Income Non-Custodial Fathers." In *The Fatherhood Movement: A Call to Action*, edited by W. Horn, D. Blankenhorn, and M. B. Pearlstein. New York: Lexington Books.

Moore, Kristin. 1995. "Nonmarital Childbearing in the United States." In *U.S. Department of Health and Human Services Report to Congress on Out-of-Wedlock Childbearing*, pp. v–xxii. Hyattsville, MD: National Center for Health Statistics.

Osborne, Cynthia, and Sara McLanahan. 2007. "Partnership Instability and Child Well-Being." *Journal of Marriage and Family* 69: 1065–83.

Palkovitz, Rob. 2002. "Involved Fathering and Child Development: Advancing Our Understanding of Good Fathering." In *Handbook of Father Involvement*, edited by C. S. Tamis-LeMonda and N. J. Cabrera, pp. 33–64. Mahwah, NJ: Erlbaum.

Pleck, Joseph H., and B. Masciadrelli. 2004. "Paternal Involvement by U.S. Residential Fathers: Levels, Sources, and Consequences." In *The Role of the Father in Child Development*, edited by M. E. Lamb, pp. 222–71. Hoboken, NJ: Wiley & Sons.

Rosenzweig, Mark R., and Kenneth I. Wolpin. 1995. "Sisters, Siblings, and Mothers: The Effect of Teen-Age Childbearing on Birth Outcomes in a Dynamic Family Context." *Econometrica* 63: 303–26.

Sawhill, Isabel, and Adam Thomas. 2005. "For Love *and* Money? The Impact of Family Structure on Family Income." *Future of Children* 15: 57–74.

Schwartz, Christine R., and Robert D. Mare. 2005. "Trends in Educational Assortative Marriage from 1940 to 2003." *Demography* 42: 621–46.

Seltzer, Judith A. 1991. "Relationships between Fathers and Children Who Live Apart: The Father's Role after Separation." *Journal of Marriage and the Family* 53: 79–101.

Shapiro, Adam, and James David Lambert. 1999. "Longitudinal Effects of Divorce on the Quality of the Father-Child Relationship and on Fathers' Psychological Well-Being." *Journal of Marriage and the Family* 61: 397–408.

Sigle-Rushton, Wendy, and Sara McLanahan. 2004. "Father Absence and Child Well-Being: A Critical Review." In *The Future of the Family*, edited by D. P. Moynihan, T. M. Smeeding, and L. Rainwater, pp. 116–55. New York: Russell Sage Foundation.

Smock, Pamela J. 2000. "Cohabitation in the United States: An Appraisal of Research Themes, Findings, and Implications." *Annual Review of Sociology* 26: 1–20.

Thomson, Elizabeth, Thomas L. Hanson, and Sara S. McLanahan. 1994. "Family Structure and Child Well-Being: Economic Resources vs. Parental Behaviors." *Social Forces* 73: 221–42.

Ventura, Stephanie J. 2009. "Changing Patterns of Nonmarital Childbearing in the United States." *NCHS Data Brief*, no. 18. Hyattsville, MD: National Center for Health Statistics.

Ventura, Stephanie, and Christine Bachrach. 2000. *Nonmarital Childbearing in the United States, 1949–99*. National Vital Statistics Report 48, no. 6. Hyattsville, MD: National Center for Health Statistics.

Wachter, Kenneth W. 1997. "Kinship Resources for the Elderly." *Philosophical Transactions of the Royal Society of London*, Series B 352: 1811–17.

Waller, Maureen R. 2002. *My Baby's Father: Unmarried Parents and Paternal Responsibility*. Ithaca, NY: Cornell University Press.

Weiss, Yoram, and Robert J. Willis. 1985. "Children as Collective Goods and Divorce Settlements." *Journal of Labor Economics* 3: 268–92.

# CHAPTER ONE

# Birth Control Use and Early, Unintended Births

## Evidence for a Class Gradient

*Paula England, Elizabeth Aura McClintock,
and Emily Fitzgibbons Shafer*

Family patterns have always differed by social class in America. Generations ago, lower- or working-class individuals married earlier than the middle class, and all classes typically started childbearing shortly after marriage. In the past, less-privileged young adults typically had a first birth at about 18–20 years of age; they do the same today except they are often not married (Ellwood and Jencks 2004; Rindfuss et al. 1996). The shotgun marriage—a marriage that occurs in response to a premarital pregnancy—has gone out of fashion (Akerlof et al. 1996), yet an unintended pregnancy often galvanizes couples to solidify a several-month-old romantic relationship and even move in together (Reed 2006). About 80 percent of nonmarital births are to romantically involved couples (England and Edin 2007, Chapter 1), but they typically break up within a few years. Each partner may go on to have another unintended birth with another partner, leading to multiple-partner fertility and complex households. As Sara McLanahan illustrates in this volume, from a child's point of view, this produces many transitions and instability in household composition. The pattern is most pronounced among poor blacks, but non-college-educated whites and Latinos are increasingly following these patterns as well.

Middle-class childbearing remains largely in marriage, and is increasingly delayed until well after marriage. As a result, class differences in the age of mothers at the birth of a first child have grown appreciably (Ellwood and Jencks 2004; Rindfuss et al. 1996). Class differences in the instability of children's circumstances have long been present because of class differences in divorce rates, but today such differences are magnified by the less durable unions into which the children of disadvantaged parents are born.

Recent academic discussions of class differences in family patterns focus on the "retreat from marriage," and many policy discussions suggest the need to encourage marriage as a way of reducing instability for less-privileged children. Cultural changes have raised the economic and relational standards for marriage (Cherlin 2004). At the same time, in recent decades, the earnings of men without a college degree have fallen, creating a situation where the poor are unlikely to ever meet their own economic standards for marriage (England and Edin 2007). The retreat from marriage has undoubtedly increased family instability and complexity, as well as the class gradient in such instability. However, we believe that the retreat from marriage has been overemphasized.

In this chapter we focus on a more causally "upstream" set of causes for class differences in family patterns. As we will show, more-advantaged youths begin engaging in intercourse slightly later and, as young adults, use birth control (contraception and abortion) more consistently. As a result, they are much less likely to become parents early, or to have unintended births at any age. While early births are not always unintended, and not all unintended pregnancies are early, the two phenomena are empirically linked: a national survey asking women about their childbearing between 1997 and 2002 found that 78 percent of births to women under age 20 resulted from unintended pregnancies, compared to 45 percent among women 20–24, and 24 percent among women 25–44 (Kissin et al. 2008). This is probably because few see the teen years as appropriate for childbearing, and because anyone who has a high propensity for unplanned pregnancies because of inconsistent contraceptive use will probably have an unplanned pregnancy shortly after the initiation of sexual activity. As Bongaarts (1978) has pointed out, sex and birth control are the proximate determinants of fertility. It follows that class differences affecting early fertility must operate through these proximate determinants. Once premarital sex is ubiquitous, unintended fertility is particularly likely to flow from lack of consistent use of birth control. Class differences in unintended fertility, then, are likely a result of class differences in birth control use.

Our focus here is on class differences, not race differences. Racial differences in family patterns are well documented in past research. To maintain the focus on class, in our analysis we combine all racial groups, statistically adjusting out of any class differences the amount that reflects the different racial composition of those in various class locations.

Our concept of class is gradational. We are interested in how the plethora of correlated measures of hierarchical position that go into what we typically mean by class or socioeconomic status—income, occupation, education, and so forth—affect behaviors that lead to early, unplanned births. Given this broad view, we use the terms "class" and "socioeconomic status" (hereafter "SES") interchangeably. We recognize that for some outcomes, predictive power is increased if discrete classes are posited (Weeden and Grusky 2005). Here, however, we utilize theories that suggest gradational processes. As we consider behavior that spans late childhood and early adulthood, both the class of one's family of origin and one's own emergent social class are relevant, although our analyses emphasize the former. Most of our own empirical analyses here use an individual's mother's education as the most readily available measure tapping class background, but we augment analyses with some other measures, and we review research using other measures as well.

Our goal is to document and suggest explanations for class differences in early and unplanned births. We combine a review of past research with a presentation of our own data analysis. The evidence from past analyses and our own analysis shows that, although their fertility goals early in life are the same as those of their more-privileged counterparts, individuals from lower-class backgrounds start having intercourse at a slightly earlier age, use contraception substantially less in their teens and early adulthood, have more teen births, abort less when they have a pregnancy, and are more likely to have unintended pregnancies. After presenting the evidence, we review three theoretical perspectives on what it is about class that leads to the behaviors proximate to early, unplanned pregnancies. The perspectives focus on (1) opportunity costs, (2) social roles, and (3) efficacy and self-regulation. We note that current evidence gives us little ability to adjudicate between these perspectives and recommend that future research focus on such adjudication.

## DATA AND METHODS

In addition to reviewing others' evidence, we provide some illustrative analyses of class differences in the behaviors leading up to early and unintended births. Drawing on three data sets, we present the analyses in a common format. We present class differences in various dependent variables by showing predicted scores for individuals whose mothers have one of three education levels: less than high school, high school, or a four-year college degree. (In one case, when reporting premarital conceptions from the Current Population Survey (CPS), a large national probability sample, we use the respondents' own education because the data do not include parental education.) In each case, the predicted scores for each education level come from a regression that uses education along with controls for race (and sometimes other variables), with controls set at their mean value.[1]

Interactions by race are common in the literature. Although we do not report the results below, we have determined that, for each of the predicted values we present, our basic conclusions about an educational gradient hold for both blacks and whites (although the magnitude of the association may differ somewhat). Thus the reader can be confident that, at least in direction, any class difference we talk about can be found in both the black and the white population (the size of the sample for other groups would not sustain separate analysis). Often, though, there are race differences in levels within class, even when there are no differences in direction in the effects of class by race. These race differences in levels are beyond our topical scope here.

### Add Health Data

We use data from the first, second, and third waves of the National Survey of Adolescent Health (Add Health), a nationally representative longitudinal survey of adolescents in grades seven to twelve at the time of the initial interview (Bearman, Jones, and Udry 2004; Chantala 2006).[2] The sample is school-based: 134 public, private, and parochial schools were selected and a sample of 27,000 adolescents was selected from these schools for extensive in-home interviews. Approximately 21,000 of these students completed the in-home interviews. Their parents were also interviewed at home. To collect sensitive information more accurately, students used an audio-computer-assisted self-interview device (audio-CASI) for several sections of the interview. The initial (Wave I) interviews were collected during the 1994–95 academic year and the second interviews (Wave II, the first follow-up) were collected about a year later. The third wave of interviews (Wave III, the second follow-up) was conducted in 2001–02.

In this analysis, all explanatory variables except the respondent's age and college status are measured at the initial interview (Wave I, average age about 14.5). Age at first sexual intercourse is measured in whichever interview the respondent first reports having had sexual intercourse (if ever—about 12 percent of respondents were still virgins in Wave III). Sexual activity and contraception use are measured in both the Wave II and Wave III interviews (at average ages of approximately 16 at Wave II and 21.5 at Wave III), and all other outcomes are measured at Wave III, when the respondents provide a full history of their lifetime sexual and romantic relationships, pregnancies, and births. Although we analyze age of first sex for both males and females (using sex-specific models), we restrict analyses of contraception, pregnancy, and abortion to women because men may not always know when their partners are using contraception (particularly hormonal contraception) and may not know about pregnancies with casual partners and/or pregnancies that ended in abortion.

We describe the measures below:[3]

*Mother's education:* This is our key independent variable. We have collapsed the more detailed categories of the original variable to classify mothers of respondents as having not completed high school, having completed high school or some college, or being college graduates. Their education is taken from the parent home interview (usually with the mother) at Wave I, and if not available there, it is taken from the respondent's report at Wave I.

*Enrolled in or graduated from college:* An alternative independent variable indicating respondents' own prospective class is whether, at Wave III, when respondents averaged about 21.5 years of age, they were either still enrolled in college or had graduated, as opposed to having never enrolled or quit. This was measured based on questions in Wave III about current enrollment and educational attainment. These results are presented in Appendix Table 1.A.2.

*High school grade-point average:* Another alternative independent variable indicating prospective class is the youth's self-reported grade-point average at Wave I (age about 14.5). These results are presented in Appendix Table 1.A.1.

We have five key dependent variables regarding sex, contraception, and early childbearing:

*Age at first intercourse:* Because individuals are likely to be most accurate in recalling the timing of recent events, we measure age at first intercourse at whichever interview the respondent first reports having had sexual intercourse. By Wave III, at age averaging about 21.5, about 88 percent of respondents have had sexual intercourse.

*Sexual activity and contraceptive consistency:* In Wave II and Wave III, we classify respondents as: sexually inactive for the past twelve months (sexually inactive includes virgins); sexually active and "always" using contraception; or sexually active and using contraception less consistently (or never). We use this three-category classification as a dependent variable in our regression models. We use regression-predicted means for these categories to calculate the proportion that is sexually active, and the proportion of the sexually active not always contracepting. We restrict this analysis to women.

*Abortion:* For women who have been pregnant, this indicates whether the respondent has ever had an abortion (rather than having the pregnancy end in birth or miscarriage). In analysis not shown, we also estimate the probability that a pregnancy ended in abortion (rather than in birth or miscarriage). We conduct this analysis for all pregnancies and, in results not shown, for unintended pregnancies. Both measures include any pregnancies before Wave III. We restrict this analysis to women.

*Teen birth:* This indicates whether the respondent gave birth to at least one child before age 20. It is taken from reports at all waves. We restrict this analysis to women.

Additional variables entered as controls:

*Race:* All models control for race. Racial groups are non-Hispanic white, non-Hispanic black, Hispanic, and other. Race is reported by the respondent and is also evaluated independently by the interviewer (relying on physical indications). We use primarily the respondent's self-report of her or his race, but when it is missing, we use the interviewer's report.

*Age:* Age is measured in years and is the respondent's age on the day of the Wave III interview.

*Mother's age at respondent's birth:* We control for the mother's age when she gave birth to the respondent. Mother's age at her first birth (i.e., if the respondent has older siblings) is not known.

*Intact family:* This measure indicates whether the respondent was living with both biological parents, or with original adoptive parents, at the first interview (at average age about 14.5). Parents are considered original adoptive parents if the respondent was adopted by a two-parent family by age 1.

Individual-level models are estimated using weighted data and adjusting for the stratification and clustered sampling design; not making these adjustments could bias the standard errors (Chantala 2006). Whether a pregnancy ended in abortion, which is measured at the pregnancy level, is clustered by respondent (correcting for the nonindependence of observations). Models estimated with unweighted data and without clustering are also consistent with the models that use weighted data and clusters.

To improve our ability to assess causal effects, all time-varying independent variables (except age) are lagged to the previous wave to ensure that predictive variables are measured temporally prior to outcome variables. However, when the outcome variable is a measure of lifetime occurrence, this temporal ordering is not ensured. That is, for cumulative occurrence variables, we use Wave I for controls, but in some cases, the event had happened before Wave I. This is a possibility for the independent variables measuring age at first intercourse, whether pregnancy ended in abortion, and whether the respondent ever had a teenage birth. About 40 percent of respondents (male and female combined) have had sexual intercourse by Wave I, but only about 20 percent of those who had had sex at least once had been pregnant by Wave I.

Age at first sexual intercourse is a metric variable, so we use a linear regression model when analyzing this outcome. We use multinomial logistic regression for the measure of sexual activity and contraceptive consistency at average ages 16 and 21.5. All other outcomes are analyzed using (binary) logistic regression models. All models include our independent variable of interest, mother's education, as well as controls for the respondent's race and age, the mother's age when the respondent was born, and whether the respondent was living in an intact two-parent family at the first interview. In the model predicting whether a pregnancy ended in abortion, we also include the respondent's age-squared. The values in Table 1.1 are predicted values from these regressions, where we show predictions for each category of the mother's education, setting all controls at their means. The values in Appendix Table 1.A.1 and Appendix Table 1.A.2 are also predicted values from regression models: Table 1.A.1 shows predicted values by respondent's grade-point average, setting all controls (including mother's education) at their means, and Table 1.A.2 shows predicted values by respondent's college graduation/enrollment status, setting all controls (including mother's education and respondent's adolescent grade-point average) at their means.

*Current Population Survey—Fertility Supplements*

To explore educational differences in premarital conceptions for past cohorts, we use data from pooled 1980, 1985, 1990, and 1995 June fertility and marriage histories in the Current Population Survey. We limit our analysis to white (N = 137,850) and black (N = 18,079) female respondents.

Female respondents were asked to give marital histories, including the dates (month and year) of any marriage and, when applicable, the dates each marriage dissolved (whether through divorce, separation, or death). They were later asked to give the date (month and year) of birth of every biological child up to five children. We considered a conception to have been before a woman's first marriage if the marriage was less than seven months before the birth. It is important to note that we have no information on pregnancies that ended in miscarriage or abortion; premarital conceptions, therefore, are those taken to term only. We note, however, that for most of the earlier cohorts in the analysis, abortion was neither legal nor widely available.

We measure cohort by year of the woman's birth. In our analysis, cohort is represented by a series of dummy variables (born before 1925; born in 1925–29; born in 1930–34; and so on through those born in 1960–64).

The CPS does not ask respondents about their mother's educational attainment. We use the woman's own education and treat it as the measure of social class available as a predictor of whether she has a premarital conception. A limitation of our analysis is that education is assessed at the time of the survey, while the first birth or marriage that is reported on may have occurred decades before the survey. Thus education may not be exogenous to conceptions; a pregnancy or birth may have led women to drop out of school.[4] We present the analysis despite acknowledging this serious limitation because it is the only source we know of that allows analysis of class disparities in premarital conceptions for pre–baby boom cohorts. Education is measured in years, which we convert into three categories: less than high school (<12); high school graduate (12–15); or college graduate (16 or more).

To assess the effects of education and cohort on the incidence of premarital conception, we estimated continuous-time hazard models predicting the competing risks of having a first conception versus a first marriage. The risk set was women who had not been married and not had a conception that was taken to term. We model age-specific effects using a flexible piecewise linear spline (Wu 1996) with knots at ages 18, 21, and 25. The models contain dummy variables for race, cohort, and education. Regressions were unweighted. Setting the race dummy at its mean, we then calculated and report predicted values by combination of cohort and education.

### National Longitudinal Survey of Youth 1979 (NSLY79)

To examine differences by class background (as assessed by respondents' mothers' education) in how many unintended pregnancies women have, we use the non-Hispanic female sample from the NLSY79, a U.S. national probability sample of individuals age 14–21 in 1979, using waves through 2002.

NLSY79 includes information about whether each pregnancy leading to a birth was intended or unintended. After a birth, women were first asked whether they were using contraception at the time they became pregnant, and if not, whether it was because they wanted to become pregnant. They were then asked: "Just before you became pregnant the (first, second, third, etc.) time, did you want to become pregnant when you did?" Births are intended if a woman reported not using contraception because she wanted to get pregnant or said, irrespective of contraceptive use, that she wanted to get pregnant or felt indifferent about getting pregnant at that time. Births are unintended if a woman said she did not want a(nother) baby at the time she got pregnant, but did want a(nother) baby at some time in the future, or if she said she never wanted a(nother) baby. We include all births women reported by the 2002 wave, when sample members were 37–44 years of age and thus had probably completed most of their childbearing.

Our analysis here is descriptive, not based on a regression model. (For a hazard model–based treatment of women's educational differences in unintended and intended pregnancies, see Musick et al. 2009.) Our analyses employ sample weights to account for oversampling of African Americans. We show the percentage of births that resulted from intended and unintended pregnancies for women whose mothers had various levels of education. We also compare early fertility aspirations for women whose mothers had different educational levels.

Our key independent variable, the respondent's mother's education, was reported by the respondent in the first wave in 1979. Mothers' education was reported in years, which we categorized into three groups: less than 12, 12–15, and 16 or more. For normative schooling transitions, we have labeled these as less than high school, high school graduate (including some college), and college graduate.

We also use the NLSY to examine class differences (measured by mother's education) in respondents' belief in their own self-efficacy. The 1979 interview includes an abbreviated (four-item) version of the Rotter Locus of Control Scale. These results are discussed but not shown.

CLASS DIFFERENCES IN BEHAVIOR LEADING TO
EARLY, UNINTENDED BIRTHS

*Age at First Intercourse*

Absent artificial insemination or divine intervention, a pregnancy requires intercourse. Thus those who begin sex earlier might have earlier births. If there are class differences in age at first intercourse, this might explain some of the class difference among young women in whether they have early pregnancies.

Most studies show that kids from higher-SES backgrounds are older when they have intercourse for the first time. Our analysis using Add Health data confirms this, but shows that the differences are quite small. Of the 88 percent who had ever had sexual intercourse by 2001, when the respondents averaged about 21.5 year of age, young men whose mothers had less than a high school education started at age 15.9, those whose moms had completed high school started at 16.2, and sons of college graduates started at 16.5 (results not shown). The analogous ages for women, shown in Table 1.1, are 16.4, 16.3, and 16.9, so daughters of mothers who did not complete high school or only completed high school are very close, while those with college-educated mothers start slightly more than a half year later. (These are means that have been regression-adjusted for race, mother's age at respondent's birth, and age of respondent in 2001 at Wave III.) Table 1.1 also shows that at Wave II, when respondents were about 16, those whose mothers graduated from college were less likely to have been sexually active in the previous twelve months: 23 percent of them versus over 30 percent of lower-SES girls.

We also tabulated how regression-adjusted mean ages of first intercourse differ by the youth's grade-point average at Wave I (results for girls are available in Appendix Table 1.A.1; results for boys are not shown). There was a monotonic relationship, with boys in the bottom third starting at 15.9, those in the middle third at 16.1, and those in the top third at 16.7; the analogous ages were 16.1, 16.3, and 16.8 for girls. We also examined differences between those who were and were not either enrolled in or graduated from college by 2001, when they averaged about 21.5 years of age. For both sexes, those not graduated or still enrolled by Wave III had started sex at about age 16 (16.1 for boys and 16.2 for girls), compared to close to 17 for those who were enrolled or graduated (16.7 for boys and 17.0 for girls). (Results nor shown.)

Past research has also found various measures of class background to affect age of first intercourse. Using earlier data from the 1970s, Jessor et al. (1983) showed that youth with lower expectations for academic achievement had sex earlier. Using Waves I and II of Add Health, Harris et al. (2002) show

TABLE I.I
*Predicted averages or percentages for selected behaviors related to early or
unintended childbearing, by mother's education*[*]

| Response of subjects | Respondent's mother's education | | |
| --- | --- | --- | --- |
| | Less than high school | High school graduate or some college | College graduate or higher |
| **At average age ~16 (Wave II)** | | | |
| % sexually active in past 12 months | 31.5 | 30.5 | 23.3 |
| % sexually active and not always using contraception | 16.9 | 16.2 | 13.6 |
| % not always using contraception among those sexually active | 54.5 | 53.5 | 58.3 |
| **At average age ~21.5 (Wave III)** | | | |
| % sexually active in the past 12 months | 79.7 | 83.0 | 78.0 |
| % sexually active and not always using contraception | 45.7 | 45.0 | 35.7 |
| % not always using contraception among those sexually active | 57.7 | 54.6 | 46.2 |
| **Measures of cumulative experience by average age ~21.5 (Wave III)** | | | |
| Average age at first intercourse (for the experienced) | 16.4 | 16.3 | 16.9 |
| % ever pregnant | 41.1 | 39.8 | 21.3 |
| % who had an abortion of those ever pregnant | 12.9 | 21.0 | 34.5 |
| % who had a teen birth | 15.9 | 14.5 | 6.1 |

SOURCE: National Longitudinal Study of Adolescent Health, Waves I, II, and III, 1996–2002.
[*]Predicted values from regression that also includes race, respondent's age, mother's age at respondent's birth, and whether respondent lived with both biological or original adoptive parents at age 14.5.

that, the higher the educational attainment of both fathers and mothers, the lower the likelihood that youth have had sex. (For other consistent findings on parental education, see Brewster et al. 1993; Manlove et al. 2009; and Miller and Sneesby 1988.) Looking at younger kids, Laflin et al. (2008) found that middle school kids whose mothers have higher education, and who themselves have higher grades or aspirations to go to college are less likely to have had sex. Longmore et al. (2001) also found that a higher level of educational attainment by the mother reduced the chances of middle school sex. By contrast, Wu and Martin (2009) find no effect of mother's education on hazard of sexual initiation after controlling for mother's age at first birth.[5]

Youth doing better in school and aspiring to more education, harbingers of a higher future class location, usually start intercourse later. Wu and Martin (2009) find that a test of cognitive skills predicted later initiation. Halpern et al. (2000) find a curvilinear relationship among high schoolers. Very low scoring youth are less apt to initiate sex, but from below the middle of the distribution upward, higher scores predict starting later. Using another data set, Halpern et al. (2000) found that youth with higher test scores were not only less likely to have intercourse, but also less likely to engage in holding hands or kissing, behaviors that pose little risk. They also find that youth with higher grade-point averages and who perceive a higher chance of going to college are less likely to have had intercourse. Deptula et al. (2006) found that higher test scores increased the perceived costs of sex among adolescents, and those who perceived more costs were less likely to begin having sex, consistent with the notion of opportunity costs.

While lower-SES youth start sex earlier in the life cycle, they do not have sex earlier within a partnership. Using the Add Health data on all relationships between Waves I and III (these relationships were happening between ages 14 and 21), we found no effect of mothers' education on whether either males or females had sexual intercourse within one week of meeting their partners. Similarly, there was no effect of mother's education on having sex within two weeks or four weeks. On the other hand, for both males and females, those in the top third of the high school grade-point average distribution at Wave I were less likely to move to sex quickly in a relationship (results not shown).[6]

In summary, whether we use measures of class background or the youth's own prospective educational attainment, it appears that the more privileged start having intercourse—and engaging in other sexual behavior—later in the life cycle. However, the differences in age at first intercourse between the child of a high school dropout and a college graduate are only about half a year, and thus should not be exaggerated.

*Birth Control: Contraception and Abortion*

Earlier sex would not necessarily lead to many pregnancies if contraception were rigorous. In Table 1.1 we also examine contraceptive use. Although fewer of those with a mother with a college degree were sexually active at Wave II when they were about 16, among those who were, those with college-educated moms were slightly more likely to fail to use contraception always (58 percent versus 54–55 percent of lower-SES girls, Table 1.1). On the other hand, when we look at whether the respondents used contraception the *first* time they ever had intercourse (using data all the way to Wave III for those who started later), we find that daughters of better-educated mothers were slightly more likely to use contraception (91 percent of daughters of college graduates compared to 86–87 percent in the other two groups; results not shown). (Exactly the same figures are found for contraception at young men's first sex; results not shown.)

At Wave III, when women averaged 21.5 years of age, over three-quarters of all three SES groups were sexually active in the previous year. At this age, although there was little class difference in sexual activity, there was a strong class gradient on contraceptive use, as shown in Table 1.1. Among the sexually active women whose mothers had less than a high school education, 58 percent did not always use contraception, compared to 55 percent of those whose moms finished high school, and 46 percent of those whose mothers were college graduates.

Among the sexually active at Wave II (at about 21.5 years of age), young women who had had a higher high school grade-point average also were more likely to use contraception always, as were those enrolled in or graduated from college at Wave III (60 percent of the latter, as opposed to 40 percent of those not enrolled or graduated). (These results are shown in Appendix Table 1.A.2, and are from predicted values from regressions analogous to those shown in Table 1.1, except that they include controls for the respondent's grade-point average and for mother's education, or for college expectations, grade-point average, and mother's education.)

Past evidence generally supports the idea that, among those who are sexually active, more-privileged youth use contraception more consistently Holmbeck et al. (1994) show that high school students with higher test scores had more knowledge of contraception and were more likely to use it when they first engaged in sex. Brewster et al. (1993) found that girls who had not been held back a grade were more likely to use contraception during their first sexual encounter. Examining males the year after they finished high school, Bailey et al. (2008) found that those who went to college were more apt to use condoms consistently, but that the protective effect of college attendance can be accounted for by high school grade-point average and sexual risk behavior during high school. However, in an analysis of 15–29-year-old sexually active males, Manlove et al. (2008) found no effect of their parents' education on condom use.

Given these SES differences in contraceptive use, it is not surprising that Table 1.1 shows a steep class gradient in whether respondents had ever been pregnant by Wave III when they were about 21.5 years of age: 40–41 percent of women whose mothers did not have a college degree, but only 21 percent of those whose mothers had a college degree.

Once a pregnancy has occurred, a class gradient appears in whether young women got an abortion, as we show in Table 1.1. Of those who had ever been pregnant, the proportion who had ever had an abortion was 13 percent among those whose mothers did not finish high school, 21 percent among those whose mothers had only a high school education or some college, and 35 percent among those whose mothers went to college.[7] We know, however, by comparing the number of abortions that providers say they perform in a year in the United States with the number reported in surveys, that abortions are underreported (Cooksey 1990). If abortions were more underreported by lower-SES women, then the differences here may exaggerate the reality. However, the limited evidence we have does not show monotonic differences by disadvantage. One study compared the socio-demographic characteristics of those reporting abortions in the 2002 National Survey of Family Growth with characteristics from a nationally representative Guttmacher Institute survey of women who had abortions in 2000–01, surveyed through providers (Jones and Kost 2007). The comparison suggested that women with household incomes below the poverty line (who are much more likely to come from low-SES families) reported 44 percent of their abortions; those with incomes 100–199 percent of the poverty line reported 39 percent; and those with incomes twice the poverty line reported 56 percent of theirs. The relationship with women's own education was also nonmonotonic. Those with less than twelve years of schooling reported 57 percent of their abortions; those with just high school 43 percent; those with some college 32 percent; and those with college degrees 54 percent of their abortions. Thus, while underreporting is very serious, there does not appear to be a clear monotonic tendency for either the more- or less-privileged to underreport more.

Some past research has used survey responses regarding abortion, despite the limitations discussed above. This research has shown that higher-SES women report a higher propensity to abort a pregnancy if conception occurs. Brazzell and Acock (1988) show that more career-oriented sexually active adolescent women are more likely to say that if they got pregnant they would have an abortion. Cooksey (1990) shows that, in the 1980s, among young women who became pregnant outside marriage, those whose parents had more education were more likely to have an abortion.

*Having an Early (Teen) Birth*

Our analysis in Table 1.1 shows that the education level of a young woman's mother influences whether she has a teen birth (that is, a birth before age 20). After adjusting for control variables, we found that 16 percent of women whose mothers lacked a high school degree had a teen birth, 14 percent of those whose mothers completed high school, and only 6 percent of those with college-graduate moms. This gradient probably results from the combined effects of when sex is started, how consistently contraception is used, and the propensity to abort if a pregnancy occurs, each of which we have detailed above. Though not shown in the table, differences by women's own college status are also dramatic; 16.4 percent of those not enrolled in or graduated from college at Wave III (average age 21.5) had had a teen birth, but only 3.8 percent of those enrolled or graduated by Wave III. Here the early births may be either cause or consequence of college attendance and completion.[8] (See also Philip Morgan's chapter in this volume on SES differences in age at first birth.)

FERTILITY ASPIRATIONS AND COMPLETED FERTILITY

To this point we have presented evidence that higher-SES kids start sex later, are more likely to use contraception at first sex and in early adulthood, and are more likely to have an abortion if pregnant. If this were all the information we had, we might conclude that those from lower-SES backgrounds simply want more children. Perhaps women destined to work in undesirable jobs reorient their aspirations to motherhood and simply want more children—even though they are likely to be partnered with poorer men and thus will be less able to "afford" children. If that were the case, then the story might be one of class differences in aspirations for early fertility, not class differences in unintended fertility. Interestingly, the data do not support this conclusion. In the NLSY79, in the first wave, in 1979, when women were 14–21 years of age, they were asked how many children they wanted to have in their lives. The median desired by women in each education group was two children. Indeed, this was true among whites, blacks, and Latinas as well. (Results not graphed; from our calculations from the NLSY79; see also Morgan's chapter here on this theme.)

As of the mid-1990s, age-specific fertility rates were such that a woman with a high school degree or less could be expected to have 2.1 children in her life, while college graduates would have 1.6 (Yang and Morgan 2003). Thus, despite desiring the same number of children, women who received more education had lower fertility, by about half a child. In fact, as Morgan (this volume) shows, less-educated women are at high risk of having more children than they wanted, while college graduates are at serious risk of having fewer than they said they wanted. Whether the two groups change their aspirations over time, or simply face situations that, in opposite ways, make meeting their aspirations difficult, is not well understood. What is clear, as we discuss below, is that having more children than they set out to among women in lower-class locations results from more unintended pregnancies, not more intended pregnancies.

UNINTENDED PREGNANCIES

Our calculations from the NLSY (not shown) indicate that women of different class backgrounds (as measured by their mothers' education) do not differ in their total number of intended births—they average 1.2 whether their mothers were high school dropouts, high school graduates, or college graduates. It is unintended births that are the entire source of the fertility difference by education; those whose mothers did not complete high school had .8 unintended births on average, while college graduates averaged only .3 such unintended births. Figure 1.1 shows the proportion of women's births that were unintended by their mother's education. Among those whose mothers had less than a high school degree, 39 percent of their pregnancies were unintended; 29 percent were unintended for those whose mothers had a high school degree; and only 21 percent were unintended for those whose mothers had a college degree. Using this same data set, and a competing hazard with multiple controls, Musick et al. (2009) use predicted education (based on a woman's parents' education and income as reported in 1979, as well as her 1980 cognitive test score (the Armed Forces Qualifying Test, her educational aspirations, and her education to date) as a determinant of the competing hazards of unintended and intended births. For whites, they find that (predicted) education lowers the risk of unintended births but increases the risk of intended births. For blacks, education lowers both risks, but does so much more strongly for unintended births. Although they find (predicted) education to lower unintended births, they do not find wages to lower unintended (or intended) fertility. Thus, overall, the evidence suggests the women's class background as well as their own education reduces unintended childbearing. Most studies of unintended pregnancy focus on women. However, Kathryn Edin, Timothy Nelson, and Joanna Reed, in this volume, provide rich qualitative data from interviews of low-income fathers, showing that few of these low-SES men report explicitly planned pregnancies.

There is reason to believe that class differences in unintended pregnancies are longstanding. Decades-old qualitative research by Rainwater (1960) found many working-class and poor couples with more children than they wanted. Operating in an era before the birth control pill, and before steril-

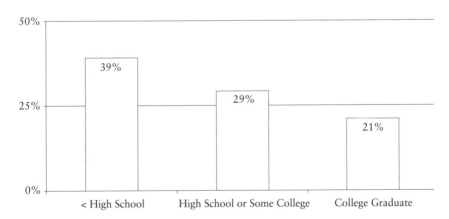

*Figure 1.1.* Percentage of women's births resulting from unintended pregnancy, by mother's education. Source: National Longitudinal Survey of Youth 1979, 1979–2002 waves. Includes all births by 2002, when respondents were 37 to 44 years old.

ization became common, the main means of birth control were condoms and
the diaphragm. Most people in all classes knew about the available methods,
and money to buy them was not mentioned as the limitation. Nor did opportunity costs seem to be a factor, since few women thought of employment
as an option unless income was desperately needed. Despite knowledge of
contraceptive methods, money to buy them, and the seeming irrelevance
of opportunity costs, education was nonetheless related to consistency in the
use of contraceptives among these married working-class couples.

Rainwater's research pertained to marital conceptions, but there is also
evidence of a longstanding class gradient on premarital conceptions. Given
the strong norms against premarital sex in decades past, and the fact that
premarital pregnancies were seen as a crisis necessitating so-called shotgun
marriages, we can safely assume that most premarital pregnancies in decades
past were unintended. It is this assumption that makes premarital pregnancies interesting for our purposes here; we can examine the class gradient on
premarital conceptions as indirect evidence of a gradient on premarital unintended pregnancies. In Figure 1.2 we array women by the cohort in which
they were born, going back to those born before 1925. The figure shows the
proportion in each cohort who had a premarital pregnancy taken to term,
separately by the women's educational levels. The premarital pregnancies
we record here include those that led to nonmarital births, as well as those

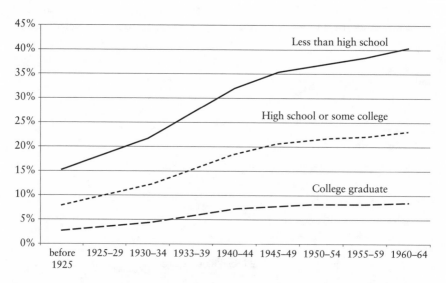

*Figure 1.2.*    Percentage of women who had a premarital conception before age 25
(and took it to term), by education and cohort. Source: CPS June Fertility Supplement, 1980, 1985, 1990, 1995. Predicted values from a competing model that
includes race and cohort.

that led to shotgun weddings (Frank Furstenberg, in this volume, discusses historical changes in whether premarital pregnancies led to marriage). Here, unlike in the analyses above, we use women's own education rather than that of their mothers to classify respondents; this is because the CPS Fertility Supplement data set used does not have information on the family of origin of the respondent. In fact, women's education is being reported at the time of the survey, while the premarital pregnancies may have occurred years before the survey. Thus, a causal interpretation that the woman's education affected her sexual or contraceptive behavior must be made with caution; it is possible that the link between education and premarital conception results from early births that interrupted women's education, rather than from women on a trajectory to attain less education being more likely to have a premarital conception. As Figure 1.2 shows, in every cohort, less-educated women were more likely to have premarital conceptions.[9] This is at least suggestive evidence that the SES of one's family—usually a precursor to one's own education—has affected the tendency to have early, unintended births for many decades.

The consistent effect of education on premarital conceptions across cohorts is interesting, perhaps even surprising, given the diversity of norms among these different cohorts regarding premarital sexual activity, the availability of birth control and abortion, the relative wages of men and women, and expectations regarding of women's employment after child-bearing. This consistency of the relationship over time makes us doubt that opportunity costs related to women's wages are the main mechanism. The forgone opportunities of women's wages are relevant only in contexts where a woman will remain employed if she doesn't have a child, but will drop out or at least reduce her hours and thereby forgo earnings if she has a child. In such situations, the higher her earnings, the more she has to lose as the result of a pregnancy. This thesis seems irrelevant to the higher rate of nonmarital conceptions at lower educational levels among early cohorts, because, at least among whites, few women of any educational level planned employment after marriage, so having a child had little opportunity cost for their earnings. Class differences in self-regulation might better explain both whether couples had the self-discipline to abstain from sex in cohorts when strong norms advocated doing so, and whether they have the "planfulness" or foresight to contracept consistently in cohorts after the sexual revolution.

If opportunity cost *is* to explain educational differences in avoiding pregnancy in the early cohorts, we need a broader notion of the relevant opportunity costs. In the early cohorts, particularly among whites, premarital births that led to shotgun marriages often interrupted the man's education as well as the woman's. Thus, where the man was on a trajectory toward higher education, the interruption of his education had high opportunity costs for the family's future standard of living. Where the man was unlikely to get more education, an earlier-than-anticipated pregnancy and marriage had little opportunity cost in economic terms. Given marital homogamy, it was higher SES-background women and their usually higher SES-background partners who faced these higher opportunity costs in the potential reduction of men's lifetime earning power if an early pregnancy caused him to stop his education in order to start supporting the family. This potential outcome may have contributed to the scarcity of premarital conceptions among the highly educated in earlier cohorts, as those with more to lose avoided pregnancies by either abstaining from sex or using birth control.

WHAT'S BEHIND THE CLASS DIFFERENCES:
THREE THEORETICAL VIEWS TO GUIDE FUTURE RESEARCH

Why would the class background or prospective class location of a youth or young adult affect the outcomes that lead to early, unintended births? We consider three theoretical views that could explain the differences we have reviewed. It is important to bear in mind that they are not mutually exclusive. Moreover, unfortunately, we see only limited evidence from research to date that would allow us to adjudicate between them.

### Opportunity Costs

In economists' rational-choice view, decisions are made according to costs and benefits. One has a child only when the expected (lifetime) benefits of having a child now with this partner minus the costs of birth control exceed the costs of childbearing (Hotz et al. 1997). In addition to the out-of-pocket costs of clothing, sheltering, and educating the child, the costs of childbearing include opportunity costs—earnings forgone while a parent, usually the mother, takes care of the child. These factors are the focus of recent economic theorizing on fertility. Consider a situation where the woman would stay home (or cut back to fewer hours of employment) for some period if she were to have a child. In that situation, the more her potential hourly earnings, the more money she (and her family) will forgo if she has a child. In this view, less-educated women have more children because they have less to lose (in forgone earnings) by taking time away from paid work for childbearing. At first glance, *unintended* pregnancy seems contrary to the rational-actor assumptions of the theory. But advocates of the opportunity cost theory do not see an inconsistency.[10] They point out that there are economic costs and noneconomic costs (e.g., "hassles" or inconvenience) of birth control. Thus we can imagine a situation in which, if contraception were costless, one would contracept and avoid pregnancy; but the opportunity costs of having a child are small enough relative to the costs of contraception that a "rational actor" decides not to use contraception, despite having a mild preference for not getting pregnant.[11]

### Social Roles

Sociologists often claim that the role makes the person. Research supporting this theory, sometimes called the "social structure and personality" view, has shown, for example, that occupations requiring complex cognitive manipulations make their incumbents smarter over time (Kohn and Schooler 1983). Applying this perspective to early childbearing, the hypothesis is that engagement in social roles that discourage early childbearing—such as school enrollment or having a job—encourages the prevention of pregnancy. This view, like the opportunity cost view, predicts that women in school or in a higher-paying job will use birth control more consistently, but for a different reason. In the opportunity cost view, those in school avoid a birth more assiduously simply because their education has increased opportunity costs. The "social roles" view sees roles as changing behavior through processes other than economic incentives. The way in which "the role makes the person" is that one develops an identity consistent with being in the role (e.g., "I am a student," "I'm a biologist," or "I have a job"), confronts expectations associated with the role (e.g., "I'm supposed to focus on school and get a degree in four years" or "I'm supposed to go to school, party, and have fun now—not have kids"), and forms network connections to others in the role who expect and encourage one to follow its expected trajectory. More generally, the view posits that being in certain roles encourages individuals to avoid pregnancy and giving birth if becoming a parent is in tension with the expectations of the role. Role expectations thus are one way that normative life-course sequences are encouraged.

Consistent with this view, women who are enrolled in high school or college are much less likely to get pregnant (Glick et al. 2006; Skirbekk et al. 2004; Upchurch et al. 2002; Blossfeld and Huinink 1991). Similarly, being employed reduces the odds of giving birth (Budig 2003). While the social expectations associated with "student" and "career" have the upside of discouraging unintended pregnancies, they also lead many upper-middle-class women to have fewer children than they initially said they wanted. This is one illustration of what gender and work/family scholars have long pointed out—that many jobs have expectations that implicitly assume a worker with no responsibilities for childbearing. Of course, being in the "role" of student and employed worker also shifts opportunity costs; thus we need clever research designs that will show us whether it is the social expectations and meanings of the role, or the economic incentives, or both, that lead these roles to affect behaviors regarding birth control.

*Efficacy and Self-Regulation*

Individuals differ in the extent to which they exhibit the follow-through needed for consistent contraception. For example, to use the birth control pill as prescribed, one must visit a doctor or clinic for a prescription, buy the pills, remember to take them on all appropriate days, and make an appointment for the next medical visit before running out of pills. This sort of follow-through requires a belief that one can control events through one's own actions. It also requires the self-regulation to make oneself follow through even when it is inconvenient.

General measures of a sense of personal control have been found to predict abstaining from sex or using condoms when having sex, especially among girls (Pearson 2006). Measures of belief in one's own efficacy specific to abstinence or contraception also predict either abstaining from sex or using contraception, rather than having unprotected sex (Pearson 2006; Longmore et al. 2003).

Class differences in efficacy may cause differences in unintended pregnancy rates, even if the less-advantaged, like their more-advantaged counterparts, do not want to get pregnant at an early age. While there is no direct evidence we know of on whether the class link to having sex without contraception is mediated by self-efficacy,[12] there is evidence that low-SES individuals have relatively low self-efficacy, the belief that one has power to affect things in one's own life (Gecas 1989; Mirowsky and Ross 2007; Boardman and Robert 2000).[13] Experiencing a lifetime of adverse events that one has limited power to change is likely to lead to a lower sense of control in the world. A low sense of efficacy may be present even in situations where one does have the ability to change the outcome. In such cases the sense of low self-efficacy itself has a causal effect.

In order to use contraception consistently one also needs to self-regulate—to discipline oneself to engage in behavior that is unpleasant or inconvenient in the present but pays off later. Effective contraception requires consistent actions that are not gratifying at the time (e.g., making appointments, visiting doctors and pharmacies, taking pills, or putting on condoms). Individual roots and consequences of self-regulation have been explored by psychologists (Baumeister and Vohs 2004), and consequences of a similar concept called "planful competence" is explored by the sociologist John Clausen (1991). What we lack is a sociological account of the social roots of self-regulation. We hypothesize that the social class of one's family of origin, as well as one's own prospective social class, may affect one's ability to self-regulate. One mechanism may be class differences in whether the parenting style is "concerted cultivation" (Annette Lareau and Amanda Cox in this volume; Lareau 2003). Concerted cultivation may include modeling self-regulation, explaining the importance of it, and serving as an external regulator until self-regulation is sufficiently developed. Although Lareau and Cox do not discuss its effects on contraception, it is a plausible extension of their perspective.

CONCLUSION

Combining our own analyses and our review of the literature, we have shown that social class background, as measured by one's mother's education, has a powerful effect on a multitude of behaviors that lead up to early and unintended births. Other measures that are harbingers in youth of one's future class location, such as grade-point average or enrollment in college, have similar effects.

Women and men whose mothers have more education initiate sexual intercourse slightly later than those whose mothers have less education. When young people have sex in high school, the evidence is mixed on whether those in higher versus lower SES groups are more or less likely to use contraception. But by early adulthood, when most individuals of all class backgrounds are sexually active, women whose mothers had more education are much more likely to use contraception regularly. If a pregnancy occurs, women with more-educated mothers are more likely to have an abortion. They are much less likely to have a teen birth. If we follow women through to middle age, when most of their childbearing is finished, we find that women with more-educated mothers, and women who themselves have more education, have slightly lower fertility and that a much lower proportion of their births are from unintended pregnancies. These differences do not come from wanting fewer children, as women of all backgrounds (defined by their mother's education) want a median of two children. Thus those from lower-SES backgrounds are more at risk of having pregnancies in situations and at times they themselves did not find appropriate.

The evidence of a class gradient on behavioral patterns affecting early and unintended childbearing is clear. What remains unclear are the mechanisms through which class background or location affects these behaviors. Little of the evidence allows us to adjudicate between the three theoretical perspectives we reviewed; this is an important task for future research. Below we review how our findings could be explained by each of the perspectives.

Those from higher-SES backgrounds have a probable trajectory toward education and good jobs. As such, they have more to lose than those for whom these outcomes seem unlikely with or without early childbearing. Thus much of the evidence we have reviewed is consistent with the idea that class affects birth control behavior through incentives, in this case taking the form of opportunity costs. However, it is clear that the relevant opportunity costs are not only women's earnings, which are often emphasized in recent literature. As we have shown, premarital conceptions were more common among less-educated women as far back as cohorts born in 1925, when few white women planned employment. In those early cohorts, if the opportunity cost of an unplanned nonmarital conception was greater, it would have been because more-educated women partnered with men with good chances for higher education, and these men's prospects would have been compromised by a shotgun marriage that interrupted their schooling and catapulted them into the role of breadwinner. Studying cohorts (from the NLSY) born from 1958 to 1965, Musick et al. (2009) find that, while women's predicted education strongly reduces unintended pregnancies, almost none of the reduction is mediated by wage rates, casting some doubt on the role of opportunity costs.

Individuals are unlikely to avoid early, unintended births without a belief in their own efficacy and substantial self-regulation. For some it takes self-regulation to follow the advice of parents and abstain from early sex. It takes considerable organization to use contraception consistently—often involving making and keeping appointments, filling prescriptions, and remembering to take pills. The fact that less-privileged women often report that they did not want to get pregnant when they did, and yet were not using contraception, suggests that the self-regulation and belief in one's self-efficacy that are needed to motivate the use of contraception have a class gradient. We reviewed literature showing a class gradient in self-efficacy beliefs, and that such beliefs affect young adults' use of contraception. Analogous evidence of a class gradient in self-regulation and its possible role in mediating class differences in consistent contraception is needed in future research. We can envision investigating the hypothesis that class differences in self-regulation explain class differences in contraception as an alternative to the view that emphasizes opportunity costs. Or, it could be incorporated into a broader rational choice view which recognizes that those who have better-developed self-regulation skills will find it less costly (in a noneconomic sense) to engage in the discipline of abstinence or contraception.

Young people and adults in social roles that are seen as inconsistent with pregnancy or birth may also be discouraged from engaging in early sex and be encouraged to use birth control if they are sexually active. Consistent with this, those women who are in school or hold jobs are less likely to get pregnant. While these findings are also consistent with the opportunity cost view, it is also likely that some of the class gradient results from the networks, norms, and identities associated with these roles, all of which discourage behavior that pulls young people into early, unintended childbearing. For example, full-time college students are likely to see having a child as simply "not what college students do"—inconsistent with either the studying or partying dimension of the expected role.

*Predicted averages or percentages for selected behaviors related to early or unintended childbearing, by female respondent's high school grade-point average*[*]

| Response of subjects | Respondent's grade-point average | | |
|---|---|---|---|
| | Lowest 33% | Middle 33% | Highest 33% |
| **At average age ~16 (Wave II)** | | | |
| % sexually active in past 12 months | 35.9 | 33.0 | 23.1 |
| % sexually active and not always using contraception | 22.6 | 18.9 | 10.5 |
| % not always using contraception among those sexually active | 62.7 | 57.0 | 45.6 |
| **At average age ~21.5 (Wave III)** | | | |
| % sexually active in the past 12 months | 84.7 | 83.9 | 78.4 |
| % sexually active and not always using contraception | 51.0 | 48.7 | 36.3 |
| % not always using contraception among those sexually active | 60.7 | 58.4 | 46.7 |
| **Measures of cumulative experience by average age ~21.5 (Wave III)** | | | |
| Average age at first intercourse (for the experienced) | 16.1 | 16.3 | 16.8 |
| % ever pregnant | 45.5 | 38.8 | 27.6 |
| % who had an abortion of those ever pregnant | 16.7 | 21.1 | 24.1 |
| % who had a teen birth | 17.4 | 12.7 | 8.6 |

SOURCE: National Longitudinal Study of Adolescent Health, Waves I, II, and III, 1996–2002.

[*]Predicted values from regression that also includes race, respondent's age, mother's age at respondent's birth, whether respondent lived with both biological or original adoptive parents at age 14.5, and mother's education.

*Predicted averages or percentages for selected behaviors related to early or unintended childbearing, by female respondent's college status*[*]

| Response of subjects | College status | |
|---|---|---|
| | Not enrolled and not graduated | Enrolled or graduated |
| **At average age ~21.5 (Wave III)** | | |
| % sexually active in the past 12 months | 83.7 | 77.3 |
| % sexually active and not always using contraception | 49.9 | 30.2 |
| % not always using contraception among those sexually active | 60.2 | 39.6 |

SOURCE: National Longitudinal Study of Adolescent Health, Waves I, II, and III, 199–2002.

[*]Predicted values from regression that also includes race, respondent's age, mother's age at respondent's birth, whether respondent lived with both biological or original adoptive parents at age 14.5, mother's education, and respondent's high school grade-point average. We do not show other outcomes that are in Table 1.A.2 in this table because many of those outcomes are already determined by the time women are enrolled in or have graduated from college.

REFERENCES

Akerlof, George A., Janet L. Yellen, and Michael L. Katz. 1996. "An Analysis of Out-of-Wedlock Childbearing in the United States." *Quarterly Journal of Economics* 111(2): 277–317.

Bailey, Jennifer A., Charles B. Fleming, Jessica N. Henson, Richard F. Catalano, and Kevin P. Haggerty. 2008. "Sexual Risk Behavior 6 Months Post–High School: Associations with College Attendance, Living with a Parent, and Prior Risk Behavior." *Journal of Adolescent Health* 42: 573–79.

Barber, Jennifer S., and Patricia L. East. 2009. "Home and Parenting Resources Available to Siblings Depending on Their Birth Intention Status." *Child Development* 80: 921–39.

Baumeister, Roy F., and Kathleen D. Vohs. 2004. *Handbook of Self-Regulation: Research, Theory, and Applications.* New York: Guilford.

Baydar, Nazli. 1995. "Consequences for Children of Their Birth Planning Status." *Family Planning Perspectives* 27(6): 228-34, 245.

Bearman, Peter, Jo Jones, and J. Richard Udry. 2004. *The National Longitudinal Study of Adolescent Health: Research Design.* Chapel Hill, NC: Carolina Population Center.

Blossfeld, Hans-Peter, and Johannes Huinink. 1991. "Human Capital Investments or Norms of Role Transition? How Women's Schooling and Career Affect the Process of Family Formation." *American Journal of Sociology* 97(1): 143–68.

Boardman, Jason D., and Stephanie A. Robert. 2000. "Neighborhood Socio-economic Status and Perceptions of Self-Efficacy." *Sociological Perspectives* 43(1): 117–36.

Bongaarts, John. 1978. "A Framework for Analysing the Proximate Determinants of Fertility." *Population and Development Review* 4: 105–32.

Brazzell, Jan F., and Alan C. Acock. 1988. "Influence of Attitudes, Significant Others, and Aspirations on How Adolescents Intend to Resolve a Premarital Pregnancy." *Journal of Marriage and the Family* 50(2): 413–25.

Brewster, Karin L., John O. G. Billy, and William R. Grady. 1993. "Social Context and Adolescent Behavior: The Impact of Community on the Transition to Sexual Activity." *Social Forces* 71(3): 713–40.

Brown, Sarah S., and Leon Eisenberg. 1995. *The Best Intentions: Unintended Pregnancy and the Well-Being of Children and Families.* Washington, DC: National Academy Press.

Budig, Michelle J. 2003. "Are Women's Employment and Fertility Histories Interdependent? An Examination of Causal Order Using Event History Analysis." *Social Science Research* 32(3): 376–401.

Chantala, Kim. 2006. "Guidelines for Analyzing Add Health Data." Vol. 2008. Chapel Hill, NC: Carolina Population Center.

Cherlin, Andrew. 2004. "The Deinstitutionalization of American Marriage." *Journal of Marriage and Family* 66: 848–61.

Clausen, John S. 1991. "Adolescent Competence and the Shaping of the Life Course." *American Journal of Sociology* 96(4): 805–42.

Cooksey, Elizabeth C. 1990. "Factors in the Resolution of Adolescent Premarital Pregnancies." *Demography* 27: 207–18.

Deptula, Daneen P., David B. Henry, Michael E. Schoeny, and John T. Slavick. 2006. "Adolescent Sexual Behavior and Attitudes: A Costs and Benefits Approach." *Journal of Adolescent Health* 38: 35–43.

Ellwood, David T., and Christopher Jencks. 2004. "The Spread of Single-Parent Families in the United States since 1960." In *The Future of the Family*, edited by Daniel P. Moynihan, Timothy M. Smeeding, and Lee Rainwater, pp. 25–65. New York: Russell Sage Foundation.

England, Paula, and Kathryn Edin. 2007. *Unmarried Couples with Children*. New York: Russell Sage Foundation.

England, Paula, Janet C. Gornick, and Emily Fitzgibbons Shafer. 2009. "How Women's Employment and the Gender Earnings Gap Vary by Education in Sixteen Countries." Unpublished Manuscript.

Gecas, Viktor. 1989. "The Social Psychology of Self-Efficacy." *Annual Review of Sociology* 15: 291–316.

Geronimus, Arline T., and Sanders Korenman. 1991. "The Socioeconomic Consequences of Teen Childbearing Reconsidered." *Quarterly Journal of Economics* 107: 1187–1214.

———. 1993. "The Socioeconomic Costs of Teenage Childbearing: Evidence and Interpretation." *Demography* 30: 281–90.

Glick, Jennifer E., Stacey D. Ruf, Michael J. White, and Frances Goldscheider. 2006. "Educational Engagement and Early Family Formation: Differences by Ethnicity and Generation." *Social Forces* 84(3): 1391–1412.

Halpern, Carolyn Tucker, Kara Joyner, J. Richard Udry, and Chirayath Suchindran. 2000. "Smart Teens Don't Have Sex (or Kiss Much Either)." *Journal of Adolescent Health* 26: 213–25.

Harris, Kathleen Mullan, Greg J. Duncan, and Johanne Boisjoly. 2002. "Evaluating the Role of 'Nothing to Lose' Attitudes on Risky Behavior in Adolescence." *Social Forces* 80(3): 1005–1039.

Holmbeck, Grayson N., Raymond E. Crossman, Mary L. Wandrei, and Elizabeth Gasiewski. 1994. "Cognitive Development, Egocentrism, Self-Esteem, and Adolescent Contraceptive Knowledge, Attitudes, and Behavior." *Journal of Youth and Adolescence* 23(2).

Hoffman, Saul D., and E. Michael Foster. 1997. "Economic Correlates of Nonmarital Childbearing among Adult Women." *Family Planning Perspectives* 29(3): 137–40.

Hoffman, Saul D., E. Michael Foster, and Frank F. Furstenberg, Jr. 1993. "Reevaluating the Costs of Teenage Childbearing." *Demography* 30: 1–13.

Hotz, V. Joseph, Jacob Alex Klerman, and Robert J. Willis. 1997. "The Economics of Fertility in Developed Countries." In *Handbook of Population and Family Economics*, edited by Mark R. Rosenzweig and Oded Stark, pp. 275–342. New York: North-Holland Elsevier Press.

Jessor, Richard, Frances Costa, Lee Jessor, and John E. Donovan. 1983. "Time of

First Intercourse: A Prospective Study." *Journal of Personality and Social Psychology* 44(3): 608–26.

Jones, Rachel K., and Kathryn Kost. 2007. "Underreporting of Induced and Spontaneous Abortion in the United States: An Analysis of the 2002 National Survey of Family Growth." *Studies in Family Planning* 38(3): 187–97.

Kissin, Dmitry M., John E. Anderson, Joan Marie Kraft, Lee Warner, and Denise J. Jamieson. 2008. "Is There a Trend of Increased Unwanted Childbearing among Young Women in the United States?" *Journal of Adolescent Health* 43: 364–71.

Kohn, Melvin, and Carmi Schooler. 1983. *Work and Personality: An Inquiry into the Impact of Social Stratification*. Norwood, NJ: Ablex Publishing.

Laflin, Molly T., Jing Wang, and Maxine Barry. 2008. "A Longitudinal Study of Adolescent Transition from Virgin to Nonvirgin Status." *Journal of Adolescent Health* 42: 228–36.

Lareau, Annette. 2003. *Unequal Childhoods: Class, Race, and Family Life*. Berkeley, CA: University of California Press.

Longmore, Monica A., Wendy D. Manning, and Peggy C. Giordano. 2001. "Preadolescent Parenting Strategies and Teens' Dating and Sexual Initiation: A Longitudinal Analysis." *Journal of Marriage and the Family* 63(2): 322–35.

Longmore, Monica A., Wendy D. Manning, Peggy C. Giordano, and Jennifer L. Rudolph. 2003. "Contraceptive Self-Efficacy: Does It Influence Adolescents' Contraceptive Use?" *Journal of Health and Social Behavior* 44(1): 45–60.

Manlove, Jennifer, Erum Ikramullah, and Elizabeth Terry-Humen. 2008. "Condom Use and Consistency among Male Adolescents in the United States." *Journal of Adolescent Health* 43: 325–33.

Manlove, Jennifer, Erum Ikramullah, Lisa Mincieli, Emily Holcombe, and Sana Danish. 2009. "Trends in Sexual Experience, Contraceptive Use, and Teenage Childbearing: 1992–2002." *Journal of Adolescent Health* 44: 413–23.

Martín-García, Teresa, and Pau Baizán. 2006. "The Impact of the Type of Education and of Educational Enrollment on First Births." *European Sociological Review* 22(3): 259–75.

Miller, Brent C., and Karen R. Sneesby. 1988. "Educational Correlates of Adolescents' Sexual Attitudes and Behavior." *Journal of Youth and Adolescence* 17(6): 521–30.

Mirowsky, John, and Catherine E. Ross. 2007. "Life Course Trajectories of Perceived Control and their Relationship to Education." *American Journal of Sociology* 112(5): 1339–82.

Morgan, S. Philip, and Allan Parnell. 2002. "Effects on Pregnancy Outcomes of Changes in the North Carolina State Abortion Fund." *Population Research and Policy Review* 21(4): 319–38.

Musick, Kelly, Paula England, Sarah Edgington, and Nicole Kangas. 2009. "Education Differences in Intended and Unintended Fertility." *Social Forces* 88(2): 543–72.

Pearson, Jennifer. 2006. "Personal Control, Self-Efficacy in Sexual Negotiation, and Contraceptive Risk among Adolescents: The Role of Gender." *Sex Roles* 54(9/10): 615-25.

Rainwater, Lee. 1960. *And the Poor Get Children: Sex, Contraception, and Family Planning in the Working Class.* Chicago, IL: Quadrangle.

Reed, Joanna. 2006. "Not Crossing the 'Extra Line': How Cohabitors with Children View Their Unions." *Journal of Marriage and Family* 68(5): 1117–31.

Rindfuss, Ronald R., S. Philip Morgan, and Kate Offutt. 1996. "Education and the Changing Age Pattern of American Fertility: 1963–1989." *Demography* 33(3): 277–90.

Skirbekk, Vegard, Hans-Peter Kohler, and Alexia Prskawetz. 2004. "Birth Month, School Graduation, and the Timing of Births and Marriages." *Demography* 41(3): 547–68.

Upchurch, Dawn M., Lee A. Lillard, and Constantijn W. A. Panis. 2002. "Nonmarital Childbearing: Influences of Education, Marriage, and Fertility." *Demography* 39(2): 311–29.

Weeden, Kim A., and David B. Grusky. 2005. "The Case for a New Class Map." *American Journal of Sociology* 111: 141–212.

Wu, Lawrence L. 1996. "Effects of Family Instability, Income, and Income Instability on the Risk of a Premarital Birth." *American Sociological Review* 61(3): 386–406.

Wu, Lawrence L., and Steven P. Martin. 2009. "Insights From a Sequential Hazard Model of Sexual Initiation and Premarital First Births." Department of Sociology, New York University, New York. Unpublished manuscript.

Yang, Yang, and S. Philip Morgan. 2003. "How Big Are Educational and Racial Fertility Differentials in the U.S.?" *Social Biology* 50(3/4): 167–87.

NOTES

1. Setting race dummies to their means is a way of getting the predicted score that would be expected on average for a population with the race composition of the sample.

2. This research uses data from Add Health, a program project designed by J. Richard Udry, Peter S. Bearman, and Kathleen Mullan Harris and funded by a grant P01-HD31921 from the National Institute of Child Health and Human Development, with cooperative funding from seventeen other agencies. Special acknowledgment is due Ronald R. Rindfuss and Barbara Entwisle for assistance in the original design. Persons interested in obtaining data files from Add Health should contact Add Health, Carolina Population Center, 123 W. Franklin Street, Chapel Hill, NC 27516-2524 (addhealth@unc.edu).

3. With the exception of two variables, mother's education and mother's age at the time the respondent was born, none of the independent variables in this analysis have much missing data. We classify mothers with missing data on education as having "high school or some college" (the modal category) and include a variable indicating that information on mother's education is missing. We classify mothers with missing data on age at respondent's birth as being 25 years old when the respondent was born (approximately the median value) and include a variable indicating that information on mother's age at birth is missing. Otherwise, we drop observations when data are missing. After dropping observations that are missing data, the sample size for the analysis of age at first intercourse is 6,441 women and

5,573 men. In Wave II, sexual activity (whether a virgin and whether sexually active in the past twelve months) and contraceptive consistency are known for 6,465 women, and in Wave III 7,290 women provide complete information on sexual activity and contraceptive use. Almost 30 percent of women have been pregnant at least once, and (after we drop those for whom data are missing) they provide information on the outcomes (whether ended in abortion) of 4,670 pregnancies. Of these pregnancies, 2,756 were unintended; this is the sample size for the analysis of whether an unintended pregnancy ended in abortion. The sample size for the analysis of whether the women have had a teen birth (coded "no" if they have never been pregnant or their first birth occurred at age 20 or older) is 7,337 women.

4. A large literature has examined the effects of teen births on whether women drop out of school. The recent sibling fixed-effect literature on effects of early births on women's education suggests that much of the correlation between having an early birth and women's education results from the fact that women on a trajectory to more education are less likely to have such births, rather than that the births cause them to drop out. These studies show that the educational outcomes of sisters, one of whom had a teen birth and one of whom did not, are much less different than naïve estimates of the effects of early childbearing from OLS regressions that ignore selection (Geronimus and Korenman 1991, 1993; Hoffman et al. 1993). Hoffman and Foster (1997) show that the socioeconomic correlates of early childbearing and nonmarital childbearing are very similar, at least for recent cohorts of women. If these findings for teen births generalize to nonmarital births in both current and past cohorts, it would be doubtful that the effect of a birth in curtailing education would explain most of the education gradient we observe on premarital conceptions. However, to the extent that nonmaritally conceived births do curtail education, our estimates of these educational gradients are upwardly biased.

5. Many studies do not contain this control. We could not add it because Add Health data do not include a measure. However, because of this finding, we controlled for the closest thing available to this in Add Health, mother's age at respondent's birth, in our models. Given that most women have only 1–3 children, and that they are reasonably tightly spaced, this should serve as an indicator of approximately when the mother began childbearing.

6. Women who had been in the lowest third of the GPA distribution had intercourse within two weeks of meeting a partner 23 percent of the time, while those in the highest third did so 19 percent of the time (net of mother's education, race, and age). For men, the comparable figures are 37 percent and 31 percent. The large difference between male and female reports is probably a result of men overreporting and/or women under-reporting.

7. Another way to look at this class gradient is to use pregnancies as the unit of analysis. Examining any pregnancies reported by Wave III, when women averaged 21.5 years of age, we find that, after controls, those whose moms had not finished high school had aborted 10 percent of any pregnancies they had, those with high school–educated moms aborted 17 percent, and those whose mothers were college graduates aborted 30 percent of their pregnancies (results not shown). A previous higher grade-point average and current college enrollment or graduation also predict being more likely to abort a pregnancy, conditional on getting pregnant.

In results not shown, we examined how many women aborted when an *unintended* pregnancy occurs (meaning that the woman says that she did not want to get pregnant when she did). Among women whose mothers did not finish high school who had an unintended pregnancy, 16 percent aborted; the figure was 25 percent among women whose mothers finished high school only, and 42 percent among women whose mothers graduated from college. These are predicted values that have been regression-adjusted for race, mother's age at respondent's birth, and age of respondent in 2001 at Wave III. Units of analysis were all pregnancies.

8. We control for race, age, mother's education, whether the respondent lived in a two-parent family at Wave I, and respondent's grade-point average at Wave I. Of course, here we cannot be sure if having a birth (or not) affected college enrollment and completion, or if being in college made women less likely to have a birth.

9. Although we doubt it is the case, it is possible that the education difference in reported premarital conceptions observed in these data simply reflects the greater resources of the more highly educated to conceal or "get rid" of unwanted pregnancies through giving children up for adoption or abortion. As reviewed above, evidence suggests that, among those who get pregnant, young women with more education are more likely to abort (Cooksey 1990). If this is true, our analysis here will underestimate premarital conceptions more for the highly educated than for the less-educated. However, the cohorts born before about 1950 had little access to legal abortion. It is possible that higher-SES women in early cohorts who got pregnant were more likely than pregnant lower-SES women to give their babies up for adoption, and not to report the birth in a survey.

10. This is consistent with economists' tendency to ignore what people say about their motivations and treat behavior as "revealed preferences." Doing so presumes good self-regulation; this is one critique of orthodox economics by the newer behavioral economics.

11. This same "cost of time" perspective also predicts that, given that one has a child, women with higher opportunity costs are more likely to stay employed full-time and purchase child care, and data support the idea that mothers with more education are more likely to be employed (England et al. 2009). In this perspective, fertility and employment are jointly chosen.

12. Pearson's (2006) Add Health analysis finds effects of parental income and education on abstaining from sex even under controls for overall and sex-specific measures of self-efficacy; thus the latter measures do not entirely mediate the class effects on abstinence. She does not find income and education effects when predicting condom use, after controlling for these two measures of efficacy, but it is unclear if this means that these measures entirely mediate the class link to condom use, or that there was no class effect.

13. In results not shown, we explored differences by NLSY respondents' mothers' education in the Rotter index of internal locus of control. Combining men and women, we found differences in the expected direction on dichotomized versions of several items in the scale. For example, 63 percent of those whose mothers did not graduate from high school, compared to 79 percent of those whose mothers were college graduates, agree more that what happens to them is their own doing (versus feeling that they do not have enough control over the direction their life is taking). The analogous percentages for feeling certain that one can make plans work were 40 percent (mom had less than high school) and 65 percent (mom was a college graduate). Using the scale as a whole, mean levels were monotonically higher for respondents whose mothers had more education.

# CHAPTER TWO

# Thinking about Demographic Family Difference

## Fertility Differentials in an Unequal Society

*S. Philip Morgan*

## STUDYING FAMILY DIFFERENCES

Literature linking ethnicity/race, religion or socioeconomic differences to demographic family differences has a long history. The reasons are many but they include substantive and theoretical ones. These differences can be substantial, e.g., in fertility timing and quantum (i.e., in the mean age at childbearing and in the number of children), in union patterns, and in co-residence patterns. Thus these differences are fruitful places to test our theories about family difference and change. Sociologists often focus on the effects of group membership, with special emphasis on groups where membership is largely ascribed (e.g., ethnicity/race and religion). Emile Durkheim's *On Suicide* (and *Suicide and the Birth Rate: A study in Moral Statistics*) provides well-known examples of using group differences in demographic outcomes to test social theory. But examples "closer to home" are numerous and also well known (e.g., Goldscheider and Uhlenberg 1969).

There are also practical and policy reasons for a focus on demographic family differences. Group survival depends on biological and social replacement—key family functions. Some groups judge that their replacement processes are insufficient, including some religious denominations (e.g., Nelson 1981) and a host of contemporary developed nations with "lowest-low fertility" (see Kohler et al. 2002). There are also concerns among slower-growing groups that faster-growing ones pose a threat. These concerns play out within and across societies. An especially problematic application of theories of differential growth spawned the U.S. eugenics movement of the early twentieth century. Echoes of this logic are at the base of some contemporary concerns about the increase in size of "other" U.S. racial/ethnic groups relative to those with a western European heritage (see Buchanan 2002). Family differences are also seen as indicators and markers of assimilation. Or the lack of convergence in family behavior can be assigned causal roles in perpetuating group differences in socioeconomic outcomes across groups.

Finally, there exists a relatively mundane reason for this extensive literature on demographic indicators: high-quality data exist. Admittedly, data do not magically appear and the reasons above partly explain why these data are collected. But there are other administrative reasons to collect data on race, religion, socioeconomic status, and fertility/family. Although far from perfect, fertility data are among the most widely collected and reliable (see Morgan and Lynch 2001). But substantial attention in government statistics to the measurement of union status, race, and socioeconomic standing also aid family research. Likewise, broad social science interest in religion leads to its inclusion in many surveys.

Past work on race, religion, socioeconomic standing, and family differences generally assumed that those factors were transitional. As Ryder (1973) put it, as these groups became more fully integrated into American life, their behavior, including fertility-relevant behavior, would resemble that of other groups. This claim is synonymous with Goldscheider's (1971) "characteristics hypothesis" for racial/religions differences. That is, the ethnicity/race or religion association with family differences was spurious—depending upon associations with socioeconomic status, region of the country, rural urban residence, etc. These factors often do play a role in understanding the association of ethnicity/race or religion and family differences at a point in time. But the relevant dimensions of ethnicity/race, religion, and family difference change over time and with social context.

Other differences might be expected to persist indefinitely because they are supported by relatively stable group characteristics—both institutional and ideological. I argue that the best examples of such stable differences are educational and socioeconomic differences in fertility timing. These timing differences consistently translate into modest but relatively stable differences in period and completed fertility (Rindfuss and Sweet 1977; Yang and Morgan 2003). Finally, there are differentials that are more dynamic, relying on intergroup interactions and the shifting salience of particular identities. This is an especially interesting and larger-than-expected set, which I will focus on at some length.

I begin by offering a theoretical frame, the *theory of conjunctural action* (TCA) that allows for uniform analysis of all three types of differentials. I then provide contemporary examples of each type. A key feature of this approach is a move away from culture-versus-structure arguments—a framing that has long hampered social science research, and especially research on the family.

## THE THEORY OF CONJUNCTURAL ACTION

My colleagues (Johnson-Hanks, Bachrach, and Kohler)and I, supported by a contract from NICHD (Explaining Family Change), have constructed a consilient theory of family change/difference. It has as its key building blocks insights and concepts from: (i) studies of macro-historical change, (ii) the study of the life course, and (iii) the disciplines of neuroscience, psychology, anthropology, sociology, history, and economics.[1] The relevance here is its provision of a single theoretical frame to account for differentials of multiple types.

The basic TCA premise is that all stimuli and experience are filtered by an individual's brain on the basis of stored (but modifiable) mental "maps," "frames," or "schemas" (hereafter schemas). Some of these schemas can be easily articulated and recognized by actors, others less so or not at all. With their neural architecture, humans are predisposed to form schemas and possess the basic characteristics for some specific schemas at birth (see Lidz and Freeman 2003). The TCA enriches social science models of explicit calculation by incorporating an explanation for behaviors resulting from reflexive, schematic, or automatic mental processes. It also sheds light on the conditions under which behaviors are the product of conscious *decision-making*, weighing the pros and cons of the various alternatives in an actor's choice set, or are *automatic* and follow mostly from an actor's established schema.

Although individuals within any social group may differ in the set of schemas they hold, many schemas are shared and mutually reinforced in social communities. Some shared schemas constitute an important element of group identity. Shared schemas are important because they allow for effective social interaction and joint actions of social groups. Moreover, shared schemas may give rise to patterned behaviors—that is, similar behavioral responses of individuals in comparable environments.

TCA also posits that society is organized materially as well as schematically. Any material form or reserve of value that has an existence outside of the schemas it manifests my colleagues and I call a "material," or material structure. Although materials are not necessarily physical objects, they invariably have a perceptible form. They are not only schools, but also curricula, lunch schedules, and teaching techniques; not only a wedding ring, but also the spoken vow of fidelity to one's spouse. Many materials have direct implications on individual behaviors by regulating the available set of behaviors or "choices," and by affecting the costs and benefits of choosing some behaviors versus others. However, an important aspect of TCA is that materials personify schemas in the world of objects; they instill and reinforce them in the minds of social actors.

The third premise of TCA, and Sewell's fundamental contribution (Sewell 1992, 2005), is that there is no opposition between schemas and materials; they are fundamentally interdependent and mutually constitutive. The product of the interaction of schemas and materials over time my colleagues and I (and Sewell) call "structures." For example, the structure called the nuclear family would not exist without examples of such families in the world *and* the ability of individuals to learn schemas about such families, store them, and use them to motivate or evaluate their own and others' family behaviors.

Fourth, schemas/materials are unevenly distributed across "social space";[2] for example, poor people are more likely to experience welfare systems and rich people are more likely to be acquainted with investment counselors. As people age and make life-course transitions—such as completing school, marrying, divorcing, or suffering from sickness—their experience of schemas/materials changes accordingly. As individuals develop cognitively and socially, they form identities, or schemas, about who they are and how persons like themselves should behave (Erikson 1959). Identity formation brings order to the individual life course by providing internal clues regarding the appropriate schema for this person at this place and time. Identity also signals to others how a person will behave and reason, and thus facilitates social interactions (for related uses of the concept of identity, see Akerlof and Kranton 2000; Smith-Lovin 2005).

Fifth, the circumstances or situations in which individuals find themselves are highly relevant to behavior: action never occurs in the abstract but rather in concrete configurations of context. In its basic form, this aspect of TCA is shared with many other social science theories in which behaviors depend on the environment that individuals encounter. Within TCA, however, the role of local contexts is more refined and flexible. In keeping with Bourdieu (1977: 78; see also Sewell 2005: 220–23), my colleagues and I use the term "conjuncture" to refer to the historically contingent, temporarily salient aspects of context that situate action. People are constantly interpreting the conjunctures they experience: they read each conjuncture by answering the question, "what is this an example of?" In this process of "construal," individuals process the range of stimuli present in any conjuncture and draw on available schemas to assign meaning to what is happening. The process of construal is often "automatic." Usually, one does not choose to read a conjuncture in one way or another (see, e.g., DiMaggio 1997; Shore 1996). However, the process of construal can produce conflicting meanings and identify choices that require one to evaluate options. The process of construal selects schemas that identify and justify possible courses of action, one of which may be weighing the costs and benefits of alternative choices.

Finally, when an individual resolves a conjuncture by taking or not taking action, the outcome of the conjuncture—an "event"—either reinforces or transforms structure. Actions consistent with existing schema and normative use of material structure reinforce it, while new or innovative behavior changes structure, albeit usually only in localized ways. Thus humans change their social context by living in it; that is, people's lives are structured, but that structure is constantly being remade through specific actions in concrete situations. This insight is of course widely shared across the social sciences. What TCA contributes to this consensus is a parsimonious mechanism through which the constant reconstitution occurs—the interplay of material and virtual structure in specific conjunctures gives rise to events that reinforce or transform the structures themselves.

When using TCA one could account for variation through exhaustive comparative social history, tracing the sequences of transformative events in the two groups. However, there is also a more direct method, comparable to classic decomposition or proximate determinate approaches. Specifically, one can observe differences (or changes) in quantifiable behavior as a result of differences (or changes) in the distribution or characteristics of *conjunctures* or in the distribution and characteristics of *construals*. This is parallel to thinking about differences in fertility rates as the result of differences in the proportion of women married or in marital/nonmarital fertility.

Conjunctures are unequally distributed across social space and social groups. For example, it is rare for a college student to face the problem (conjuncture) of having the father of her baby convicted of a drug crime. This conjuncture, however, may be familiar among poor, urban black women. The distribution of conjunctures can also change over time or across the life course. For example, labor force participation places women in new conjunctures where family and work obligations may conflict. Given that action relates to the specific configuration of factors at play at the time, changes in the distribution of conjunctures will alter the distribution of demographic events that result from them.

How people *construe the conjunctures* they face matters directly for the kinds of demographic outcomes that result, and changes in the process of construal can lead to changes in demographic rates. For example, remaining in an unhappy marriage may be seen as "staying faithful to your wedding vows," as "not being true to yourself," or as being a "rational decision" given the costs of separation and the implications of those costs for one's standard of living. This largely automated process of identifying "what is going on here" or "what this is an example of" makes certain courses of action in any conjuncture appear plausible, or even natural, while others do not even surface as options.

DIFFERENTIALS AS TRANSITIONAL PHENOMENA

The TCA emphasis on the duality of structure makes it clear why differentials likely will emerge and then shrink during periods of dramatic secular change. The decline in fertility is a classic case of dramatic secular change—once begun it continues until low fertility is reached (see Bongaarts and

Watkins 1996). High fertility as a societal structure is supported by schemas that support large families and by materials that reduce child costs or that increase the cost of birth control. The fertility transition, the transition to low fertility, has occurred wherever economies have become economically advanced. However, the spread of economic development is not even across geographic areas or social groups. And even if it were, the "fit" between economic and fertility transitions is not well calibrated, the reason being that the influence of economic development on fertility must operate through changed conjunctures and construal. These changes eventually do occur and satisfy Coale's (1973) preconditions for a fertility decline—that controlling fertility will be construed as a legitimate choice and that conjunctures will contain material conditions that suggest/motivate/facilitate a desire for fewer births (i.e., factors that affect motivation for childbearing are antinatalist and increase the availability of methods to realize lower fertility).

For example, urban fertility predictably declines before rural fertility because urban material conditions are less conducive to childbearing—child labor is less valuable/useful, schooling is available and possibly required, kin support for childbearing is more remote, birth control is more accessible, etc. Schemas supportive of small families are also more prevalent in cities—the package of ideas that Thornton (2001,2005) calls "developmental idealism" or a related set that Goode (1963) called the ideology of the conjugal family. Thus, using the language suggested above, the conjunctures faced by urban dwellers are different from those in rural areas, and their construal will likely also be different. Over time these rural/urban differences abate as institutions, resources (i.e., materials), and schemas become more homogenized.

But the social landscape is multidimensional, and some barriers to (or facilitators of) the diffusion of schema or materials must compete with indigenous schema and materials. The fertility literature is full of such examples: the spread of fertility decline in Europe often stalled (on a decadal time scale) at national borders with a language shift (see Coale and Watkins 1986). Such a pattern suggests that the diffusion of schemas was slowed by communication difficulties or by competition from indigenous structures. In contrast, Chinese diaspora populations across Asia were consistently in the vanguard of fertility decline. These early declines suggest an existing schematic predisposition toward birth control among Chinese (see Greenhalgh 1988).

Of contemporary import in the United States are debates around the higher fertility of Hispanic populations (versus non-Hispanic). A century ago, concerns about the high fertility of eastern and southern Europeans raised concerns about the rapid growth of these populations, and about their slow assimilation into the "American way of life" as measured by their fertility levels. In retrospect, we know that the convergence toward native fertility levels (by previous generations of migrants from eastern and southern Europe) occurred rather swiftly (on a generational or decadal time scale). Of course, history need not repeat itself; the "new immigrants" are different from earlier waves on a number of relevant dimensions (see Massey 1995). Concern is heightened because period estimates of generational differences show no evidence of decline. But Parrrado and Morgan (2009) show that this apparent stagnation (or even increase in fertility among the second and third generations) is an artifact of the differential pace of fertility decline among the first and subsequent generations. If the data are arrayed by generation, one can observe the expected declines across generations. Thus contemporary evidence (like that in the past) suggests that many of the immigrant differentials in U.S. fertility are transitional—they will disappear as these groups "became more fully integrated into American life" (Ryder 1973).

DIFFERENTIALS AS SUSTAINABLE STRUCTURE

The conceptualization of differences as the product of different schemas/materials, conjunctures, and construal makes it clear that such differences may be transitional or not. As examples, let us consider the longstanding differential in fertility by education (or socioeconomic status) or between the United States and most other developed countries. Let us focus here on pervasive and persistent educational differentials in U.S. fertility (see Rindfuss and Sweet 1977; Yang and Morgan 2003).

Table 2.1 reflects ongoing work with the 1979 National Longitudinal Survey of Youth (NLSY79; for details see Morgan and Rackin 2010: Table 4). The birth cohorts (1957–64) included in this survey had nearly completed childbearing at the most recent survey wave (2006). This remarkable survey asked men and women their fertility intentions sixteen times between 1979 and 2006 and also monitored their actual fertility behavior. Below, for

TABLE 2.1
*Intended and achieved parity by educational level: U.S. women born 1957–64\**

| Education at age 24 | Parity at age 24 | Intent at age 24 | Parity at age 41+ | Net error | Gross error | N |
|---|---|---|---|---|---|---|
| Less than high school | 1.70 | 2.44 | 2.55 | 0.09 | 0.74 | 591 |
| High school | 0.95 | 2.20 | 2.05 | -0.15 | 0.81 | 1688 |
| 13–15 years | 0.46 | 2.16 | 1.76 | -0.40 | 0.97 | 909 |
| 16+ years | 0.09 | 2.21 | 1.67 | -0.54 | 0.98 | 595 |

\* Data are from the 1979 National Longitudinal Survey of Youth. See Morgan and Rackin 2010 for a description of the data.

women only, Morgan and Rackin show the mean achieved fertility at age 24, mean stated intentions for more births at age 24, and completed fertility (as of 2006) when women were in their mid-40s.

Note these differences:

1. The less-educated begin childbearing earlier. On average, the least-educated have 1.70 children by age 24; the most-educated have only .09.

2. There are very modest differences in 2004 intended parity—the number of children intended by the end of the childbearing years. High school graduates and those with sixteen or more years of schooling have nearly identical mean intentions (2.20 and 2.21 children, respectively).

3. There are, however, sizable differences in completed fertility (for these women in their 40s). The more-educated have fewer children than they intended and the least-educated have more. Specifically, on average, the most-educated have only 1.67 children and the least-educated 2.55.

4. There are large differences in the "net error"[3]—a measure of the degree to which the group "missed its fertility target." For instance, consider two high school graduates who intended to have two children; if the first had only one child and the second had three, then their "net error" is compensating, and "on average" (or as a group) these women met their target. Table 2.1 shows that the less-educated women had a small positive net error—on average they had .09 *more* children than their stated intention at age 24. In contrast, the most-educated women had, on average, .54 *fewer* children than intended.

5. There are large and similar "gross errors" for each educational group.[4] For the example above, the average gross error for the two high school graduates would be one child each. In fact, the gross error is approximately one birth (.82 to 1.02) for each of the educational groups shown in Table 2.1.

While these estimates come from a narrow range of birth cohorts, I argue that they have persisted for several decades and could well persist indefinitely. (These socioeconomic differences in early childbearing and whether a birth is unplanned, and the roots of contributing differences in birth control practices, are also discussed by Paula England et al. in this volume.) These differences are inherent in the life experiences (conjunctures) faced by women with such different life trajectories. Specifically, the data above and much other evidence suggest that aspects of American family schemas are widely shared: the desire for a committed long-term union and a small number of children. But the conjunctures faced and/or people's construals are dramatically different. Let's fix the conjuncture as "an unintended pregnancy by a 19-year-old." For a woman with little education and little opportunity for further education, postponing fertility (by having an abortion) is much less likely than for a woman in school and with brighter educational prospects. Edin and Kefalas's (2005) interviews with disadvantaged women provide a description of schemas that are both pronatalist and not. In the former, motherhood is rationalized and/or glorified as doing the right thing (by not having an abortion) and as a challenge that is a welcome anchor in an uncertain world. But the alternative schema—that waiting for maturity before becoming a mother is a good strategy, with benefits for mother and child—was also widely reported and discussed. Among those studied by Edin and Kefalas, decisions to abort were probably as common as decisions to carry the birth to term. Construal (i.e., how a pregnant young woman thinks about her pregnancy), is determined by clues from the environment and from the young woman's identity. In Edin and Kefalas's data, having a boyfriend and/or a mother supportive of a birth were strong factors in the pronatalist construal. Such support for early-age childbearing is common within the communities studied by Edin and Kefalas. The contribution by Kathryn Edin and her colleagues to this volume complements this past work by focusing on the construals disadvantaged men make of a pregnant partner, or of a new baby when the union between the parents is shaky.

For young women with brighter educational and career prospects (than those studied by Edin and Kefalas), the available schemas are largely the same. But the environmental clues are dramatically different. There are few teen-mother role models in their environment, and the construals of key others (boyfriends and mothers) are likely to favor postponement. Thus abortion is chosen as the best solution to an unfortunate circumstance.

More relevant to the table above is the behavior of women in their mid-20s and older. Here a useful thought experiment is to fix the schema as "more- and less-educated women want two children on average." But the conjunctures faced by these groups of women are different. Specifically, the more-educated have a larger number and more attractive set of alternatives to motherhood than the less-educated). A strategy of continued postponement among the more-educated is translated, in time, to lower levels of childbearing. These differential sets of conjunctures are linked to current inequalities that are embedded in the U.S. political economy. The large gross errors for all educational groups show that meeting intentions is difficult for all groups; similar schemas regarding appropriate intended family sizes are played out in very different sets of conjunctures.

This example does not suggest that socioeconomic fertility differences are immutable. In fact, a different policy regime might reduce (or increase) some differences in these diverse environments. A 2009 article (comparing

Great Britain and France credits the political economy with producing larger differences by education (like those shown in Table 2.1) in Great Britain than in France (see Rendall et al. 2009).

DYNAMIC DIFFERENTIALS

Above I explained that both secular change and instances of substantial stability in family structure are linked to a changing economy or to a relatively stable class structure. Here I argue that differentials can be influenced by intergroup relations. Specifically, group identity intensifies with increasing tension/competition/conflict (hereafter competition) with another group. In a particular context and in the conjunctures people face, there are numerous bases for identity; those activated are those most relevant in particular situations. Thus, heightened group competition makes group identity more salient—more likely to be used in construal or to influence the set of conjunctures faced.

The description of differentials as "dynamic" does not require that they be constantly changing. Rather it signifies that their existence rests upon a continuing dynamic that stresses differences linked to identity and, for purposes here, to family behavior. See, for example, claims that Muslim minority populations have higher fertility than co-resident majority populations throughout South Asia (Morgan et al. 2002; Dharmalingam and Morgan 2004).

In the United States, fertility and fertility timing differences are exacerbated by what demographers refer to as contraceptive failures—i.e., timing and number failures. The latter are also referred to as unwanted births. Unwanted and mistimed births are partly anchored in the timing differences linked to socioeconomic and educational differences. Those of lower socioeconomic standing start childbearing earlier and, other things equal, reach intended family size sooner. This longer period of risk (after reaching intended family size but prior to menopause) produces higher levels of contraceptive failure.

But I argue that the long and shrill abortion debate in the United States has "raised the bar" substantially for choosing an abortion. The same process has valorized mistimed and unwanted childbearing. It has contributed to religious and political fertility differentials. What am I talking about?

A new Gallup Poll, conducted May 7–10 [2009], finds 51% of Americans calling themselves "pro-life" on the issue of abortion and 42% "pro-choice." This is the first time a majority of U.S. adults have identified themselves as pro-life since Gallup began asking this question in 1995.

The same three abortion questions asked on the Gallup Values and Beliefs survey were included in Gallup Poll Daily tracking from May 12–13 [2009], with nearly identical results, including a 50% to 43% pro-life versus pro-choice split on the self-identification question.

. . . [B]y ideology, all of the increase in pro-life sentiment is seen among self-identified conservatives and moderates; the abortion views of political liberals have not changed.

It is possible that, through his abortion policies, Obama has pushed the public's understanding of what it means to be "pro-choice" slightly to the left, politically. While Democrats may support that, as they generally support everything Obama is doing as president, it may be driving others in the opposite direction. (http://www.gallup.com/poll/118399/more-americans-pro-life -than-pro-choice-first-time.aspx)

The up-tick in support for the pro-life position, the focus of the news story above, is of secondary interest. More important are two other features of this account: first, the multi-decade duration of the debate and the large majority of Americans who do *not* approve of abortion in *any* circumstances. Second, note the acknowledgment of the dynamic nature of the debate. As noted in the discussion above on socioeconomic differences, the TCA focus on schema is very useful here. The right-to-life (pro-life) and right-to-choose (pro-choice) schema are both pervasive. For some people, the schema applied is very close to their identity. It is a marker of who they are. But for many Americans "how they think about abortion" is contingent on the particular conjuncture—the circumstances facing the individual.

There is a huge literature on the pro-life/pro-choice social movements. Our interest here is in its salience for family and especially fertility. I stress two aspects. First, the availability of abortion has valorized mistimed/unwanted births. Women have a choice, or at least claim one, when they become pregnant. I made this point above when discussing socioeconomic differences, but the argument need not be based on the paucity of competing opportunities. Take the family of Sarah Palin as an example, and I would argue, an important one. Sarah Palin's last pregnancy may or may not have been "unwanted" by the demographer's definition. But her decision to give birth to a Down syndrome child was an example of "practicing what she preached," as was her teenage daughter Bristol's decision to have a child. The Palins are the upscale poster family for the pro-life position. Peter Sprigg (2008) of the Family Research Council wrote:

While having sex outside of marriage is bad, deliberately destroying an innocent human life through abortion . . . is far, far worse. That is why conservative celebration of Bristol's decision to carry her child to term. . . . outweighed disappointment over her sexual behavior. Her announced intention to marry the father is also a plus, despite the unfortunate circumstances.

This situation only underscores the sincerity of the Palin family's pro-life convictions. Earlier this year, Gov. Palin gave birth to her son Trig—despite knowing that he had Down syndrome, a diagnosis that leads to abortion eighty percent of the time. Now, the Palins have again chosen life. When pro-abortion zealots say, "You don't understand the agonizing personal circumstances that lead to abortion," Sarah Palin can answer, "Yes, I do—but I chose life."

Even absent the religious overtones, the "choice" to have the child valorizes it. Note recent popular movies *Knocked Up* and *Juno*. Quoting from a review of *Juno*:

> "Juno" . . . shares with "Knocked Up" an underlying theme, a message that is not anti-abortion but rather pro-adulthood. It follows its heroine—and by the end she has earned that title—on a twisty path toward responsibility and greater self-understanding. (Scott 2007)

My references from popular culture are purposeful. These are the images that "we" see, and they promote worldviews (particular schema), wittingly or not. Note two pieces of evidence that deserve serious research attention. First, based on national vital statistics data, Ventura et al. (2008) show a shift in pregnancy outcomes between 1990 and 2004 (the last year with available data). Specifically, births increased from 61 to 64 percent of all pregnancies while the share of abortions declined. Over roughly this same period of time, unwanted births increased—from 9 to 14.1 as a percentage of all births (Chandra et al. 2005). Together these facts suggest that people's resolution of an unintended pregnancy (a classic example of a conjuncture) is shifting toward having a child. I suspect that the visibility of pro-life schema plays a role, as do closely related access to abortion information and services (the "material" component of structure).

A second way that the abortion debate can affect family behavior is by helping to crystallize broader schemas. In other words, abortion positions can take on larger significance as a signal of the centrality of motherhood in women's lives. Luker (1985) made this case over two decades ago. She argued that much of the passion in the abortion debate flows from the more global debate that it fosters around the competing interests in women's lives.

Morgan and Kohler (forthcoming) use the TCA frame and posit the following three foundational schemas that are broadly relevant in the United States (and likely in many low-fertility contexts):

1. Part of a normal adult life is marriage and a family—where family is defined as an opposite-sex partner and a few (usually two) biologically related children.

2. Adult life is reflexive and constructed; its goal is a meaningful and satisfying life.

3. Difficult tasks can be attacked by hard work and appropriate strategic decisions, including timing and sequencing.

The key feature of these foundational schemas is their generality; nevertheless, they have clear implications for specific behaviors. For example, the first schema characterizes marriage and family as a key aspect of the normative life course, a schema that is pervasive, longstanding, and codified in many materials. The second schema privileges a meaningful and satisfying life, consistent with Giddens's (1991) description of the deinstitutionalized modern life course that offers—particularly young adults—an increasingly broad range of options and opportunities.

The third schema is a pervasive one (or perhaps two) for problem solving: work hard using appropriate strategies. Its application is ubiquitous from mathematics (decompose complex equations into simpler ones that can be solved in a step-like fashion) to art (where dancers learn steps one at a time and then recombine them, or painters learn techniques with which they innovate).

These foundational schemas can be employed in various ways. They can compete directly, as when individuals face key tradeoffs between family and career. Individuals struggle individually, decision by decision. However, when persons' lives (the set of conjunctures they face) repeatedly bring these schemas to the fore, then common solutions are found to these common conjunctures. Quinn (2005) calls these solutions "cultural models"; I continue to refer to them as schemas but acknowledge their less abstract and more "operational" nature. We (Morgan and Kohler, 2011) propose that three foundational schemas and the conjunctures faced by middle- and upper-middle-class women have produced derivative, operational schemas for "constructing a life."

A first derivative schema, which I will call *family-first*, gives priority to family decisions. This life course is constructed, voluntarily chosen, but is built on traditional and often religious values. Adherents would say that this course is not always the easiest path, but that hard work and proper strategies can solve the day-to-day problems. More important, hard work and a family-centered life produce the greatest happiness over the long run. It is through sacrifice and hard work that one becomes mature and is fulfilled. A second schema, *individual-first*, places independence and self-actualization first, at least first sequentially. Family remains very important, but families stand the best chance of being fulfilling once persons are ready for them. Independence and self-actualization build the person that can, in time, create a good family—one that provides fulfilling experiences for all of its members. Note that these two very different operational schemas (Quinn's cultural models) emerge from the same foundational schemas and common twenty-first-century conjunctures. Understanding change and variation need not depend on different foundational schema but instead on how they are woven together in particular environments and conjunctures.

Given this construction it is easy to see why abortion is "ground zero" for contemporary debates about appropriate schema or "cultural models."

But abortion is only symptomatic of deeper and broader differences. Understanding them is crucial for understanding two of the most interesting contemporary fertility differences.

First, religious denominational differences in fertility (Catholic vs. non-Catholic, for instance) have largely disappeared. In their place are differences in "religiosity"—pan-religious categories. This differential would be operationalized by survey items such as: "How important is religion in your life?" Morgan and Hayford (2008) show that those who say religion is "very important" (vs. somewhat or not important) intend more children and have higher fertility rates—about .5 children more per woman. In the contemporary context, this is a large differential! Moreover, much of this difference can be explained by the general and more traditional family orientation of the more religious (the family-first versus individual-first cultural model).

Second, this debate about appropriate cultural models has, in the U.S. context, taken on political hues—actually bright colors: red and blue. Lesthaeghe and Neidert (2006, 2009) show a striking geographic differential in fertility (and other "second demographic transition" behavior). At the state level, the correlation between the total fertility rate (in 2002) and voting for George W. Bush for president in 2004 is .78! Republican and conservative have been strongly connected to the family-first cultural model. Lesthaeghe (1995) has long argued that the individual-first model is secularly ascendant (at the expense of the family-first model). Perhaps he will be proven correct in the long term, but the family-first schema has shown considerable tenacity in the United States. The likelihood that persons think of themselves as "conservative" (or Republican or religious) is increased by contemporary political debates. Activating this aspect of identity in turn leads to construals that generate the demographic differences associated with these identities.

In sum, Shorter (1975) envisioned a future "perfect contraceptive society" produced by an openness and responsibility about sexuality coupled with an increasing availability of effective contraceptives (and abortion). What has been lost in this supposed secular march toward rational reproduction are the broader meanings of particular kinds of birth control or of birth control at all (on these points see Johnson-Hanks 2006; and Tavory and Swindler 2009).

CONCLUSION

In purely descriptive terms, there are three types of family differences: those that are transitional, those that are relatively stable and those that are dynamic. I propose a consistent theoretical framework that can account for each in terms of the same basic concepts—structure resulting from schematic and material components. Stability and change in structure (i.e., demographic family differentials), in turn, are due to changes in these two components. More specifically, schemas and materials influence the conjunctures that persons face and their construal of them. I provide a range of examples using the literature on fertility and fertility related differences. I argue that this framework is a powerful way to think about changing families in an unequal society.

REFERENCES

Akerlof, George, and Rachel Kranton. 2000. "Economics and Identity." *Quarterly Journal of Economics* 115: 715–33.

Buchanan, P. J. 2002. *The Death of the West*. New York: Thomas Dunne Books.

Bongaarts, J., and S. C. Watkins. 1996. "Social Interactions and Contemporary Fertility Transitions." *Population and Development Review* 22(4): 639–82.

Bourdieu, Pierre. 1977. *Outline of a Theory of Practice*. Cambridge, UK: Cambridge University Press.

Chandra A., G. M. Martinez, W. D. Mosher, J. C. Abma, and J. Jones. 2005. "Fertility, Family Planning, and Reproductive Health of U.S. Women: Data from the 2002 National Survey of Family Growth." National Center for Health Statistics. *National Vital Statistics Reports* 23(25).

Coale, A. 1973. "The Demographic Transition Reconsidered." In *International Union for the Scientific Study of Population Conference, Liege* 1: 53–72.

Coale, A. J., and S. Watkins. 1986. *The Decline of Fertility in Europe*. Princeton, NJ: Princeton University Press.

DiMaggio, P. D. 1997. "Culture and Cognition." *Annual Review of Sociology* 23: 263–87.

Dharmalingam, A., and S. P. Morgan. 2004. "Pervasive Muslim/Hindu Fertility Differences in India." *Demography* 41: 529–46.

Durkheim, E. 2006. *On Suicide*. London, Penguin.

———. 1996. *Suicide and the Birth Rate: A Study in Moral Statistics*. Ottawa, Ontario: Barclay D. Johnson.

Edin, K., and M. Kefalas. 2005. *Promises I Can Keep: Why Poor Women Put Motherhood before Marriage*. Berkeley, University of California Press.

Erikson, E. H. 1959. *Identity and the Life Cycle*. New York: International Universities Press.

Giddens, A. 1991. *Modernity and Self-Identity*. Stanford, CA: Stanford University Press.

Goldscheider, C. 1971. *Population, Modernization and Social Structure*. Boston: Little, Brown.

Goldscheider, C., and P. R. Uhlenberg. 1969. "Minority Group Status and Fertility." *American Journal of Sociology* 74(4): 361–72.

Goode, W. J. 1963. *World Revolution and Family Patterns*. New York: Free Press of Glencoe.

Greenhalgh, S. 1988. "Fertility as Mobility: Sinic Transitions." *Population and Development Review* 14: 629–74.

Hayford, S., and S. P. Morgan. 2008. "Religiosity and Fertility in the United States: The Role of Fertility Intentions." *Social Forces* 86(3): 1163–88.

Johnson-Hanks, Jennifer. 2006. *Uncertain Honor: Modern Motherhood in an African Crisis*. Chicago: University of Chicago Press.

Johnson-Hanks, Jennifer, Christine Bachrach, S. Philip Morgan, and Hans-Peter Kohler. 2011 forthcoming. *Understanding Family Change and Variation: Structure, Conjuncture and Action*. Springer: New York.

Kohler, H.-P., F. C. Billari, et al. 2002. "The Emergence of Lowest-Low Fertility in Europe during the 1990s." *Population and Development Review* 28: 641–80.

Lesthaeghe, R. 1995. "The Second Demographic Transition in Western Countries: An Interpretation." In *Gender and Family Change in Industrialized Countries*, edited by K. Oppenheim Mason, A.-M. Jensen, and W. T. Mason, pp. 17–62. Oxford, UK: Clarendon.

Lesthaeghe, R., and L. Neidert. 2006. "The Second Demographic Transition in the United States: Exception or Textbook Example?" *Population and Development Review* 32: 669–98.

———. 2009. "U.S. Presidential Elections and the Spatial Pattern of the American Second Demographic Transition." *Population and Development Review* 35(2): 391–400.

Lidz, J., S. Waxman, and J. Freedman. 2003. "What Infants Know about Syntax but Couldn't Have Learned: Experimental Evidence for Syntactic Structure at 18 Months." *Cognition* 89: B65–B73.

Luker, K. 1985. *Abortion and the Politics of Motherhood*. Berkeley, CA: University of California Press.

Massey, D. S. 1995. "The New Immigration and Ethnicity in the United States " *Population and Development Review* 21: 631–52.

McPherson, Miller. 1983. "An Ecology of Affiliation." *American Sociological Review* 48: 519–32.

———. 2004. "A Blau Space Primer: Prolegomenon to an Ecology of Affiliation." *Industrial and Corporate Change* 13: 263–80.

Morgan, S. Philip, and Hans-Peter Kohler. 2011. "Fertility Change and Variation." In *Understanding Family Change and Variation: Structure, Conjuncture and Action,* by Jennifer Johnson-Hanks, C. Bachrach, S. P. Morgan, and H. P. Kohler. New York: Springer.

Morgan, S. P., and S. M. Lynch. 2001. Demography's Success and Its Future: The Role of Data and Methods. *Demography and Epidemiology: Frontiers in Population Health and Aging. Annals of New York Academy of Sciences* 954: 35–51.

Morgan, S. P., and H. Rackin. 2010. "The Correspondence of Fertility Intentions and Behavior in the United States." *Population and Development Review* 36: 91–118.

Morgan, S. P., S. Stash, et al. 2002. "Muslim and Non-Muslim Differences in

Female Autonomy and Fertility: Evidence from Four Asian Countries." *Population and Development Review* 28(3): 515–38.

Morgan, S. Philip, Christine Bachrach, Jennifer Johnson-Hanks, and Hans-Peter Kohler. 2008. "Theory Development by Parenthood Group: A Theory of Conjunctural Action." In *Designing New Models for Explaining Family Change and Variation*, S. P. Morgan (PI), Chapter 3. Contract Report (N01 HD-3-3354) to NICHD. Durham, NC: Duke University.

Nelsen, H. M. 1981. "Religious Conformity in an Age of Disbelief: Contextual Effects of Time, Denomination, and Family Processes upon Church Decline and Apostasy." *American Sociological Review* 46(5): 632–40.

Parrado, E., and S. P. Morgan. 2008. "Intergenerational Fertility among Hispanic Women: New Evidence of Immigrant Assimilation." *Demography* 45: 651–71.

Quinn, N. (1999). "Culture and Contradiction: The Case of Americans Reasoning about Marriage." *Ethos* 27(1): 89–103.

Rendall, M. S., O. Ekert-Jaffe, et al. 2009. "Universal versus Economically Polarized Change in Age at First Birth: A French-British Comparison." *Population and Development Review* 35(1): 89–115.

Rindfuss, R. R., and J. Sweet. 1977. *Postwar Fertility Trends and Differentials in the United States*. New York: Academic Press.

Ryder, N. B. 1973. "Recent Trends and Group Differences in Fertility." In *Toward the End of Growth: Population in America*, pp. 57–68. Englewood Cliffs, NJ: Prentice-Hall:

Scott, A. O. 2007 (Dec. 5). "Seeking Mr. and Mrs. Right for a Baby on the Way." http://movies.nytimes.com/2007/12/05/movies/05juno.html.

Sewell, William H. 1992. "A Theory of Structure: Duality, Agency, and Transformation." *American Journal of Sociology* 98: 1–29.

———. 2005. *Logics of History: Social Theory and Social Transformation*. Chicago: University of Chicago Press.

Shore, Bradd. 1996. *Culture in Mind: Cognition, Culture, and the Problem of Meaning*. New York: Oxford University Press.

Shorter E. 1975. *The Making of the Modern Family*. New York: Basic Books.

Smith-Lovin, Lynn. 2005. "Affect Control Theory." In *Handbook of Social Theory*, edited by George Ritzer. Los Angeles: Sage.

Sprigg, P. 2008 (September 1). "Sarah Palin's Amazing Grace." Press release. Washington, DC: Family Research Council.

Tavory, I., and A. Swidler. 2009. "Condom Semiotics: Meaning and Condom Use in Rural Malawi." *American Sociological Review* 74: 171–89.

Thornton, A. 2001. "The Developmental Paradigm, Reading History Sideways, and Family Change." *Demography* 38(4): 449–67.

———. 2005. *Reading History Sideways: The Fallacy and Enduring Impact of the Developmental Paradigm on Family Life*. Chicago: University of Chicago Press.

Ventura, S. J., J. C. Abma, W. D. Mosher, and S. K. Henshaw. 2008. "Estimated Pregnancy Rates by Outcome for the United States, 1990–2004. *National Vital Statistics Reports* 56, no. 15. Hyattsville, MD: National Center for Health Statistics.

Wilson, E. O. 1998. *Consilience: The Unity of Knowledge*. New York: Knopf.

Yang, Y., and S. P. Morgan. 2003. "How Big Are Educational and Racial Fertility Differentials in the U.S.?" *Social Biology* 50(3/4): 167–87.

NOTES

1. The fullest development of our ideas is presented in *Understanding Family Change and Variation: Structure, Conjuncture and Action*[0] (Johnson-Hanks, Bachrach, Morgan, and Kohler, 2011 forthcoming); the discussion below draws heavily from Chapter 3 of our NICHD contract report (Morgan et al. 2008, Chap. 3, "Theory Development by Parenthood Group: A Theory of Conjunctural Action"; see pp. 36–41).

2. A. McPherson and colleagues (1983, 2004) argue that many aspects of patterned social behaviors can be understood by treating individuals as located in an n-dimensional space defined in terms of characteristics that shape patterns of social life, such as income, education, and ethnicity/race..

3. The net error is the sum of the signed differences between intended and achieved parity. The values in Table 2.1 are the average net error per woman.

4. Gross errors are the sum of the absolute differences between intended parity (at age 24) and completed parity (at age 41+). Values in Table 2.1 are the average error per woman.

# CHAPTER THREE

# Between Poor and Prosperous
Do the Family Patterns of Moderately Educated
Americans Deserve a Closer Look?

*Andrew J. Cherlin*

Most experts agree that the severe recession that began in 2008 was the worst economic downturn since the Great Depression. While this crisis had an effect across all social classes, the job losses were particularly acute among the less-educated. Many of the jobs these workers were doing will never return because of the transformation of the American economy. The bankruptcy and restructuring of General Motors, for example, is likely to leave the firm with one-tenth the number of factory workers it employed in 1970 (Vlasic and Bunkley 2009). Indeed, the collapse of GM and Chrysler marked the symbolic end of an American labor aristocracy. For decades the workers on the automobile assembly lines and in other heavy industries were our country's blue-collar aristocrats. With their relatively high pay and generous fringe benefits, they were the envy of the rest of the working class. Their steady earnings allowed them to marry and support their families, if not royally then at least comfortably. Sons often followed fathers into the vast plants. (Few women held these kinds of jobs until recently.)

Now, after waves of layoffs, plant closings, and union givebacks, they are an endangered species. They are not alone. The kinds of jobs that provide a good, steady income to high school–educated adults are in decline, with some exceptions such as the health care industry. In my home city of Baltimore, the sprawling Sparrows Point works of Bethlehem Steel employed 30,000 workers in the 1950s, most of whom had no more than high school educations. Along with veterans' benefits such as low-interest home mortgages, their wages allowed them to buy a piece of the American dream—a modest home, a car, all the latest appliances. Today the factory employs fewer than 2,500 workers who, because of technological advances, produce about as much steel as the plant did in its heyday (Reutter 2001; Connolly 2007). The disappearance of these jobs is a sad development for the would-be workers and for those who, in better times, might have married them and helped to raise their children.

But it is also symptomatic of a larger problem: widening differences in the family lives of Americans according to their level of education. A half-century ago most people, rich or poor, grew up in the same kind of families: two married parents and their biological children. But today the kind of family you live in depends on your education and your income. A number of social scientists have written about this development. It is often characterized as a demographic divide between the less-educated and the better-educated (McLanahan 2004). The most common dividing line is having a four-year college degree, which corresponds to the idea that a college education is needed to succeed in the new American economy and that those who succeed are more likely to marry and to stay married. (To simplify my prose, I will use the term "college degree" to mean a four-year bachelor of arts or sciences degree.)

This contrast between the fortunes of the college-degree and the non-college-degree populations provides a valuable perspective on the current state of American family life. As for the latter group, most of the attention has been paid to the least educated among them: the disproportionately minority population without high school degrees who can be found in central city, concentrated-poverty neighborhoods. These are among the most disadvantaged Americans. They are also the ones whose family lives center least on marriage and most on single parenting. For example, Kathryn Edin, who with Timothy Nelson and Joanna Reed describes the romantic relationships of economically disadvantaged men (Chapter 4 this volume), has explained why low-income women are often willing to have children without marrying (Edin and Kefalas 2005). Sara McLanahan has painted a broad picture of the non-college-degree population, for the most part not differentiating among them, in her valuable study of "fragile families," which she discusses in Chapter 5 (see also Carlson, McLanahan, and England 2004; Carlson and Furstenberg 2006).

Annette Lareau, who in Chapter 6 presents follow-up interviews to her well-known study of social class differences in parenting styles and educational experiences (Lareau 2003), defined three classes. Middle-class children had at least one parent with a professional or managerial occupation; working-class children had a parent with a lower-level white-collar or a skilled blue-collar position, and poor children had parents who relied on public assistance or did not participate regularly in the labor market. But perhaps because of the constraints of her modest-sized qualitative sample, she combined the latter two categories in most of her analyses, in which she writes of the "concerted cultivation" of the middle-class parents and the "accomplishment of natural growth" among the working class and the poor.

Without denying the importance of studies of the poor or of broad-brush studies of the families of non-college-educated individuals, I would suggest that we may be overlooking the emerging family patterns of people in the middle. Frank Furstenberg makes a similar point in Chapter 8 in this volume, when he writes, "In fact, it is remarkable how much of our research concentrates on either the top (people like us) or the bottom of the social structure." This middle group is less easy to define, less concentrated in central cities, and therefore harder to observe, but of great interest nevertheless. It is the group we used to call blue collar, back when mostly male chambray-shirted workers manned factories by the millions. We still sometimes use the label working class to refer to them. Given the importance of education in the economic prospects of Americans today, I would define this group as people who have graduated from high school or have a general educational development (GED) certificate and who may have taken some college courses but who do not have a college degree. Since I am not convinced that they constitute a coherent social class, I will simply call them the "moderately educated." I will call individuals without a high school degrees or a GED the "least-educated" and those with college degrees the "most-educated." The moderately educated are a large group. Among women age 19 to 44 in the 2002 National Survey of Family Growth (NSFG), the moderately educated constituted 62 percent of the sample—far more than the least-educated and the most-educated combined.

A word on the GED: much research shows that the economic payoff to attaining a GED is minimal, except for high school dropouts with low skills (Cameron and Heckman 1993; Tyler 2005). Consequently, some researchers would include women who have a GED but no high school diploma in the "less than high school degree" educational group. But in the 2002 NSFG, which I draw upon in this chapter, the percentage of women who can be classified as high school graduates but whose highest degree is in reality a GED is modest: 10 percent of all high school graduates among women age 35 to 44 (the age range included in Figure 3.1), 9 percent among women 19 to 44 (see Figure 3.2), and 9 percent among women under age 40 (see Figure 3.3). Therefore, the placement of GED-only women in the "high school degree" category by me (Figure 3.1) and by Kennedy and Bumpass (2008) (Figures 3.2 and 3.3) is unlikely to affect the percentages that are depicted.

PAST LITERATURE

To be sure, much has been written by sociologists about working-class families. A literature dating back to the 1950s and 1960s described sex-segregated family lives in which husbands socialized among men and wives socialized among women, such as in the Italian-American neighborhood in Boston studied by Gans (1962) in 1957 and 1958. Wives also were said to retain a strong attachment to their mothers, according to a study of working-class families in London in 1955 (Willmott and Young 1957). Thus marriage required little of the friendship and companionship between husbands and wives that was becoming such an important part of the middle-class family. Moreover, people often complained to observers about marriage. E. E. LeMasters, for instance, hung out between 1967 and 1972 at a working-class tavern patronized mostly by construction and trade workers—whom he called, in the title of his book, *Blue-Collar Aristocrats* (LeMasters 1975). He reported that men complained about the institution of marriage—specifically, the constraints it put on them. They enjoyed socializing with their male friends, but they complained that their wives wanted them to spend more time at home. When LeMasters talked to their wives, he found that they complained about the unfair division of labor: they took care of children and the household, sometimes had jobs too, and had to satisfy their husbands' sexual demands even if they were not in the mood. They said they gave too much and received too little in return. Nevertheless, as LeMasters noted, the men provided their families a decent standard of living. He wrote:

> Thus a wife does not leave a blue-collar elite man for trivial reasons. Unless he becomes an alcoholic, or abuses her and the children, she tends to be philosophical about his spending too much time at the tavern. "I wish he would come home from work earlier," one wife said, "but he's a lot better husband than some others I could name." (p. 46)

Lillian Rubin also reported on sex-segregated lives in the earlier of two books she published on working-class families, based on interviews she did in 1972 (Rubin 1976). In the economic realm, these husbands and wives believed that men should earn money and women should care for the children and the home. Even though low incomes often led wives to work at least part-time outside the home, the ideal remained the breadwinner-homemaker family. Being the sole earner was a source of pride for men, an ideal to strive for. One husband is quoted as saying: "She doesn't have to work. We can get by. Maybe we'll have to take it easy on spending, but that's okay with me. It's worth it to have her home where she belongs." (p. 179)

In fact, Rubin's book, published a year after LeMasters's book and aptly titled *Worlds of Pain*, presented an unremittingly negative picture of working-class life: Husbands were trapped in stultifyingly boring work, scrimping and saving for recreational vehicles that sat unused in their driveways fifty weeks a year. Their resentful wives, caring for children and keeping house with little or no help, were stuck home while their husbands enjoyed themselves at the tavern or bowling alley. Life was grim and unsatisfying.

But this picture of working-class families is now well out of date. Gans, Young, and Willmott, and later Rubin, reissued their books with new introductions and postscripts. All of them reported that the distinctiveness of the working-class family had faded somewhat. The sex-segregated family circle is no longer as central to the sons and daughters of the Italian-Americans Gans studied, he concluded in 1982. The more prosperous (compared to the 1950s) next generation did not need as often to borrow money, clothes, or food from their parents and siblings. It was harder for the sons and daughters to socialize because they did not live as close to one another as family members of their parents' generation did. Moreover, resistance had grown to the conformity that the family circle demanded. According to Young and Willmott, writing in 1986, migration out of the working-class neighborhood of London they studied had loosened the bond between the daughter and her mum.

Both Gans and Rubin also observed that the strict division of roles between wife and husband had weakened, although most men still did substantially less of the child care and housework. Rubin noted that even when the women in her original study were working outside the home, they defined themselves primarily as wives and mothers. Paid work was something they did to help their families, but it was not an important part of their identity. Many shared their husbands' views that, ideally, they ought to stay home. By 1992, wrote Rubin in a new introduction to her book, these attitudes had changed: women viewed employment as a proper activity, necessary to maintain their families' lifestyles and also a source of satisfaction and self-esteem.

In fact, Rubin published a new book in 1994, based on reinterviews with thirty-six of the same couples as well as interviews of new couples in the early 1990s (Rubin 1994). In it, she seemed almost nostalgic for the economic stability that the blue-collar jobs of the 1960s and 1970s had provided to the families whose grim lives she had described in the earlier book. She noted the harmful effects of the worsening job market for the non-college-educated—especially for the kinds of blue-collar jobs that husbands used to hold—on the morale of men and their families. A woman who had a job as a hotel desk clerk told Rubin six months after her husband was laid off as a welder:

> We did okay for a while, but the longer it lasts, the harder it gets . . . I tell him maybe he has to get in a different line of work because maybe they don't need so many welders anymore. But he just gets mad and tells me I don't know what I'm talking about. (p. 121)

Her husband later told Rubin:

> I can't go out and get one of those damn flunky jobs like my wife wants me to. I've been working all my life, making a decent living, too, and I got pride in what I do. I try to tell her, but she doesn't listen. (p. 122)

This literature reminds us that one should be careful not to romanticize the working-class marriages of the past and not to overlook the inequalities and tensions that were so common among them. It also suggests that in some ways the family lives of the so-called working class have become *less* distinctive: the companionate marriage, with its friendship-based and couple-centered lives has become common. The dual-earner model is widespread. Yet in others ways, new developments in the last few decades have fostered the emergence of distinctive patterns among this middle group.

MULTIPLE PARTNERSHIPS

In my own work, I began to think of the moderately educated as distinctive when I was compiling data for a book on the multiple unions that Americans tend to have (Cherlin 2009). In Chapter 5, McLanahan discusses the phenomenon of "multiple partner fertility," that is to say, having children with more than one partner. Americans do have more partners than adults in most other Western countries (Cherlin 2009). Using the 2002 NSFG data, I calculated, according to education and race/ethnicity, the percentage of 35-to-44-year-old women who had already experienced three marital or cohabiting partnerships. For example, a woman may have been married, ended that marriage, moved in with another man, ended that relationship, and moved in with a third man. (A cohabiting relationship that led to marriage was counted as one partnership, not two.) You might expect that the less education people have, the more partnerships they would form and dissolve, and that African Americans and Hispanics would have more partnerships than whites. But that is not what the data show.

Figure 3.1 displays the percentages for women by education and race. Looking first at education, we see that the highest percentage was for women with high school degrees, and the second highest percentage was for women without high school degrees. To be sure, the difference between the two groups is modest, but we can conclude that multiple unions were at least as common among high school graduates as they were among the women who had not graduated from high school. Additional tabulations that distinguish between marriages and cohabiting unions show that high school graduates had the largest percentage of two or three marriages of any educational group and the second highest percentage (after the less-than-high-school group) of multiple cohabiting unions. In addition, the bottom half of the figure shows that the race/ethnicity with the highest number of multiple partners was non-Hispanic whites by a substantial margin over African Americans and Hispanics. Thus, having multiple partnerships was not a minority-group pattern. Further analyses showed that non-Hispanic whites were most likely to have had multiple marriages, whereas Hispanics were more likely to have married once, and African Americans were much more likely than either group to have never married.

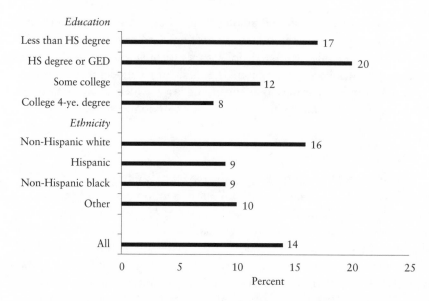

*Figure 3.1.*   Percentage of women age 35 to 44 who had had three or more residential partnerships. Source: Cherlin 2009, Chart 14, p.211.

Consequently, if one is looking for a profile of the typical woman with many unions it would not be a black or Hispanic high school dropout but rather a white woman with a high school degree. This subgroup is most likely to have had multiple marriages as well as a substantial number of cohabiting unions. My sense is that this group includes many young women and men who are seeking the conventional married lifestyle. This is particularly true among non-Hispanic whites, who are more likely to turn a cohabiting relationship into a marriage than are African Americans (Manning and Smock 1995). But they are doing so in a social and economic climate in which marriage seems less attainable and in which cohabitation, in their thoughts, becomes the best alternative to it. So in addition to marrying, they also form cohabiting unions and are sometimes willing to have children in those unions even if they think that conditions that would allow for marriage do not yet exist.

These racial-ethnic and educational differences held in further statistical analyses. I estimated three sets of regression equations, each of which included indicators of education, race-ethnicity (Hispanic, African American, or non-Hispanic white), race, age, and religious attendance. The first was a Poisson regression model based on the number of partners a woman has had; the second was a logistic regression model based on a woman's having had three or more partners versus having had two or fewer; and the third was a logistic regression model based on a woman's having had two or more partners versus having had one or none. The results of all three were very similar: women with more education had significantly fewer partners; high school graduates (who did not attend college) had the most partners. Hispanics and African Americans had significantly fewer partners than non-Hispanic whites; women who attended religious services at least once a month had significantly fewer partners than women who attended less often; and older women had significantly more partners.

WHAT IS NEW?

Yet we must ask whether this phenomenon represents something new about the conditions of moderately educated families rather than merely reflecting a twenty-first-century version of the same struggles that sociologists have written about for decades. The strongest evidence that we are seeing something new, I would suggest, is the transformation of the American economy that has occurred since the iconic working-class literature appeared. In particular, the key development is the sharp decline during the past two decades of the kinds of decent-paying blue-collar jobs that used to sustain what was called the working class. Today it is much more difficult for moderately educated workers to play the role of the steady provider. These men and women tend to do the types of work that economists call routine jobs or middle-skill jobs—those that require some skill but not a college degree. Well before the economic crisis of 2008–09 accelerated the process, these jobs were moving to other countries or shrinking into computer chips. Think not only of factory workers but also of bookkeepers, clerks, and telephone operators. These are the kinds of jobs that someone with a high school education could do. Since about 1990 these routine jobs have been disappearing so fast that the wages of Americans who perform them have been edging closer to the wages of the least-educated workers, who hold low-skilled manual jobs such as waiter, janitor, and gardener. Manual jobs that serve the personal needs of others cannot be outsourced overseas or automated easily; professionals still need people to take their lunch orders, clean their offices, and cut their lawns. But manual jobs do not pay well.

Put another way, the middle may be dropping out of the American labor market. Autor, Katz, and Kearney (2006) provided evidence of what they labeled the "polarization" of the labor market by comparing wage-ratios at different points in the distribution of wages. They showed that the so-called 50:10 ratio—the average wage of a worker at the fiftieth percentile in hourly wages compared to the average wage of a worker at the tenth percentile—dropped sharply between 1987 and 2004. If we take the numerator as indicating the typical wage earned by someone in the middle of the wage distribution and the denominator as indicating the typical wage of someone near the bottom of the distribution, then the declining ratio suggests that the wages offered for routine work have been edging closer to the wages offered for manual work. In contrast, the 90:50 ratio—the average wage at the nine-tieth percentile compared to the fiftieth—continued to grow. This latter result means that the earnings of people with high-skilled professional and manage-rial jobs have continued to grow relative to the wages of other workers.

The result is a labor market with a prosperous top, a sinking middle, and a growing low-wage bottom. People with college degrees can usually find well-paying professional or managerial jobs, but what is left for every-one else is a declining demand for routine work and a steady demand for low-paying manual work. This is the twenty-first-century economic reality that young adults must contend with as they try to establish their own fam-ily lives. The wages of men without college degrees have fallen since they peaked in the early 1970s, and the wages of women without college degrees have failed to grow. In fact, high school–educated young men today may be the first generation in memory to earn less than their fathers did. By 1996, the average 30-year-old husband with a high school degree earned 20 per-cent less than a comparable man in 1979 (Levy 1998).

There is, however, a less negative view of the occupational outlook for the moderately educated. Not all occupations in the middle are declining. The demand in the health industry, for instance, is high for jobs such as respiratory therapists and radiology technicians. Skilled trade workers such as electricians have seen an increased demand for their services. Paralegals are in demand. Most of the occupants of these positions do not have college degrees, but nearly all have some advanced education or intensive training beyond a high-school degree. Holzer and Lerman (2007, 2009) claim that substantial demand still exists for high school–plus workers such as these and that further growth in demand is likely. There still are selective oppor-tunities, they suggest, for young adults with a vocational certificate, on-the-job training, or an associate of arts degree. They urge support for training programs and career-oriented education as a way to substantially improve the occupational and earnings prospects of young adults who cannot or will not obtain a four-year college degree.

Perhaps, then, the moderately educated are themselves heterogeneous, with the high school–plus group having greater opportunities than those whose education or training stopped at high school graduation. Looking back at Figure 3.1, we can see that the percentage of women with three or more partnerships was substantially lower for the "some college" group than for the "high school degree or GED" group. The latter may be more vulnerable economically and more likely to have multiple partnerships as a result. Still, Holzer and Lerman do not claim that all workers in the high school–plus category have good labor market prospects; rather, they argue against the view that few workers except those with four-year college degrees can be expected to find decent, stable jobs.

The second reason why the current condition of the families of moderately educated individuals represents a new development is the growing importance of cohabitation. It was simply not acceptable to for couples to live together without being married in the days when LeMasters, Gans, and Rubin (in her earlier book) were writing. Now that cohabitation is an option, it has altered the behavior of couples. Although young men are no longer expected to be the sole earners for their families, they still are expected to be the main earners. If they do not have steady jobs with decent pay, they are not as attractive as marriage partners. A generation or two ago, the couple might have dated and might have had sex, but they would not have lived together. Today the choice set has changed. A young woman whose partner does not yet have steady work might be reluctant to marry him, but she might well cohabit with him. Moreover, because they live in an era when the stigma of childbearing outside of marriage has faded, some of these cohabiting couples are willing to have children together even though they are not willing to marry.

Figure 3.2 shows the percentage of women age 19 to 44 in the 1995 and 2002 NSFG samples who had ever cohabited. It shows, first, just how common cohabitation has become among the moderately educated. By 2002, 63 percent of women with a high school degree had cohabited, as had almost

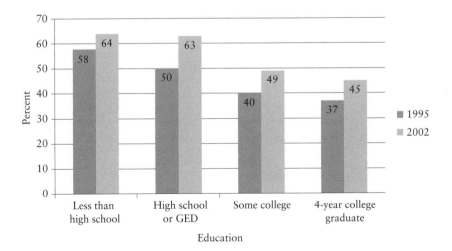

*Figure 3.2.* Percentage of women age 19 to 44 who had ever cohabitated. Source: Kennedy and Bumpass 2008; Open access journal. See: http://www.demographic -research.org/info/copyright_notice.htm.

half of those with some college education but no four-year degree. The figure also shows that, between 1995 and 2002, cohabitation increased fastest among high school graduates: note that in 1995, high-school graduates cohabited less often than women who had not completed high school; but by 2002 high-school graduates had caught up.

Amid all the concern about "out-of-wedlock births," it is not widely known that since the early 1980s, the percentage of children born to women living alone has hardly increased. Rather, most of the growth in the share of children born to unmarried women has been to women who are in cohabiting relationships (Bumpass and Lu 2000; Kennedy and Bumpass 2008). The most recent data suggest that perhaps half of all births to unmarried mothers occur in cohabiting unions (Kennedy and Bumpass 2008). Since more than one-third of all births are nonmarital (U.S. National Center for Health Statistics 2009), we can estimate that about one out of six (one-half of one-third) American children are being born to cohabiting couples. And the greatest growth of these cohabiting couples with children can be found among the moderately educated. Figure 3.3 shows the trend during the 1990s, as indicated by the 1995 and 2002 NSFG samples. In both surveys, women without high school degrees had the highest percentage of births occurring in cohabitations. But between the two surveys, the greatest growth in births to cohabiting couples occurred among the two middle categories: high school degree recipients and those with some college, among whom the percentages doubled. By the latter period nearly one-fourth of births to women with high school degrees occurred within cohabiting relationships. Recall that moderately educated women are far more numer-

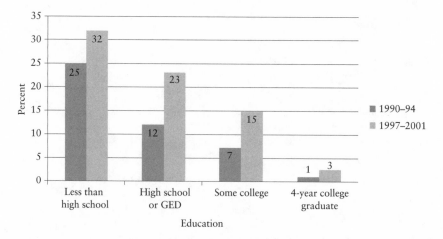

*Figure 3.3.*   Percentage of births that occurred to cohabiting women under age 40. Source: Kennedy and Bumpass 2008.

ous among the 19-to-44 age group than are the least- and most-educated. Therefore, we can say with confidence that the growth of childbearing in cohabiting relationships has been driven by an increase in the number of the moderately educated.

A third relevant way that family life among the moderately educated has changed is the growing segmentation of the marriage market. A century ago, a Catholic college graduate was more likely to marry a Catholic high school graduate than to step outside of his or her religion and marry a Protestant college graduate. That is no longer true. Schooling has become the great sorting machine of the marriage market (Kalmijn 1991). Today, college graduates are increasingly marrying each other. By pooling their incomes, they can consolidate their gains in the new economy. At the other end of the educational gradient, people without high school degrees are marrying each other, if they marry at all, because everyone one else seems to shun them (Schwartz and Mare 2005). In between are those whose highest degree is from high school or perhaps a two-year college, who are also increasingly marrying each other and, in doing so, constituting a third segment of the marriage market. They marry more than the least-educated but less than the most-educated (Kennedy and Bumpass 2008).

The marriages that do form among the least-educated and moderately educated Americans are precarious. Over the past two or three decades, the divorce rate has fallen for women with college degrees, while remaining steady or going up for women without them. As a result, large differences now exist in the risk of divorce. According to estimates by Raley and Bumpass (2003) from the 1995 NSFG, 34 percent of the first marriages of women without a high school degree will end in divorce or separation within five years—a very high break-up rate for just five years of marriage. The break-up rates are still substantial for the marriages of people in the middle: 23 percent for those who ended their education after high school, and 26 percent for those who took some college courses but do not have a four-year degree. Among women with college degrees, on the other hand, just 13 percent of marriages will end in divorce or separation within five years.

A pair of surveys of married couples in 1980 and 2000 that asked similar questions suggests considerable strain over money and work among a group whom the researchers call young, dual-earner, working-class couples (Amato, Booth, Johnson, and Rogers, 2007). In both surveys, many wives reported that they were working because their families needed the money, not to develop careers, and many of them said they wanted to work fewer hours or not at all. Wives thought that the amount of housework and child care they did was unfair compared to how much their husbands did. Husbands, for their part, complained that their wives came home from work irritable and tense and that their jobs interfered with the life of the family. They were less supportive of their wives' employment. Both wives and husbands were more likely to say that they had problems in their marriage because one of them gets angry easily, is critical or moody, or will not talk to the other one. They were also more likely to say that the thought of getting a divorce or separation had crossed their minds or that they had discussed the idea with family members or close friends. Overall, in both surveys working-class, dual-earner couples had the most stressed, least happy marriages of any group in the Amato et al. (2007) study—worse than poor couples and much worse than middle-class couples. Whereas dual-earner marriages were the least troubled among the middle class, they were the most troubled among the working class.

MONEY AND MARRIAGE

The best in-depth information we have about how cohabitation is changing the family lives of young adults with moderate levels of education come from a qualitative study of 115 adults age 21 to 35 in the Toledo, Ohio, area who were currently cohabiting or who had recently cohabited. The researchers characterized the sample as "largely working class and lower middle class (i.e., generally high school graduates and those with some college or technical school training)" (Manning and Smock 2005). The study showed the great importance that these young adults attach to the man's labor market position in making decisions about whether to marry. About three times as many women as men said that their cohabiting partners needed to do better in the job market before they would consider marrying them (Smock, Manning, and Porter 2005). The authors write:

> For example, Henry, a 33-year-old information systems manager, reflects: "Had I been . . . in a financial position where I was able to take care of myself and a family, then it might have moved things along quicker." Jamal, 27 years old, says, "What would make me ready? Knowing that I could provide. . . ." Victor, a 27-year-old male, states that "the male's financially responsible for like, you know, the household, paying the bills."

Young adults who experience these financial worries are increasingly cohabiting rather than marrying. Young men who are out of school and working, but whose incomes are unstable—they may be working part-time or at a series of short-term jobs, are more likely to start a cohabiting relationship than are men with steady, full-time earnings or men with no earnings (Oppenheimer 2003). Smock et al. (2005) noted that the idea of marrying *after* economic stability has been achieved contrasts with the situation Rubin (1976) reported, in which working-class couples married relatively young and then struggled economically for several years.

The Toledo young adults frequently mentioned the wedding as a factor in their decision-making, even though the researchers did not raise the topic (Smock et al. 2005). Several young adults said that they did not want to "go downtown" to get married—meaning a ceremony by a justice of the peace, perhaps at city hall—but rather would wait until they had saved enough money for a wedding party with friends and family. This attitude suggests that marriage has become a symbolic step for many young couples, one that is celebrated publicly when the couple is on adequate financial footing and their relationship is going well emotionally. It is consistent with the idea of marriage as a capstone experience, which I have discussed elsewhere (Cherlin 2004). Whereas marriage was once the first step into adulthood, it is now often the last. Overall, cohabitation seems to be emerging as the lifestyle of choice for couples in which the man is doing well enough that they can envision marrying some day but not so well that they feel they can marry now.

A DISTINCTIVE MIDDLE?

I have argued that the family lives of the moderately educated are distinct from the lives of those with more education and less education. What distinguishes the family lives of the moderately educated from the college-degree population is the willingness of the former to have children in cohabiting unions or without a live-in partner. Far fewer women with college degrees have children outside of marriage than in any other educational group. Yet the moderately educated marry in larger numbers and are more likely to have children within marriage than are the least-educated. Because their family lives encompass both cohabitation and marriage, the moderately educated have more unions than the least-educated (who are less likely to marry) or the most-educated (who are less likely to cohabit). A similar dynamic leads to more multiple unions among non-Hispanic whites than among Hispanics, many of whom are in a first marriage, or among African Americans, who are much less likely to have ever married. Thus, white, moderately educated individuals have the greatest amount of turnover in married or cohabiting partners.

One wonders whether changes in marriage, cohabitation, and fertility among the moderately educated point to a broader decline in what we might call the working-class lifestyle. Lamont (2000) interviewed working-class men and concluded that, among whites at least, they constructed a moral world for themselves based on a "disciplined self." It centered on working hard every day, often with their hands, and being a steady provider to their wives and children. It created a lifestyle that family and friends saw as respectable. This work ethic and sense of responsibility became a central part of a worker's self-worth, Lamont argued, and workers used it to differentiate themselves from middle-class professionals, whom they viewed as lacking personal integrity and sincerity. (Black workers, Lamont writes, also constructed a moral sense of self, but it centered not on discipline but rather on sharing with others in need—what she called a "caring self.")

But what happens when the conditions that allowed workers to achieve a disciplined self, rooted in manual work, no longer exist? Lamont restricted her interviews to men who had been continuously employed for at least five years in occupations such as mechanic, heating system specialist, and letter carrier. What occurs when young men cannot easily find continuous, full-time employment in these kinds of occupations? We might expect to see a weakening of the disciplined self. And one consequence of that weakening, the evidence in this chapter suggests, is a decline in marriage and a rise in cohabitation. More speculatively, another consequence could be a decline in attendance at religious services. Many mainstream churches center their activities on married couples and their children (Edgell 2006). Working-class couples who are married and have steady incomes can participate in these churches and receive reinforcement for their lifestyle. Yet when a transformed economy makes marriage and steady work more difficult to obtain, those who in better times might have married and attended church may be reluctant to show up.

To be sure, we should not romanticize the typical working-class lifestyle of the mid-twentieth century. The older literature that I have reviewed shows that blue-collar family life had many flaws. And not everyone need marry or participate in organized religion. Nevertheless, if what we are seeing are signs of a large group of moderately educated Americans, cut off from steady, decent-paying jobs, from marriage, and possibly from other core social institutions, there might be cause for concern. This social disengagement could portend not only a growing economic gap but also a growing social gap between the moderately educated and the college-educated middle class.

Yet it must be said that the family lives of the moderately educated are still in flux. The most recent data that I can cite in this chapter are from 2002, and some data come from surveys that are five or ten years older than that. The comparisons between the information in the 1995 and 2002 NSFG samples suggest that rapid change in the place of cohabitation and in fertility was occurring in the 1990s and early 2000s. If the pace of change was maintained in the late 2000s, these data may no longer be a reliable guide to educational differences in family life. The propensity of the moderately educated to incorporate marriage into their lives could have weakened and have approached the lesser place of marriage among the least-educated. We must await newer sources of information to say with confidence what family lives are like today.

For now, the best available data suggest that moderately educated couples, the would-be heirs to factory jobs that faded away, are still trying to raise children together, still shooting for the American dream of marriage, kids, good jobs, and a home. Yet they are increasingly frustrated by the job market. Those who can only find short-term employment with little stability and a limited future tend to live together in brittle, easy-to-end cohabiting unions. Although they still marry, stable, long-term marriage often eludes them. Their lives belie our image of the American family as a great engine of equality that provides children, rich or poor, with the upbringing they need to be successful. Instead, their experiences show that the American family, rocked by changes in our globalized and automated economy, is increasingly dividing us rather than uniting us.

REFERENCES

Amato, Paul R., Alan Booth, David R. Johnson, and Stacy J. Rogers. 2007. *Alone Together: How Marriage in America Is Changing.* Cambridge, MA: Harvard University Press.

Autor, David H., Lawrence F. Katz, and Melissa Kearney. 2006. "The Polarization of the U.S. Labor Market." *American Economic Review* 96: 189–94.

Bumpass, Larry L., and Hsien-hen Lu. 2000. "Trends in Cohabitation and Implications for Children's Family Contexts in the United States." *Population Studies* 54: 19–41.

Cameron, Stephen V., and James J. Heckman. 1993. "The Nonequivalence of High School Equivalents." *Journal of Labor Economics* 11: 1–47.

Carlson, Marcia J., and Frank F. Furstenberg, Jr. 2006. "The Prevalence and Correlates of Multipartnered Fertility among Urban U.S. Parents." *Journal of Marriage and Family* 68: 718–32.

Carlson, Marcia, Sara McLanahan, and Paula England. 2004. "Union Formation in Fragile Families." *Demography* 41: 237–61.

Cherlin, A. J. 2004. "The Deinstitutionalization of American Marriage." *Journal of Marriage and Family* 66: 848–61.

———. 2009. *The Marriage-Go-Round: The State of Marriage and the Family in America Today.* New York: Alfred A. Knopf.

Connolly, Allison. 2007 (June 21). "15 Days for Sparrows Point." *Baltimore Sun.*

Edgell, Penny. 2006. *Religion and Family in a Changing Society.* Princeton, NJ: Princeton University Press.

Edin, Kathryn, and Maria J. Kefalas. 2005. *Promises I Can Keep: Why Poor Women Put Motherhood before Marriage.* Berkeley: University of California Press.

Gans, Herbert J. 1962. *The Urban Villagers: Group and Class in the Lives of Italian-Americans.* New York: Free Press.

Holzer, Harry J., and Robert I. Lerman. 2007. "America's Forgotten Middle-Skill Jobs: Education and Training Requirements in the Next Decade and Beyond." Washington, DC: Urban Institute. ehttp://www.urban.org/url.cfm ?ID=411633 [July 9, 2009].

———. 2009. "The Future of Middle-Skill Jobs." Center on Children and Families

Brief no. 41. Washington, DC: Brookings Institution. http://www.brookings
.edu//media/Files/rc/papers/2009/02_middle_skill_jobs_holzer/02_middle
_skill_jobs_holzer.pdf [July 9, 2009].

Kalmijn, Matthijs. 1991. "Shifting Boundaries: Trends in Religious and Educational Homogamy." *American Sociological Review* 56: 786–800.

Kennedy, Sheela, and Larry Bumpass. 2008. "Cohabitation and Children's Living
Arrangements: New Estimates from the United States" *Demographic Research*
19: 1663–92.

Lareau, Annette. 2003. *Unequal Childhoods: Class, Race, and Family Life*. Berkeley:
University of California Press.

LeMasters, E. E. 1975. *Blue-Collar Aristocrats: Life-Styles at a Working-Class Tavern*. Madison: University of Wisconsin Press.

Levy, Frank. 1998. *The New Dollars and Dreams: American Incomes and Economic
Change*. New York: Russell Sage Foundation.

Manning, Wendy D., and Pamela J. Smock. 1995. "Why Marry? Race and the
Transition to Marriage among Cohabitors." *Demography* 32: 509–20.

———. 2005. "Measuring and Modeling Cohabitation: New Perspectives from
Qualitative Data." *Journal of Marriage and Family* 67: 989–1002.

McLanahan, Sara. 2004. "Diverging Destinies: How Children Are Faring under the
Second Demographic Transition." *Demography* 41: 607–27.

Oppenheimer, Valerie K. 2003. "Cohabiting and Marriage during Young Men's
Career-Development Process." *Demography* 40: 127–49.

Raley, R. Kelly, and Larry L. Bumpass. 2003. "The Topography of the Divorce
Plateau: Levels and Trends in Union Stability in the United States after 1980."
*Demographic Research* 8: 245–59.

Reutter, Mark. 2001 (October 19). "Shadow of Steel's Lost Empire." *Baltimore Sun*.

Rubin, Lillian B. 1976. *Worlds of Pain: Life in the Working-Class Family*. New
York: Basic Books.

———. 1994. *Families on the Fault Line*. New York: Harper Collins.

Schwartz, Christine R., and Robert D. Mare. 2005. "Trends in Educational Assortative Marriage from 1940 to 2003." *Demography* 42: 621–46.

Smock, Pamela J., Wendy D. Manning, and Meredith Porter. 2005. "'Everything's
There Except Money": How Money Shapes Decisions to Marry among Cohabitors." *Journal of Marriage and Family* 67: 680–96.

Tyler, John H. 2005. "The General Educational Development (GED) Credential:
History, Current Research, and Directions for Policy and Practice." *Review of
Adult Learning and Literacy* 5: 45–84.

U.S. National Center for Health Statistics. 2009. "Births: Final Data for 2006."
*National Vital Statistics Reports* 57, no. 7. (http://www.cdc.gov/nchs/data/nvsr
/nvsr57/nvsr57_07.pdf) [January 31, 2009].

Vlasic, Bill, and Nick Bunkley. 2009 (April 28). "G.M.'s Plan Envisions a Much
Smaller Automaker." *New York Times*. (http://www.nytimes.com/2009/04/28
/business/28auto.html?ref=us [April 28, 2009].

Willmott, Peter, and Michael Young. 1957. *Family and Kinship in East London*.
Harmondsworth, UK: Penguin Books.

# CHAPTER FOUR

# Daddy, Baby; Momma, Maybe

Low-Income Urban Fathers and the
"Package Deal" of Family Life

*Kathryn Edin, Timothy Nelson,*
*and Joanna Miranda Reed*

Economically disadvantaged fathers are far less likely to marry before having children than middle-class fathers are, and they have them far earlier (Nock 2007). When they do marry, they are more likely to divorce (Martin 2004). In the absence of a marital tie, the government assigns them financial obligations, which most do not satisfy fully (U.S. Census Bureau 2007). Thus, such men's fathering behavior attracts a good deal of attention from both scholars and policymakers.

Little attention is paid, however, to these men's roles as romantic partners. Qualitative studies have been an exception to this trend, both the classic community studies (i.e., Drake and Cayton 1945; Liebow 1967; Hannerz 1969; Hollingshead 1949; Moreland 1958; Powdermaker 1939; Rainwater 1970; 1960) and more recent qualitative work (Nelson, Clampet-Lundquist, and Edin 2002; Furstenberg 2001; Hill 2007; Reed 2007; Roy 2008; Waller 2008; 2002; Wilson 1996). As these studies have repeatedly shown, economically disadvantaged men do engage in romantic relationships; this is the context into which most of their children are born (though some children are the product of nonrelationships, i.e., one-night stands) (Augustine, Nelson, and Edin 2009). New survey research reveals that fully eight in ten nonmarital children now enter the world with a mother and father who describe themselves as "romantically involved"; up to half of those parents live together, and at least 70 percent of both mothers and fathers say there is at least a 50-50 chance they'll marry each other. Yet it is also true that fewer than a third of such couples are still together by the time the child turns 5(Center for Research on Child Wellbeing 2007). Low-income couples who marry before having children are fragile as well—much more so than middle-class married couples are—but they still function as partners for a considerable period of time (Martin 2004; McLanahan 2004).

We offer the reader two portraits of the romantic partnerships of such men. The first is of a relatively large group of very economically disadvantaged white and black men (with earnings below the poverty line for a family of four in the formal economy over the prior year) who live in poor and struggling working-class neighborhoods throughout the Philadelphia metropolitan area and have biological children, most of them outside of marriage. All were fathers of at least one minor child outside of a marital tie when we interviewed them. The second comes from a longitudinal, qualitative study of forty-eight unmarried couples who were first interviewed just after the birth of a nonmarital child and followed through the child's fourth birthday. These couples are not sampled according to their economic status or neighborhood characteristics, though most (like the population they represent) are nonetheless quite disadvantaged.

By exploring in depth the texture of their romantic lives and worldviews, we show that the function of the romantic tie for the father role departs radically from the traditional 1950s "package deal" conception of family life. Furstenberg and Cherlin (1991), and more recently Nicholas Townsend (2002), point to the family behaviors of men who came of age in an earlier generation, arguing that for these men fatherhood flowed through, and was contingent upon, men's relationship with the children's mother (see also Liebow 1967). Furstenberg and Cherlin coined the term "package deal" to explain the very low rates of father involvement among the divorced fathers they observed. In this view, the tie between the mother and father is central and serves to bind men to their obligations to their children—obligations they would otherwise ignore (e.g., in the case of divorce).[1]

Two of us (Edin and Nelson) and a multiracial team of graduate students spent seven years observing and interviewing low-income fathers residing in high-poverty neighborhoods in Philadelphia and its poorest inner suburb, Camden, New Jersey. All three of us, along with a large research team, participated in a four-year qualitative study of forty-eight unmarried couples, a subsample of respondents to a large representative survey of nonmarital births in three cities, Chicago, Milwaukee, and New York. We began interviewing these couples in the hospital right after the mother had given birth to a nonmarital child. The fathers in both studies were not only quite economically disadvantaged and fathering outside of a marital tie; they also came of age several decades later than the divorced men Furstenberg and Cherlin (1991) observed, or the 1972 high school graduates Townsend (2002) was writing about. Our average respondent reached adulthood (21) in the mid- to late 1990s.

For the men we have studied, notions of family life are radically different than the portrait that Furstenberg, Cherlin, and Townsend provide. In our story, the *father-child* relationship is typically what is viewed as central, and is what binds men to couple relationships—relationships that might not have otherwise formed or been maintained (see also Edin et al. 2007; Reed 2007; Roy 2008). This is not to say that such men are child-centric to the degree that mothers are (Edin and Kefalas 2005), only that in the realm of family relations, "Daddy, baby; momma maybe" is a fair representation of the worldview of many of the fathers we studied.

## METHOD

### The Philadelphia/Camden Fathers Study (PCFS)

We began the Philadelphia/Camden Father's Study with two and a half years of participant observation in one of the eight low-income communities (census tract clusters where at least 20 percent of the population lived in poverty in 1990) selected for the study. Based on this fieldwork, which began in 1995, we constructed an interview guide that we administered in systematic, repeated, in-depth interviews with 110 white and African American men between 1997 and 2002. We sampled equal numbers of blacks and non-Hispanic whites. To offer more of a life-course view, roughly half of our fathers were under 30 and the rest were older. During the prior year, the earnings of all of them were below the poverty line for a family of four in the formal economy. In the course of our conversations with these men, we collected detailed life histories. Our data come from these life histories (e.g., "Tell me how it was for you coming up," "Tell me the whole story of that relationship from the time you first met until now"), and from their answers to questions formulated to capture their worldview (e.g., "What should fathers do for their children?" "In your view, what makes for a good father?").

### The Time, Love, and Cash among Couples with Children Study (TLC3)

As part of the Fragile Families and Child Wellbeing Survey, a birth cohort study of mostly nonmarital children that is representative of births to women living in large cities, we conducted repeated, in-depth interviews with a stratified random subsample of couples in three cities. We targeted even numbers of blacks, Hispanics, and non-Hispanic whites. We excluded parents who were not romantically involved at the time of the child's birth and whose household income was more than $60,000 per year (30 percent of the survey sample). After conducting the survey in the hospital, couples who agreed to also participate in TLC3 were interviewed in their homes around the time when their child reached the following benchmarks: two to three months of age, and the first, second, and fourth birthdays. In each wave, the couple was interviewed together and each parent was also interviewed separately. Response rates were high, both in the initial wave and over time. Eighty-three percent of those asked agreed to participate; 100 percent of these completed couple interviews and 91 percent completed individual interviews at the time their babies were born (baseline). Round two response rates were 75 percent for couples and 81 percent for individuals from the original sample. Rates for round three were 69 percent for couples and 85 percent for individuals, and for round four 61 percent and 81 percent of the original sample, respectively. Couple response rates were lower, in part because about a third of the couples broke up during the course of the study. In our conversations with these parents, we collected detailed relationship histories and asked nearly identical questions about parents' worldviews as we had asked of the PCFS fathers. For added richness, we draw from both the individual and couple narratives here.

In the pages that follow, we begin with an analysis of the PCFS data, followed by a parallel analysis of the TLC3 couple-level data. The PCFS findings capture the worldview of a very disadvantaged group of fathers (by virtue of their income and neighborhood context) living in a single metropolitan area (Philadelphia/Camden). The TLC sample, drawn from three cities (Chicago, Milwaukee, and New York), imposed only modest income—and no neighborhood—criteria restrictions. The sample also captured an unusually large proportion of cohabiters. Thus the TLC3 sample is considerably more advantaged, both economically and in terms of their relationship characteristics, than the fathers in PCFS. A limitation of the samples is that they are both from large urban areas.

FINDINGS

*The Philadelphia/Camden Father's Study*

In PCFS, we asked each father to tell us "the whole story" of how he got together with the mothers of each of his children, and how these relationships developed over time. Typically, the pre-pregnancy narrative was noticeably succinct: the couple met, began to "affiliate," and then "came up pregnant." Men seldom even mentioned, much less discussed, any special qualities of their partners or any common tastes or values that drew the two together. Usually, the woman lived on his block, hung out on his corner, worked at the same job, was a friend of his sister, or the girlfriend of a friend, and she was simply willing to "affiliate" with him. Hanging out on the stoop, an occasional outing to a bar or a club, a window-shopping trip to a hot venue such as the downtown Gallery or the popular South Street strip, and fantasizing about shared children is what constituted romance (see also Townsend 2002: 42).

In the case of couples with a first birth together, the length of the courtship before conception was usually exceedingly brief—typically well under a year. As Furstenberg points out in Chapter 8 of this volume, exceedingly brief courtships were also a feature of the 1950s postwar marriage boom, often because a baby was on the way. Not surprisingly then, a common feature of men's narratives about the period before pregnancy is the ambiguous nature of the relational tie (see also Augustine, Nelson, and Edin 2009; Edin et al. 2007; Reed 2007; Roy 2008). Only rarely did such couples "fall in love," get engaged, or get married *before* conceiving a child together, though some did so later. Instead, they meet, they "associate," "affiliate," "communicate" begin to "kick it," "talk to each other," "get with each other," or "end up together." Then, "one thing leads to another." Consistent with England, McClintock, and Shafer's account in Chapter 1 of this volume, planned pregnancies were rare, yet the contraceptive practices that couples usually engaged in initially seldom continued for long (see also Edin and Kefalas 2005; Edin et al. 2008; Augustine, Nelson, and Edin 2009). Then the inevitable occurred: the woman "comes up pregnant" (see also Davis, Gardner, and Gardner 1941: 127).

John, a 24-year-old white father of one, described the sequencing of his relationship with his child's mother in this way: "Actually she was dating a friend of mine and somehow . . . she wanted me. . . . Eventually, I just got stuck with her for a little while." John didn't feel that he had found the ideal match—he "got stuck" with his baby's mother "for a little while." No language of love or even attraction (except her attraction to him) entered into this narrative, although there may well have been attraction involved. Nor does the phrase "a little while" indicate much commitment.

Thirty-nine-year-old Amin, a black father of two, described the development of his relationship with his youngest son's mother, a coworker in the dietary department of a local hospital, in this way: "She was attractive to me when I first saw her and I made my approach and we begin to socialize and communicate and then from there we began to affiliate at some point and time we became intimate and my son was born." As Amin told it, attraction, affiliation, and intimacy quite naturally—and inevitably—led to a son being born.

Despite the vague and bureaucratic language often used to describe these relationships (e.g., "affiliation"), almost no father had much trouble pinpointing when his relationship with his baby's mother began; they knew the point at which they got "together" with their baby's mother (though a small number of pregnancies do occur outside of relationships). Being together generally means that the couple is spending regular time together and defines the relationship as something more than a casual encounter or a one-night stand. Unlike a mere "hook-up," which has no distinct beginning or end, the termination of these relationships generally involve a "breakup." Furthermore, those who maintained outside liaisons usually viewed their own behavior as "cheating," though this did not mean that such relationships did not occur.

The verbs "affiliate," "associate," and "get with" suggest a bond that is more than a casual liaison, but not exactly a boyfriend/girlfriend relationship. Few of these men were consciously "courting" or searching for a life partner. Indeed, there is little evidence that they were even attempting to discriminate much based on who would be a suitable mother for their child. Many recalled that they did very much want children and fairly soon, even if not right then. Yet, as was the case with Furstenberg's 1950s couples (Chapter 8, this volume), who were propelled by an impending pregnancy into so-called lifelong marital commitments with partners they barely knew, the partnering process was far more haphazard than discriminating.

Bruce was a white father of 2-year-old twins. At 42, Bruce met a "new girl," Debbie. He didn't use protection because "Every time I had any kind of relationship there is no babies born so I didn't believe in safe sex. Next thing I knew, this girl Debbie, she was pregnant." Debbie made the announcement that she was seven weeks pregnant after the two had been together for only four months. Bruce told her, "'I am shooting blanks, you can't be pregnant . . . !' Then we went for a DNA test and that was when she found out that I was the father and she was the mother." Here a "family" was formed through a pregnancy brought to term in a relationship that was neither casual nor serious. Yet for Bruce, and most other men in our study, this was not viewed as a problem.

Tim, a white 23-year-old father of two, got a woman pregnant after only two months of being "together." "She used to go out with my friend. My friend was trying to get back with her, and I ended up getting with her. . . . We were only together for about two months, and she was getting pregnant. . . . I didn't mind at all." Tim didn't choose his baby's mother; he "ended up" with her. Yet he "didn't mind" when he learned she was pregnant.

Children, while usually desired, were only rarely explicitly planned, according to the narratives of men in PCFS (see Augustine, Nelson, and Edin, 2009). Yet contraception and other attempts to avoid pregnancy faded quickly as the couple began "affiliating." According to England and her co-authors, these fertility patterns are typical of less-educated men (Chapter 1, this volume). Once she became pregnant and decided to take the pregnancy to term (this decision is generally ceded to the woman), the bond between the two typically coalesced into more of a "relationship," though often in dramatic fits and starts (see also Edin and Kefalas 2005).

David, a black 30-year-old, was the father of five children by three women. In the months just before conceiving his fifth child, he was both "with" Deborah and "seeing" Kathy on the side. He went to Kathy whenever he and Deborah argued (though Deborah didn't know about Kathy). Which woman he should choose became a dilemma. However, when Deborah ended up pregnant, he decided to "do what was right" and chose her.

> [When I was first with Deborah] I had a girlfriend on the side too. Kathy. She's somebody that I met at a NA meeting. We got close and we were helping each other [with our addictions]. One thing led to another, and we got intimate. . . . Me and Deborah would get into an argument, she'd tell me to leave, I'd go stay with Kathy. (So how did you end it with Kathy?) Deborah got pregnant, and I had to do what was right, stand by Deborah.

Monte, a white 21-year-old, had three children by the same woman.

> I had just come out of a juvenile institution. I think I just turned 17 . . . and I started going with her friend. And then one day she came around and we started talking, then I went with her and left her friend, and me and her got together and started having kids together and then we got closer and closer. Then we started living together.

Monte's story illustrates well a typical sequence of events among men in our study: attraction and a moderate level of couple cohesion produced a pregnancy that was taken to term. It was at this point that the real relationship commenced; it was an outgrowth of the pregnancy, not the impetus. "Getting closer and closer" and then "living together" were things these couples generally accomplished *after* they conceived children, not before.

For Jack, a 33-year-old white father of two, his babies' mother was just one of several "girls" he met on a weekend home from college. She was already married to someone else, but left her husband for Jack that very day. Three months later she was pregnant, yet Jack saw nothing remarkable about the process by which he first became a father.

> [After high school] I went to college. . . . My grades weren't great but I was getting through. I was going back home every other weekend. . . . Met some girls. In turn, met my [baby's mother]. Shortly afterwards, she became pregnant, so I quit school, got a job.

Kahlid, a 28-year-old black father of one, said that it was just a few months into the relationship with his child's mother that the pair conceived. Despite the fact that the outside observer might read his narrative as a classic example of putting the cart before the horse, Kahlid, like Jack, viewed the sequence of events leading up to the pregnancy as unexceptional.

> (How long were you and your girlfriend together before she got pregnant?) Six, seven months. (What went through your mind?) I was happy! I came [over after] work and she said that she was getting symptoms and I was like, "What you talking about?" Morning sickness, throwing up, like this. So she went to the hospital. She took the test and she says she was pregnant . . . and

I was excited. It was my first child. And she was going to keep the baby, and I was happy. I knew I had to keep a job and take care of my responsibilities.

Evidence from the Fragile Families survey—the longitudinal birth co-hort survey that is representative of nonmarital births to couples living in large cities we mentioned earlier—offers additional support for the idea that the couple relationship is often galvanized by pregnancy (Rainwater 1970: 210–11). First, recall the high rate of couple cohesion at the time of a typi-cal nonmarital birth (80 percent). Second, roughly six in ten couples giving birth outside of marriage cohabit between the time of conception and the child's first birthday (Center for Research on Child Wellbeing 2007).

The glories of the delivery room are the high point of many fathers' life histories in PCFS. But the arrival of a child introduces a sharp contra-diction. On the one hand, fathers' narratives offer evidence that they are making some effort to sustain a relationship with their babies' mothers—often motivated by the desire to live with or be intensely involved with the children. But they also recognize, at least in part, that they are trying live out the dream of being part of a real "family unit" against almost impos-sible odds. Thus, while working to solidify these relationships, they are also often deeply fatalistic about their chances of staying together over the long term. This fatalism, which, as we will show, is fueled by men's fears about their ongoing ability to provide and their utter conviction that their babies' mothers will leave them if they fail, often rendered men's relational efforts half-hearted.

With only a few exceptions, fathers emphatically said that their rela-tionship with their children ought not be contingent on their relationship with their child's mother—and outright rejected the package deal. Yet they nonetheless realized that due to normative and legal practices governing the custody of nonmarital children, as well as their own limited economic prospects, their relationship to the mother was their conduit to the child.

Lavelle was the 34-year-old black father of a 4-year-old girl he called Little Toya. Little Toya's mother, also named Toya, didn't inform him that he'd become a father until his child was nearly 2. Lavelle, who had no other children, fell head over heels in love—with Little Toya. Nonetheless, once "Big Toya" made it clear she was going to restrict access to his daughter—to "try and play it off as a package deal," in Lavelle's words—he made consid-erable efforts to invest in a romantic relationship he had had little interest in previously.

Over the two-year period that we observed Lavelle "dealing" with Toya, we watched as he first tried to get visitation (she told him she would not allow her daughter to visit or go on outings with him unless she could come too), then proposed marriage (she turned him down, saying she didn't want to lose her freedom, her welfare benefits, or her Section 8 certificate), and then finally convinced her to let him call her his fiancée. What did he get out of the deal? She was willing to spend weekends with him in Camden (she lived about thirty minutes away), with Little Toya in tow. Lavelle confided that he would never have chosen Toya if she hadn't given birth to his child.

> I would have had to get visitation to see her [which is why] I'm still with the mother. 'Cause she wants to play it off like a package deal: "You can't go here without me." "You can't take her here without me." "You can't take her there without me." [First,] I said, "Okay, then I'm going to get visitation so I can take her when I want to take her. . . ." It is [difficult negotiating with Toya about little Toya]. She [feels] she gave birth to her so it's her way or the highway.

Self, a South Jersey black youth who was 21, knew he was to become a father as soon as his girlfriend learned of the pregnancy, but had such a fractious relationship with his baby's mother during the pregnancy that he didn't even visit the child until almost a year after she was born. The emotional connection he built with his daughter on the week-long visit was so compelling that he abandoned plans to attend college in Florida and decided instead to move in with the mother of his child.

> Almost a year after the child was born, finally I went to go visit her. . . . I was going to go away and whatnot. But [after that week], we decided that we would stay together. . . . I decided not to go to school, I decided to stay. We made the decision that I would search for proper employment and stay in the city and we would work together.

Across the income distribution, most couples now stay together, at least in part, because they share common interests and values. Owing to the lightning speed of the courtship period, disadvantaged couples who bear children together often find they have little in common, as we show below. But childbirth offers a vital new shared interest—a child—and this often brings some measure of emotional closeness. Consider the story of 38-year-old Tony, father of one.

> (How do you think the birth of Alyssa affected your relationship?) Um, I think in the beginning it brought us a lot closer together. (Why would it bring you closer together?) It just—being with this little baby that's just a part of both of us—it was amazing.

Bucket, a black father of two children by the same woman, described how the birth of his first child made things even a "little better."

> (How'd you all get along during the rest of the pregnancy?) We had a good time man. While she was pregnant, I couldn't go *nowhere*. Shoot! She wanted me to do this, wanted me to do that. I was like a puppy anyway. I waited on

her. I did certain things that she wanted me to do. I was *glad* man. (How did the birth of your child affect your relationship with her?) It didn't affect it at all. See like, when the baby was born and we had a *baby*, it seemed like things got a little better and stuff.

Yet men like Bucket have powerful reasons *not* to invest in the relationship as well. The ethnographic literature typically focuses on how much women mistrust men. What is less well known is how little men trust women (for exceptions, see Waller 2008; Hannertz 1969: 100–102; Liebow 1967: 137–60; Rainwater 1970: 209). The chief source of power (outside of physical violence) in these relationships is control over the child. In the context of a nonmarital birth, women have much greater power in this regard. Because men view children as their most precious resource (Nelson and Edin, forthcoming), they are, on the one hand, eager to hang on, and expect to be actively involved in parenting the child. Furstenberg, in Chapter 8 of this volume, shows that this desire for paternal engagement is consonant with their partner's expectations. Yet they are often very apprehensive about their ability to satisfy the economic demands they also know their children's mothers will place on them over time, and most are convinced that a woman's love for a man will come to an abrupt halt the minute he fails to provide (see also Drake and Cayton 1945: 564–99; Rainwater 1970: 216).

Men on the economic edge, even those in multi-year partnerships with several children, often obsessed about the younger guy with the nicer car who had a better job and might turn their partner's head. Most were convinced that, for women, "there is no source of commitment in a relationship." Donald was certain that a woman would dump any man if he failed to provide. This black 37-year-old found himself always "feuding and fightin'"—with his child's mother during their eight-year on-again-off-again relationship, which he blamed on the fact that she was too controlling, plus the fact that "I was not committed to really being with her" (see also Roy 2008; Waller 2008). Reading between the lines of his narrative, we can assume that spotty employment and drug use were probably also a cause. After their breakup, Donald's ex-partner went on to have two additional children by two other men and had just married a third man, who was trying to play the role of father to his 14-year-old daughter while her mother was trying to push Donald out of their lives. Listen to the deep cynicism in Donald's view of women:

> Yeah, their whole thing is, "What can you give me?" and "What can I get from you and how fast can I get it?" More or less money-wise. There is no commitment to a real relationship. Particularly in black women, their whole goal is let me see how much I can get for it and how good I can look and you know. . . . To be honest, yeah, I do [have a theory]. A lot of them are caught

up in, "I want to look good." "I want to be independent." "I don't want to be dependent upon you." "I want to be able to be with you, but not like that." There is no source of commitment in a relationship. [It is not] just men [that aren't committed], but anybody [nowadays]. In a relationship it is about, "We are in it 50-50 commitment," and so forth. They are not here. Their thing is, "When things go bad, I am out of here." To me, that was my experience and I am not taking it [anymore].

Amin (introduced earlier), was similarly convinced that money was necessary to sustain a relationship and that "situations"—such as unemployment—would almost certainly bring a relationship to an end. Because he lacked confidence that he could remain stably employed, Amin felt that he couldn't even contemplate marriage, and worried he might not even be able to sustain a long-term relationship.

So you just have to explain to individuals that this is your situation for the present time and I would appreciate it if you would bear with me and understand that you know that when I was able to provide, this is what I did. And there are periods where things are going to be rough and the things are going to be not as plentiful. So I am hoping that you would bear with me and understand. . . . My confidence level was a good advantage and my relationship with my former girlfriend was at an advantage [when I was working full-time] because when you have money and you are helping to support a family, women feel a lot better about a man when he is doing that. . . . When a woman is a woman and she accepts a man for who he is and not necessarily what he does and doesn't have, then she will stand by a man regardless. But when a woman starts to allow the fact that he is not bringing as much money into the home affect her relationship and her attitude towards him then that is a problem. . . . And that is another reason why I have not considered marriage because . . . there is not too many women out there that is really ready themselves to honestly fulfill the covenant of the words that you recite when you are at the podium.

Jeff, a black 47-year-old father of two, also believed a woman's love was contingent on money. He also saw this mercenary strain in his daughter.

[My daughter's mother taught me that] love is like running water. It turns off and on. I really believe that behind the fact that they can love you when you're doing, but when you don't do, they don't love. . . . My daughter had told me on numerous occasions that this [or that] individual does more for her than I do and I felt hurt. Regardless if this person is doing something for you or not, he can't fill my shoes. I'm still your father regardless. If I give you a million dollars or I give you a penny, I'm still your father.

Bill, a white 31-year-old father of six, similarly emphasized the nearly ubiquitous belief that love and engagement are not enough; relationships take money. Bill was deeply in love with his girlfriend of a decade and the mother of all of his children, but he had just lost his job tending bar and she had kicked him out. While working to get back into her good graces, Bill feared that in the meantime she would be wooed by a "younger guy."

> I hear a lot of people say that love is good but I am telling you, money will rule over a relationship real quick. [If that is gone, the love is gone] and a lot of women will do that to you, they do, and I don't know what it is. Don't get me wrong, there might be maybe two relationships out of a hundred that will survive without money. . . . It is all about that fashion statement too. . . . Women don't want to be sitting around thinking, even if a man works part-time and he is doing what he has to do, he could be the greatest man in the world and a woman will overlook that for somebody driving in a new car, a young guy. He might have a little bit of money now, but sooner or later down the line he could wind up like I am at anytime, no guarantees at all. Yo, that concerns me a lot. I love my girlfriend a lot. I call her my wife because we have been together for ten years off and on and we have six kids and I still say she is my wife basically, even though we are not married.

Tom, a white father of three, believed that when a man is "down and out" a woman could easily be attracted away by a guy who was doing better or "has a nicer car." In his case, a slowdown at work while the mother of his younger two children was pregnant the second time led to unbearable conflict.

> I was working every day and I was paying the bills. I did everything that I possibly could. I came home, I took care of the kids, I would put the kids to bed, just so we would have some [alone] time. . . . Her father had got me a job doing the roofing. . . . We saved money and we moved into the house and things were good and we were splitting the rent. Then I lost the job and I couldn't afford them payments anymore. . . . Yeah, it got real slow and the winter time came and there was just no work, so I didn't know what to do. I couldn't collect unemployment because I wasn't on the books. . . . She was already pregnant with the second baby and that is when I couldn't deal with her anymore and we couldn't get along.

We asked Tom, "Only money? No other problems?"

> Exactly. Only money. [It was] only a money issue. That is what I don't understand, why don't they understand, why don't they understand . . . ? They might see other people doing better or a guy that has a nicer car and I am sure that plays on their conscience. "I can have that. That could be me. Why am I [with *this* guy]?' And it is all about money in my eyes. I can see it.

Monte, the white father we introduced earlier, doesn't cite specific fears that are behind his mistrust of women; he just doesn't trust them period. Girls that appear "honest and nice" might start "act[ing] like a fool" without warning. As soon as a couple begins living together, a woman's "real self starts to come out," Monte says. That's why he isn't taking a chance on love.

> I'm just afraid [to trust women], you know. You can't judge a book by its cover, you know. I've known these girls who are so honest and nice, but I've also learned that when you meet a girl and she's real nice and honest and everything like that, when, [after] talking and getting to know each other and you're there every day and all night with each other, things start to change. Her real self starts to come out. So I'm not taking that chance. It just ain't worth it.

### The Time, Love, and Cash among Couples with Children Study

George and Tamika met through a chance encounter at a downtown department store. They started talking at the jewelry counter, a conversation that lasted for hours. Tamika, a black 29-year-old, wasn't so sure about George, who was also black and 30. After he began deluging her with phone calls, flowers, and presents, the two did begin seeing each other now and then. Meanwhile, George was seeing other women as well, but he knew he wanted to "settle down" with Tamika. It had been two months since they had last seen each other when Tamika called George and told him she was pregnant. She too was shocked by the pregnancy—she had thought she was infertile so they had never used contraception. George said they went through "that scary stage" of considering abortion before deciding to have the baby. They broke up once during the pregnancy, according to George, because of Tamika's "hormones." When they reconciled, they decided to "step up" their relationship and try to stay together for the sake of the child. Tamika moved into George's apartment just before Kaylee, Tamika's first child and George's second, was born.

"I had doubts, first of all [about] living with somebody . . . because that was something I said I would never do," reported Tamika a few months into cohabitation with George. Ideally, she said, parents should marry before they have a baby. She and George had their ups and downs in the four months they lived together after Kaylee's birth. George said that they moved in together because "we just wanted to put the baby in the best situation. And that was over here as opposed to her mom's house because there wasn't much space."

When we spoke with Tamika a few months later, she and Kaylee had moved back to her mother's house because "we wasn't really getting along," but she and George were still together and continued to see a lot of each other. George talked about getting married, but Tamika held back—"there's a lot of personal things with him that he needs to work on. And money-wise also, I think he's bad with his money. . . . He has a lot that he needs to clean up. I don't know what it would take [for us to get married]."

They were still living apart when we spoke with them the following year. Tamika said she was considering giving him another chance, because he was "trying really hard," and by the time we spoke with him they were living together again. They had recently been robbed at gunpoint while out one evening with their daughter, and the trauma of this experience in large part motivated them to try and make things work. George still talked about wanting to marry Tamika, but she was far from sure that he was the one. She said, "I just know that if [Kaylee] wasn't around, I wouldn't have been with him. But you know, because she was there, I wanted to stay together."

Around Kaylee's third birthday, things had reached the nadir with Tamika and George. Their renewed attempt at cohabitation had not gone well. Tamika was planning to move back to her mother's house, and George planned to move to another city, where his mother lived, and visit Kaylee on weekends. Tamika was relieved, she said, to finally realize that "it is OK, that I am not a bad person that this is not going to work out." She felt that they were incompatible from the start, and alleged he had a bad temper that erupted during arguments and that she was now afraid of him. She also said George was resigned to the relationship ending, although he still would like to get married. He told us that she "closes [me] out," and felt he had tried very hard to please her, but "nothing is enough."

The last time we spoke with them, George lived in another city and had visited Kaylee once or twice during the past year. He said that he felt bad about the breakup with Tamika but had started to date other women. Tamika was dating an ex-boyfriend. She said this relationship ended the first time because he had got someone else pregnant, but now he really wanted to marry her. She said they would have to "work out some personality conflicts" before she considered marriage.

From the above narrative it is clear that George and Tamika's relationship had a very rocky start. Although he pursued her, he was still seeing other women. She had reservations about the relationship almost from the very beginning. This is a couple who might never have gotten together except for the fact that Tamika got pregnant with Kaylee. The couple's subsequent decision to move in together and to "step up" the relationship was undertaken purely as an experiment, for the sake of the baby. It became clear very quickly, particularly to Tamika, that this impetus was not going to be enough to sustain the relationship, especially given her dissatisfaction with George's behavior. This story of a relationship in its infancy put to the test by a quick and unexpected pregnancy followed by a longer period of relational problems is echoed in the next example, though with even more volatility and a less conclusive ending.

Jazz, a black 21-year-old, and Keisha, who was 19, joked that their relationship "was supposed to be a one-night stand." Just after that first meeting with Jazz, Keisha became pregnant with another man's child but quickly miscarried. Meanwhile, she and Jazz had already gotten "together." When Jazz was put on house arrest, he moved in with Keisha and her mother to serve his sentence. Soon after that, Keisha learned she was pregnant by Jazz.

Jazz's legal troubles, financial problems, and weak willpower when it came to other women made her leery about taking their pregnancy to term, but in the end she decided to have the baby. Keisha said it was hard for her to stay with Jazz, but she did because "I guess this baby, I wanted him to have a father." Jazz offered to pay for an abortion, and was not involved with Keisha during the pregnancy, but had a dramatic change of heart right after his son, Jalani, was born.

> I didn't never want any kids because I didn't want to put those kids in a world and take them through the things my mama and them took me through. But now that I got them it's a blessing. . . . He makes me feel proud to be a father . . . and he'll show his love for me and that makes me really happy.

After Jalani's birth, Jazz and Keisha moved into his uncle's house. Here they could have their own room—more space than the two had had at Keisha's mother's house during Jazz's house arrest. Keisha was glad they were living together and said when a couple has children together, "I would say moving in together would be a good idea. 'Cause all the bills would either be put together and you would get help with them." She still had a general mistrust of men, though, and of Jazz in particular, and said men couldn't be counted on for long.

Keisha preferred to stay together with Jazz, but wasn't sure what would happen. Jazz said that his and Keisha's relationship "is cool but . . . she isn't the type I'd marry. . . . Just ain't what I'm looking for right now." Keisha thought she might marry him, but only "on the terms that he is a good man to me." Financially things were tough: Keisha was on welfare, and Jazz was working only sporadically. He found that there wasn't much money left over after buying the things the baby needed, yet he remained optimistic. "We can go without for a long time," he asserted.

The couple had ongoing problems with mistrust, and Jazz admitted he had cheated from the beginning of the relationship. "I ain't going to lie. I have cheated. I don't think she will cheat. . . . [Our] last argument was about . . . jealousy, that's all. I was jealous, and she was jealous. I made her even more jealous than she made me." The following year they were still a couple and living together, moving between different relatives. But Jazz suspected Keisha of cheating on him because a man called and she wouldn't tell Jazz who it was. In response, Jazz got so angry he pulled the phone out of the wall.

Keisha suspected that Jazz was cheating again when she realized she was pregnant with their second child. Neither she nor Jazz had wanted to have another child, but decided to bring the pregnancy to term. Despite their problems, Keisha said she thought they might marry in the future, if Jazz could spend more time with the family and work on improving communication with her. Jazz said he was not interested in marriage, but wanted to stay together with Keisha. Although their relationship began casually, Jazz told us he fell in love with Keisha after their first child was born. "This was the first woman that I had loved or had feelings for. Because [before] I was more like a bachelor. I be your friend . . . we can be sex partners. That will basically be it."

By the third year of the study, Jazz and Keisha had a new baby boy, Dajon, and Keisha was pregnant with their third child. Seeking a better life outside of Chicago, Keisha and Jazz moved to Iowa, along with Jazz's sister, and the two were able to afford their own place for the first time. Nine months later, Jazz was arrested for selling drugs and no family member was able to make bail. Stunned by this course of events, Keisha had "no idea" whether she and Jazz were still together or not. She was willing to give him another chance once he was released, but said "he's gonna need to grow up and get a [real] job . . . [start] being a man and paying the bills."

When we caught up with Jazz, he was living in a halfway house while serving the rest of his sentence. Explaining his descent into crime, he said, "times got rough" and "I tried to make some fast money." He felt that "a lot of time has been lost" and wanted to turn his life around. He had just gotten a job at a nearby meat processing plant where he made $11 an hour and was very optimistic about a future with Keisha, who had visited him regularly while he was incarcerated. He claimed he wanted to get married now, mostly as a tribute to Keisha's loyalty. "She's been there for me through thick and thin and not only that. I know how she feel about me. We got kids together. We a family . . . and we love each other the way we do. Every woman got their dream. They want to get married. . . . I feel I owe that to her."

We spoke to Jazz one last time a few months later. He had been released from the halfway house and the family was living together again. Keisha and Jazz were now both working at the local meat processing plant. They liked Iowa and saw "lots of opportunities here," but for Jazz it was "maybe too quiet." He claimed things between the two were going well, but also that old problems related to past infidelities and the resulting mistrust had resurfaced. "Like we might call each other a couple of names . . . , I might get jealous because I feel she's around a certain male." In a recent trip to Chicago, Jazz confided, he had had an affair with an old school friend, the same woman he had been with during Keisha's pregnancy with Jalani.

Jazz and Keisha's story exemplifies the mistrust that often pervades relations between men and women in poor neighborhoods (and also shows that there is some basis for this). This mistrust makes maintaining a relationship initiated in the face of an unexpected pregnancy a nearly impossible strain, especially when motivated primarily by the desire for the baby to "have a father," in Keisha's words. But even when not plagued by such serious problems as infidelity and mistrust, couples whose relationships are forged "for the sake of the baby" often have difficulty maintaining their relationships, much less moving forward to marriage, as the story of Suzanne and Myron shows.

Suzanne and Myron met through mutual friends right after high school graduation. Suzanne, a white 22-year-old, and Myron, who was 23, had been together off and on for about four years and had just gotten back together when Suzanne learned she was pregnant. She was "shocked" about the pregnancy, and Myron was "in denial phase" until she started showing. They brought their son, Joey, home from the hospital to Suzanne's mother's foreclosed house, where they planned to live rent-free until the bank evicted them. When we met them the first time, both Suzanne and Myron said they wanted to get married but that it was not the right time and were wary of taking such a big step before they felt ready.

Before she got pregnant, Suzanne lived with her mom and stepfather, and Myron stayed there sporadically. Suzanne said that, ideally, she would have wanted to get married and then have a baby, "but I didn't have those thoughts when I was 18 . . . I just think we got too serious too fast." Myron thought couples should move in together only once they got engaged, but that a baby can change things. "If [our son] was born of course I'd move in, even if we weren't engaged." Although Myron thought there was a 90–95 percent chance he and Suzanne would marry, having a child together is not a good reason to do so, in his view. "I want to keep Joey completely out of that, we should get married because mommy and daddy love each other not because we have [him]."

Suzanne agreed, saying, "living together, well it was kind of just something that happened . . . because of Joey. I mean we want to be together. And if there weren't some financial issues and stuff and just the circumstances, we'd probably already be married." (What circumstances?) "I'm not ready to commit to him until his past, until he's done working on it. . . . I think he has to mature in some different ways." Myron said that he loved Suzanne, but disliked that she was jealous and needy; as evidence, he described how she found the phone number of a female work colleague in his bureau drawer and "started going nuts." It was completely innocent, she learned, and they eventually resolved it, "but it kind of scared me for a little bit because every time I imagine us breaking up I imagine me not being around my son all the time, this and that. It kind of scares me."

When we visited them again, Myron said that Suzanne really wanted to get married and was "looking at rings." Rings were expensive, he countered, and he told Suzanne that they should save the money and try to buy a house and get a ring later. He also wanted her to work with a counselor about her "need" problem before they married . For his part, he was working on keeping to a monthly budget and said he was getting better with finances. He believed he would be happier if they married because then they would be "doing things right, the way things are supposed to be done." Suzanne also wanted to marry, but still had mixed feelings about Myron. "Myron and I are very committed to each other," but he was still "living too much of the single life" and had serious credit problems due to overspending in the past.

By the third year of our study, Myron and Suzanne had just had their second child, a daughter. They had also joined a church and were actively discussing what their wedding would be like. When they were married, Myron said, "she won't constantly ask me when are we getting married," and "[we will be] more respected in society." He admitted they hadn't made marriage a priority before, but now wanted to do it "the right way," with a reception, rings, and all the trimmings. Suzanne said she felt like they were married already; "we just haven't gone through the whole ceremony and everything." She predicted that nothing would change in terms of their daily lives, but "I probably would be a little bit happier if we were married."

The final time we spoke with this couple, Suzanne had enrolled in community college and Myron was working for the local cable company. They had recently moved to a brand new duplex where they "just got by" on his income of around $2,800 a month. Suzanne claimed she lived alone, and was thus able to claim food stamps for her and the children, but Myron had to comply with the child-support system. Suzanne was thinking of going back to work, and they were considering moving to Texas to be closer to some family members. They were still "working out the details" of the wedding, according to Suzanne.

COMMON THEMES

Despite the fact that TLC3 is a more advantaged sample than PCFS, only a small minority of pregnancies in both samples was explicitly planned, and many occurred within the first few months of the couple being "together." This is consistent with mothers' reports in Edin and Kefalas's (2005) companion interviews in the PSFS neighborhoods, though mothers are more likely to characterize the pregnancies as at least "semi-planned" while fathers are more likely to say they were "just not thinking" at the time their partner became pregnant (see also Edin et al. 2007). This difference may reflect subtle differences in intentionality between mothers and fathers, or mere social desirability bias (i.e., mothers might find it less socially acceptable to admit they were "just not thinking" when they became pregnant).

Once mothers learned they were pregnant, sharing the news with the father-to-be and deciding what to do about it were important defining moments for the couple. The pregnancy often prompted many of the men in PCFS, as well as some of the couples in TLC3, to think of themselves as a couple for the first time, or to reconsider a partner who had fallen out of favor. The decision whether to have the baby was usually left to the mother, with fathers typically agreeing to "support what she wants to do."

Pregnancy is a challenging time for most fathers' romantic relationships. In TLC3, several couples broke up owing to frequent arguments and other more serious problems, including infidelity and violent encounters, and then reconciled for the sake of the baby. In PCFS, where economic pressures were greater, such troubles were even more likely to break the couple up before the birth. Edin and Kefalas's (2005) interviews with mothers, described above, also highlighted pregnancy as a particularly volatile time. Among the couples in TLC3, however, both mothers and fathers typically blamed their problems during pregnancy on her "hormones" rather than on any fundamental problems with the relationship. This definition of the problem allowed the TLC3 couples to hang on to the idea that once the baby was born, everything would return to "normal"; this is despite the fact that many of these relationships were defined as "real relationships" only after the pregnancy had occurred. Naturally, the same problems tended to resurface soon after the child's birth and the mother and child's return home from the hospital. This is perhaps one reason why half of unmarried couples break up within one year of a child's birth (Center for Research on Child Wellbeing 2007). As Furstenberg points out (Chapter 8, this volume), breakup (e.g., divorce) was also exceedingly common among shotgun marriages of the 1950s.

As in PCFS, many TLC3 couples' troubles momentarily disappeared after the "magic moment" of their child's birth, as the fact of a shared child brought some measure of cohesion. Fathers who were still romantically involved, even if things were rough during the pregnancy, saw the baby as sufficient reason to renew their efforts to stay together with the mother. Especially for the somewhat more advantaged TLC3 sample, moving in together was an important part of the process of reorganizing their relationship around the baby. Of those who were living together when the TLC3 team interviewed them the first time, just a few months after their baby was born, nearly three-quarters (73 percent) had moved in together during the pregnancy or just after the child's birth.

Cohabitation in response to pregnancy was more common among TLC3 couples than among fathers in PCFS, reflecting the fact that the TLC3 couples were somewhat more economically advantaged and their relationships were, on average, a little more serious to begin with and became "family-like" to a greater degree with pregnancy and birth. While entry into a "real relationship," sometimes symbolized by the move to cohabitation, may have indicated a growing level of commitment to the romantic partner, it also reflected a father's wish to be an involved parent. Usually, among fathers, the impulse to parent is at least as strong as, if not stronger than, the desire to remain partnered for the sake of the relationship. Work done by Edin and Kefalas (2005) on a companion sample of mothers in the PCFS communities shows that mothers share the desire for fathers to be involved, but view his involvement as a desirable, yet optional, complement to their mothering activities.

Cohabitation allows an unmarried father equal access to his child and a major caretaking role. Therefore, even among cohabiting couples, there was often ambiguity over whether the couple bond or the father-child bond was the primary motivating factor. In TLC3, this ambiguity sometimes led mothers to be unsure of how to gauge the depth of their partner's commitment. For their part, fathers in PCFS often worried that the women in their lives only wanted them for as long as they could provide, and underplayed the importance of their emotional contributions to their partner and parenting role.

These relationships, even those elevated to an especially high status by cohabitation, are quite different from marriage. While couples articulated a common view of the expectations, obligations, and roles they associated with marriage, they rarely discussed their expectations for a cohabiting relationship. Instead, unspoken assumptions were usually revealed only when they were violated by the partner, and if the transgressions were deemed serious enough, the relationship would end—though sometimes there was room for trial and error. Many of these more serious problems these partners faced centered on expectations of sexual fidelity. The twin problems of infidelity and sexual jealousy played a leading role in most breakups in both studies and were often the proverbial "last straw" that led parents to end relationships already plagued by multiple problems (see also Hill 2007).

In sum, for this group of mostly disadvantaged men parenting children outside of marriage, multiple and serious problems such as infidelity, sexual mistrust, substance abuse, domestic violence, criminal activity, and incarceration abound in their narratives about their experiences as romantic partners, though these men were far less likely than the mothers in TLC3 or Edin and Kefalas's female respondents to name violence as a cause of breakup (2005; see also Hill 2007).[2] Despite their desire to form strong relationships with their children, men found that in the aftermath of the breakup, staying in regular contact with their progeny was surprisingly difficult. A full discussion of barriers to father-child involvement is beyond the scope of this chapter.

What is evident from the narratives presented here is that the haphazard nature of the way that these families are formed places enormous pressure on already disadvantaged young people who don't know each other very well, but who nonetheless attempt to form "real" relationships, sometimes via cohabitation. Although pregnancy and birth do typically prompt relationship investment among men, their precarious economic situations and their mistrust of women prompt disinvestment. Men's behavior is usually the most proximate cause of a relationship's demise. Another significant factor is the ambiguous nature of the relationships themselves, where expectations are seldom revealed until they are violated. And though men may have believed they could have a direct relationship with their children with or without the mothers—"daddy baby, momma maybe"—accomplishing this feat is far more difficult than most had imagined.

REFERENCES

Augustine, Jennifer March, Timothy Nelson, and Kathryn Edin. 2009. "Why Do Poor Men Have Children?" *Annals of the American Academy of Political and Social Science* 624 (July): 99–117.

Center for Research on Child Wellbeing. 2007. "Parents' Relationship Status Five Years after a Non-Marital Birth." Princeton, NJ: Center for research on Child Wellbeing, Research Brief 39 (August).

Davis, Allison, Burleigh B. Gardner, and Mary R. Gardner. 1941. *Deep South: A Social Anthropological Study of Caste and Class*. Chicago: University of Chicago Press.

Drake, St. Clair, and Horace R. Cayton. 1945. *Black Metropolis: A Study of Negro Life in a Northern City*. New York: Harcourt Brace.

Edin, Kathryn, and Maria J. Kefalas. 2005. *Promises I Can Keep: Why Poor Women Put Motherhood before Marriage*. Berkeley: University of California Press.

Edin, Kathryn, Paula England, Emily Fitzgibbons Shafer, and Joanna Reed. 2007. "Forging Fragile Families: Are the Pregnancies Planned, Unplanned, or In-Between?" In *Unmarried Couples with Children: The Unfolding Lives of New Unmarried Urban Parents*, edited by Paula England and Kathryn Edin. New York: Russell Sage Foundation.

Grail, Timothy S. 2007. "Custodial Mothers and Fathers and Their Child Support: 2005." *Current Population Reports* P60-234. Washington, DC: U.S. Census Bureau.

Furstenberg, Frank F., Jr. 2001. "The Fading Dream: Prospects for Marriage in the Inner City." In *Problem of the Century*, edited by Elijah Anderson and Douglas Massey, pp. 224–47. New York: Russell Sage Foundation.

Furstenberg, Frank F., Jr., and Andrew J. Cherlin. 1991. *Divided Families: What Happens to Children When Parents Part*. Cambridge, MA: Harvard University Press.

Hannerz, Ulf. 1969. *Soulside: Inquiries into Ghetto Culture and Community*. Chicago: University of Chicago Press.

Hill, Heather D. 2007. "Steppin' Out: Infidelity and Sexual Jealousy." In *Unmarried Couples with Children*, edited by Paula England and Kathryn Edin. New York: Russell Sage Foundation.

Hollingshead, A. B. 1949. *Elmtown's Youth: The Impact of Social Classes on Adolescents*. New York: Wiley.

Liebow, Eliot. 1967. *Tally's Corner*. Boston: Little, Brown.

Martin, Steven P. 2004. "Growing Evidence for a Divorce Divide? Education and Marital Dissolution Rates in the United States since the 1970's." New York, NY: Russell Sage Foundation Working Papers: Series on Social Dimensions of Inequality.

McLanahan, Sara. 2004. "Diverging Destinies: How Children Fare under the Second Demographic Transition." *Demography* 41(4): 607–27.

Moreland, John Kenneth. 1958. *Millways of Kent*. Chapel Hill: University of North Carolina Press.

Nelson, Timothy, and Kathryn Edin. Forthcoming. *Fragile Fatherhood: What Being a Daddy Means in the Lives of Low-Income Men*. New York: Russell Sage Foundation.

Nelson, Timothy J., Susan Clampet-Lundquist, and Kathryn Edin. 2002. "Sustaining Fragile Fatherhood: How Low-Income, Non-Custodial Fathers in Philadelphia Talk about Their Families." In *The Handbook of Father Involvement: Multidisciplinary Perspectives*, edited by Catherine Tamis-LeMonda and Natasha Cabrera, pp. 525–53. Mahwah, NJ: Lawrence Erlbaum Associates.

Nock, Stephen. 2007. "Marital and Unmarried Births to Men." Department of Health and Human Services Publication (PHS) 2006-1978. Hyattsville, MD: U.S. Department of Health and Human Services.

Powdermaker, Hortense. 1939. *After Freedom*. New York: Viking Press.

Rainwater, Lee. 1960. *And the Poor Get Children: Sex, Contraception, and Family Planning in the Working Class*. Chicago: Quadrangle Books.

———. 1970. *Behind Ghetto Walls*. Chicago: Aldine Press.

Reed, Joanna. 2007. "Anatomy of the Break-Up: How and Why Do Unmarried Parents Break Up?" In *Unmarried Couples with Children*, edited by Paula England and Kathryn Edin. New York: Russell Sage Foundation.

Roy, Kevin M., Nicole Buckmiller, and April McDowell. 2008. "Together but Not 'Together': Trajectories of Relationship Suspension for Low-Income Unmarried Parents." *Family Relations* 57(2): 198–210.

Townsend, Nicholas W. 2002. *The Package Deal: Marriage: Work and Fatherhood in Men's Lives*. Philadelphia: Temple University Press.

Waller, Maureen R. 2002. *My Baby's Father: Unmarried Parents and Paternal Responsibility*. Ithaca, NY: Cornell University Press.

———. 2008. "How Do Disadvantaged Parents View Tensions in Their Relationships? Insights for Relationship Longevity among At-Risk Couples." *Family Relations* 57(2): 128–43.

William Julius Wilson. 1996. *When Work Disappears: The World of the New Urban Poor*. New York: Knopf.

NOTES

1. Townsend, drawing on in-depth interviews with a group of Bay Area men who graduated from high school in 1972, showed that though fathers desired, in the abstract, to forge direct, intimate relationships with their children, their "package deal" definition of family life, in which fatherhood was part of a package that included marriage, breadwinning, and homeownership, limited them to demonstrating care through their breadwinning activities rather than forming the intimate father-child relationships they desired.

2. For a detailed analysis of breakups among TLC3 couples, see Reed 2007.

# CHAPTER FIVE

# Family Instability and Complexity after a Nonmarital Birth

Outcomes for Children in Fragile Families

*Sara McLanahan*

Nonmarital childbearing increased dramatically in the United States during the latter half of the twentieth century, changing the context in which American children are raised and giving rise to a new family form—*fragile families*—defined as couples who have a child outside marriage. As shown in Figure 5.1, the proportion of all children born to unmarried parents grew from about 4 percent in 1940 to nearly 40 percent in 2006, an increase of almost tenfold (Ventura 2009). Although the rate of increase was similar for whites and nonwhites, the impact was more dramatic for nonwhites because they started from a much higher base.

Some analysts argue that the changes in family formation are a sign of progress, reflecting an expansion of individual freedom and the growing economic independence of women (Coontz 1998). To support their claim, they note that similar trends are occurring throughout Western industrialized countries. Others are less sanguine. Pointing to the high poverty rates of single mothers, they argue that the increase in fragile families does not bode well for children and may even be perpetuating economic and racial disparities in future generations (Garfinkel and McLanahan 1986; McLanahan and Percheski 2008).

To resolve this academic debate and to provide policymakers with better information about the long-term implications of the rise in nonmarital childbearing, a team of researchers at Columbia and Princeton Universities designed and implemented a large national survey, "Fragile Families and Child Wellbeing." Between the spring of 1998 and fall of 2000, we interviewed approximately 5,000 parents who had recently given birth in hospitals in large cities, including a large oversample of unmarried couples (approximately 3,600). When weighted, the data are representative of all births in large U.S. cities with populations of 200,000 or more people. (A more detailed description of the study design is provided in Reichman et al. 2001.)

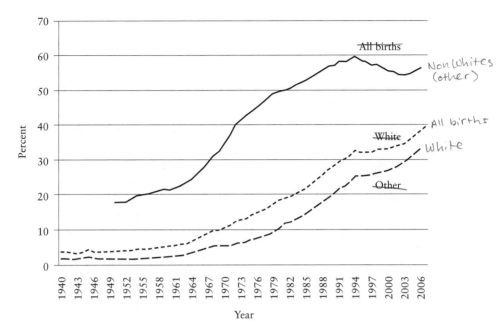

*Figure 5.1.* Trends in the proportion of all births to unmarried couples. Source: CDC/NCHS, National Vital Statistics System 2009.

THE QUESTIONS

The study was designed to address a number of basic questions about the nature and consequences of fragile families for parents and children. Our first set of questions was:

*What is the nature of parental relationships at birth? What are parents' capabilities? What happens to relationships over time?*

At the time we began the study, numerous (and often conflicting) stories existed about the nature of parental relationships and capabilities in fragile families. At one extreme were analysts who argued that unmarried parents were similar to married parents in terms of their relationships and capabilities. This perspective relied heavily on a Scandinavian model where relationships between unmarried parents are typically quite stable. Other analysts argued that parental relationships in fragile families were just as committed as relationships in married-parent families, but capabilities were much lower, giving rise to the label "poor man's marriage." Still others argued that births to unmarried parents were the product of casual unions with minimal commitment on the part of fathers.

• • •

A second question was whether this new family form was affecting parents' future resources and ability to raise their child:

*How do family structure and stability affect parents' economic and psychological resources?*

We knew from existing research that marriage was positively associated with adults' physical and mental health, as well as with their economic well-being (Waite and Gallagher 2002). Hence an important question for our research team was whether the benefits and costs associated with marriage would extend to parents in cohabiting unions. We also wanted to know whether marriages that occurred after a nonmarital birth produced the same benefits as marriages that occurred before birth. Finally, we were interested in whether family instability per se, net of family structure, affected parental resources, especially parents' mental health. Prior research on divorce and remarriage suggested that change itself can have short-term negative effects (Hetherington 1989), and we suspected that unmarried parents might be exposed to higher levels of instability than married parents.

• • •

A third set of questions centered on whether family structure and stability affected parental investments in children and the quality of parental investments:

*How do family structure and stability affect the level and quality of parental investments in children?*

Past research indicated that nonresident fathers spend less time with and less money on their children (Garfinkel et al. 1998). As noted above, however, nearly all of this research was based on divorced fathers who had lived with their children for some period of time. Whether the process would be similar for unmarried fathers was unclear. The quality of mothers' parenting in fragile families was also of interest. Based on our reading of the literature on divorce and single parenting, we expected family instability to be associated with lower-quality mothering in the period immediately following a change in family structure (Hetherington 1989) and perhaps over the longer term if mothers were exposed to ongoing financial stress (McLoyd 1990).

• • •

Finally, and most important, we were interested in how children were faring in fragile families:

*How do family structure and stability affect children's cognitive and socio-emotional development?*

A large literature suggested that family structure was associated with a wide range of negative outcomes in children. According to this literature, children who grow up with two biological parents are more likely to complete high school and less likely to engage in risky behaviors than children who grow up with only one biological parent (McLanahan and Sandefur 1994). Again, since most of this research was based on children of divorced parents, important questions remained as to whether these findings could be generalized to children in fragile families.

FINDINGS

In the next section, I summarize findings related to each of the questions listed above. Most of these findings are based on research conducted by members of the Columbia-Princeton research team, including graduate students and postdoctoral fellows at both institutions. A more extensive discussion of the methods and findings from each of these studies is available at the Fragile Families website.

### Parents' Relationships, Attitudes, and Capabilities

One of the biggest surprises to emerge from the Fragile Families Study was the finding that a large proportion of unmarried parents were in committed or quasi-committed relationships at the time their child was born. Over 50 percent of the couples were cohabiting at birth, and another 32 percent were in non-cohabiting romantic relationships. In total, over 80 percent of unmarried parents were romantically involved, and another 8 percent said they were "just friends." Less than 10 percent of mothers said they had "little or no contact" with their child's father. When we looked at these figures by race and ethnicity (not shown here), we found that the proportion of parents that were romantically involved was similar for whites, blacks, and Hispanics, although black couples were less likely to be cohabiting than whites and Hispanics (see Table 5.1 and Figure 5.2.

Not only did the vast majority of unmarried parents report being in a romantic relationship at birth, but most of these parents also had high expectations for a future together. As shown in Table 5.1, 92 percent of cohabiting mothers and 95 percent of cohabiting fathers thought their chances

TABLE 5.1
*Parents' relationship quality at birth of their child*

| Parents' responses about relationship quality | Mothers | | | Fathers | | |
|---|---|---|---|---|---|---|
| | Married | Cohabit-ing | Single | Married | Cohabit-ing | Single |
| Chances of marriage (50-50 or better) | -- | 91.8 | 52.2 | -- | 95.2 | 74.6 |
| Supportiveness scale (1–3) | 2.7 | 2.7 | 2.4 | 2.7 | 2.7 | 2.6 |
| Any violence (%)* | 4.5 | 7.0 | 7.6 | -- | -- | -- |

S O U R C E : Data from the Fragile Families and Child Wellbeing Study (weighted by national sampling weights).

*Responses from the one-year interview.

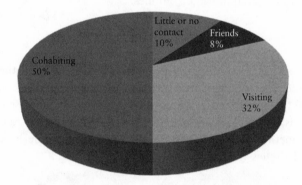

*Figure 5.2.*   Unmarried parents' relationship status at child's birth. Source: Data from the Fragile Families and Child Wellbeing Study (weighted by national sampling weights).

of marrying the other parent were "fifty-fifty" or better. A non-trivial proportion of non-cohabiting parents were also optimistic about marriage: 52 percent of mothers and 75 percent of fathers thought their chances were fifty-fifty or better. Part of the reason non-cohabiting fathers were more positive than mothers is that we only interviewed about 50 percent of these men, and the ones we interviewed were undoubtedly more committed to their relationship with the mother than the ones who did not participate in the study. Nevertheless, even when we looked at couples for whom we had interviews with both parents, fathers were more optimistic about their chances of marriage than mothers.

We also asked parents a set of questions about the quality of their relationships (see Table 5.2). To measure the positive dimension of relationship quality, we asked how often (very often, sometimes, or hardly ever) the other parent was "fair and willing to compromise," "loving and affectionate," "critical or insulting," and "encouraging." To measure the negative dimension, we asked mothers whether they had ever been "hit or slapped," "hit with a fist or object" or "cut, bruised, or seriously hurt" by the father.

Both cohabiting and married parents reported very high levels of supportiveness (3 = "very often"). Non-cohabiting parents reported slightly lower levels, with mothers being less positive than fathers. In response to the question about domestic violence, unmarried mothers reported substantially higher levels of violence than did married mothers, although violence was low among both groups. Our numbers for domestic violence are lower than those reported in other studies for several reasons. First, we asked mothers about the behavior of a specific partner—the baby's father—whereas prior studies typically ask women whether they have *ever* experienced domestic violence. Second, most of the mothers in our study were in a romantic relationship with the father at the time of the interview, whereas prior studies have typically asked women about relationships that have ended. Additional analyses comparing mothers' reports about violence before and after their relationship ended indicated that mothers underreported violence by as much as 50 percent when they were living with the father. A third reason our estimates may be lower than those reported by other studies is that our measure did not include items such as "pushing and shoving," which are the most common forms of violence and are typically included in other surveys.

Finally, we asked parents about the extent to which the fathers were involved during the pregnancy and immediately after the birth of the child. According to the mothers, over 95 percent of cohabiting fathers provided financial support or other types of assistance during the pregnancy, visited the mother and baby at the hospital, and planned to be involved in raising the child. Similar proportions of mothers indicated that the father's name would be on the child's birth certificate, and 99 percent said they wanted the father to be involved. Even non-cohabiting fathers showed substantial

TABLE 5.2

*Percentage of unmarried couples with high levels of father involvement*

| Father's involvement | Cohabiting | Romantic | Single |
|---|---|---|---|
| Gave money/bought things for child | 96.5 | 84.0 | 27.9 |
| Helped in another way | 97.7 | 74.6 | 21.9 |
| Visited baby's mother in hospital | 96.5 | 71.4 | 29.2 |
| Child will take father's surname | 92.9 | 73.8 | 37.2 |
| Father's name is on birth certificate | 96.1 | 80.3 | 51.6 |
| Mother says father wants to be involved | 99.4 | 98.6 | 73.9 |
| Mother wants father to be involved | 99.3 | 98.5 | 70.7 |

SOURCE: Data from the Fragile Families and Child Wellbeing Study (weighted by national sampling weights).

involvement. Over half of these men provided financial and other types of support during the pregnancy, and over half visited the mother in the hospital. Most striking perhaps was the large proportion of non-cohabiting fathers who indicated that they wanted to help raise their child, and the equally large proportion of mothers who wanted the fathers involved. The responses to these questions further confirm the findings that the vast majority of relationships between unmarried couples are not casual and that most unmarried fathers want (and are expected) to play a role in raising their children.

Some analysts have argued that social norms about marriage and single motherhood have changed dramatically during the past few decades, with marriage becoming less of a valued status and single motherhood becoming more acceptable. Other researchers have argued that distrust of the opposite sex has increased dramatically among men as well as women. To examine whether the parents in our study held views that were consistent with these arguments, we asked several questions about the benefits of marriage, the efficacy of single motherhood, and the trustworthiness of the opposite sex.

As shown in Table 5.3, nearly two-thirds of the unmarried mothers and over three-quarters of the unmarried fathers agreed with the statement that "it is better for children if their parents are married." Although most unmarried parents placed a high value on marriage, they were not as positive as married parents. More important perhaps, a very high proportion of unmarried mothers—80 percent of cohabiting mothers and 88 percent of single mothers—agreed with the statement that "a mother living alone can raise a child just as well as a married mother." Mothers' responses to the two questions about marriage and single motherhood were strongly associated with marital status, with married mothers reporting more support for marriage

TABLE 5.3
*Parents' attitudes toward marriage at birth of their child (percent)*

|  | Mothers | | | Fathers | | |
|---|---|---|---|---|---|---|
| *Parents' opinions* | *Married* | *Cohabit-ing* | *Single* | *Married* | *Cohabit-ing* | *Single* |
| Marriage is better for kids | 83.4 | 68.1 | 61.2 | 90.5 | 78.8 | 77.4 |
| Single mother can raise child alone | 59.5 | 80.4 | 88.2 | 33.8 | 48.8 | 56.7 |
| Men/women cannot be trusted to be faithful | 10.4 | 18.1 | 33.1 | 4.5 | 12.7 | 20.6 |
| Men/women are out to take advantage | 11.6 | 15.4 | 22.7 | 5.1 | 15.5 | 20.6 |

SOURCE: Data from the Fragile Families and Child Wellbeing Study (weighted by national sampling weights).

and less support for single motherhood than unmarried mothers. Fathers' responses to the questions about marriage and single motherhood showed a similar marital status gap, with fathers being more positive about marriage and less positive about single motherhood than mothers. These responses indicate that although most unmarried parents believe that marriage is the ideal setting for raising children, they also believe that a single mother can do the job alone. The fact that parents hold both views at the same time is consistent with the argument that marriage is an ideal but not a necessity. Cherlin argues (2005), for example, that marriage has become a "capstone rather than a normative life transition." And Edin and her colleagues (Edin and Kefalas 2005; Gibson, Edin, and McLanahan 2007) argue that couples are reluctant to marry until they have reached an imaginary "marriage bar," which they associate with a middle-class lifestyle and view as essential for maintaining a stable marriage.

The findings reported in Table 5.3 also support the claim that gender distrust is common among unmarried parents. A third of unmarried mothers who were living alone agreed with the statement that "men cannot be trusted to be faithful," as compared with only 10 percent of married mothers. Unmarried mothers were also more likely to agree with the statement that "men are out to take advantage of women." Unmarried fathers were also less trustful than married fathers, although the overall level of mistrust was lower among fathers than among mothers.

### Low Capabilities

Although many parents in fragile families were hopeful at the time of their child's birth, their ability to support a family was less positive. As shown in Table 5.4, unmarried parents were more likely to be in their teens than married parents. Despite their youth, unmarried parents were also more likely to have already had a child by another partner. Fertility differences were even larger when we conditioned on whether parents were having a first birth (results not shown). Among women having their first child, 33 percent and 53 percent of cohabiting and single mothers respectively, were in their teens, as compared with 8 percent of married mothers; among mothers having a higher-order birth, over 60 percent of unmarried mothers had had a child with a different father as compared with 18 percent of married mothers. The prevalence of *multi-partnered fertility*, defined as having children by more than one father, is one of the important new findings to emerge from our study, and this phenomenon is expected to have important implications for many aspects of family life, including parenting relationships, parenting, and child well-being (Carlson and Furstenberg 2006). Finally, unmarried parents were much less likely than married parents to have lived with both

TABLE 5.4
*Parents' demographic characteristics at birth of their child (percent)*

|  | Mothers | | | Fathers | | |
|---|---|---|---|---|---|---|
| Parents' characteristics | Married | Cohabit-ing | Single | Married | Cohabit-ing | Single |
| Age (mean) | 29.3 | 24.7 | 22.6 | 31.8 | 27.7 | 25.6 |
| Teen parent | 3.7 | 17.7 | 34.3 | 0.4 | 17.0 | 34.2 |
| First birth | 35.3 | 39.4 | 51.0 | 34.7 | 42.7 | 60.0 |
| Child with another partner | 11.7 | 38.8 | 34.5 | 27.1 | 64.2 | 76.4 |
| Race |  |  |  |  |  |  |
| White, non-Hispanic | 48.9 | 25.9 | 18.0 | 50.6 | 21.1 | 12.5 |
| Black, non-Hispanic | 11.7 | 29.1 | 49.1 | 13.8 | 33.0 | 58.4 |
| Hispanic | 28.6 | 41.0 | 30.1 | 29.4 | 43.0 | 22.5 |
| Other | 10.8 | 4.0 | 2.8 | 6.1 | 2.8 | 6.6 |
| Immigrant | 28.7 | 22.5 | 14.1 | 25.9 | 21.8 | 11.9 |
| Two parents growing up | 61.9 | 44.2 | 35.2 | 68.1 | 47.4 | 36.1 |

SOURCE: Data from the Fragile Families and Child Wellbeing Study (weighted by national sampling weights).

of their biological parents growing up, with single moms being the least likely to have experienced a traditional family.

The education gap between married and unmarried parents was striking, with very little overlap at the high and low ends of the distribution. More than a third of married parents had a college degree, but less than 3 percent of unmarried parents did so. In contrast, 49 percent of single mothers and 45 percent of their partners lacked a high school diploma, but less than 20 percent of married parents had not graduated from high school. Not surprisingly, unmarried parents had much lower earnings and much higher poverty rates than married parents.

The data for health, mental health, and risky behaviors presented a similar picture, with unmarried parents reporting poorer overall health, more health limitations, more depression, and more drug use than married parents (DeKlyen et al. 2006). Although fathers' drinking was not significantly different for married and unmarried fathers (averaging cohabiting and single fathers), unmarried mothers were more likely to report drinking during pregnancy than married mothers (Table 5.5). Finally, unmarried fathers (both cohabiting and single) were much more likely than married fathers to have been incarcerated at some point in their lives. The results for incarceration underscore the large disparities between married and unmarried fathers and highlight the important role of penal institutions in the lives of fragile families.

Two important points emerge from the findings discussed thus far. First, there is very little support for the claim that fragile families and married-parent families are equally viable settings for raising children. Thus, even at the very beginning of study, we can see that there is reason to be concerned about the parents and children in the fragile families. Second, these data highlight the fact that there is enormous selection in nonmarital childbearing. Married and unmarried parents are drawn from very different populations, and these differences must be taken into account in any comparison of the two groups. Otherwise, differences due to human capital and demographic characteristics may be erroneously attributed to differences in marital status.

### Stability and Instability

Despite their "high hopes," most unmarried parents were unable to maintain stable unions. Only 15 percent of all our unmarried couples were married at the time of the five-year interview, and only a third were still romantically involved. (Recall that over 80 percent of parents were romantically involved at birth.) Among couples who were cohabiting at birth, the picture was somewhat better: after five years, 26 percent were married to each other and another 26 percent were living together. Less than half had ended their romantic relationship. Interesting, among couples who reported "no roman-

TABLE 5.5

*Parents' human capital at birth of their child (percent unless otherwise indicated)*

| Parents' human capital | Mothers | | | Fathers | | |
| --- | --- | --- | --- | --- | --- | --- |
| | *Married* | *Cohabit-ing* | *Single* | *Married* | *Cohabit-ing* | *Single* |
| Education | | | | | | |
| Less than high school | 17.8 | 41.0 | 48.8 | 18.8 | 40.0 | 44.9 |
| High school or equivalent | 25.5 | 39.2 | 34.1 | 21.4 | 39.8 | 34.2 |
| Some college | 21.1 | 17.3 | 14.3 | 30.3 | 17.6 | 17.2 |
| College or higher | 35.7 | 2.4 | 2.4 | 29.5 | 3.6 | 3.8 |
| Income | | | | | | |
| Earnings (mean) | $25,619 | $11,434 | $10,764 | $38,568 | $20,461 | $15,893 |
| Worked last year | 79.3 | 83.4 | 79.4 | 95.7 | 91.0 | 84.3 |
| Poverty status | 14.0 | 32.5 | 53.1 | 13.2 | 33.7 | 34.1 |
| Not working at birth | -- | -- | -- | 5.7 | 17.0 | 34.0 |
| Health* | | | | | | |
| Poor/fair health | 10.4 | 14.4 | 17.1 | 8.1 | 15.4 | 12.9 |
| Health limitations | 7.1 | 9.1 | 11.1 | 5.4 | 10.5 | 14.1 |
| Depression | 13.2 | 16.2 | 15.7 | 8.1 | 9.2 | 18.0 |
| Heavy drinking | 2.0 | 8.0 | 7.7 | 25.1 | 32.0 | 21.1 |
| Illegal drugs | 0.3 | 1.7 | 3.1 | 1.6 | 6.0 | 12.4 |
| Prior incarceration** | -- | -- | -- | 7.3 | 34.1 | 39.3 |

SOURCE: DeKlyen et al. 2006.

-- Not applicable.

* Analyses based on baseline and one-year data.

** Information gathered for fathers only.

tic relationship" at birth, 4 percent were married at year five, 7 percent were cohabiting, and 2 percent were in a romantic relationship with each other.

Several factors were identified as important predictors of whether parents stayed together. Fathers' earnings, mothers' education, pro-marriage attitudes, and relationship quality were all positively associated with a greater likelihood of marriage, whereas being black, fathers' multi-partnered fertility, and mothers' distrust of men were associated with less marriage (Carlson, McLanahan, and England 2004).

Our findings regarding the predictors of marriage were generally consistent with what we expected to find, with one exception: fathers' multi-partnered fertility was a stronger predictor of union instability than mothers' multi-partnered fertility. Although we suspected that multi-partnered fertility might reduce union stability by increasing household complexity, we expected mothers' multi-partnered fertility to be a more important predictor than fathers' fertility since mothers' prior children were more likely to be living with the couple. In-depth interviews with a subset of couples in the Fragile Families Study provide some insight into this puzzle. According to these interviews, jealousy is a serious problem for many couples, and fathers' contact with children in other households often contributes to jealousy (see Monte 2007 and Chapter 4 in this volume).

We also looked at whether the factors that predicted marriage could also explain race/ethnic differences in marriage after a nonmarital birth. While these individual-level factors did explain some of the difference, none of them was as important as the difference in the availability of marriageable men, where "marriageable" is defined as having a job. Indeed, race/ethnicity differences in the ratio of marriageable men to all women in the population can account for a large part of the marriage gap between blacks and whites and between blacks and Hispanics as well (Harknett and McLanahan 2004).

Comparing family structures at birth and age 5 provides only a partial picture of the degree of instability in fragile families since it ignores changes in residential partnerships between waves and changes in nonresidential (dating) partnerships (Osborne and McLanahan 2007). To gain a more comprehensive picture of the extent of instability in fragile families, we counted the total number of residential and dating changes over the entire five-year period. Both the beginnings and endings of relationships were counted, so a mother who started and ended a relationship would be counted as having experienced two transitions. If a single mother moved in with the biological father of her child, the move was not counted as a transition. Since our data did not contain complete partnership or fertility histories, our estimates are likely to understate the true level of instability, especially turnover in dating relationships. Nevertheless, we found very high levels of instability.

As shown in Tables 5.6 and 5.7, whereas 56 percent of unmarried mothers reported at least one residential change, nearly three-quarters reported at least one residential or dating change. Similarly, whereas only 10 percent of unmarried mothers experienced three or more residential transitions, nearly half experienced as many residential or dating transitions combined. Partnership stability among single mothers living alone is very rare: only 15 percent reported no change in relationship status, and nearly all of these women had moved in with the biological father.

Finally, to document the growing complexity in fragile families, we looked at the proportion of mothers who had a child with a new partner between the birth of the focal child and the five-year interview (results not shown). For mothers who were single when their child was born, the number was 33 percent; for mothers who were romantically involved with the father but living apart, it was 23 percent, and for mothers who were cohabiting with the father it was 14 percent.

TABLE 5.6
*Number of residential transitions at year 5 by parents'*
*baseline relationship status (percent)*

| Parents' relationship | No residential transitions | 1–2 residential transitions | 3 or more residential transitions |
|---|---|---|---|
| Married at birth | 81.5 | 17.0 | 1.5 |
| Unmarried at birth | 43.9 | 45.9 | 10.2 |
| Cohabiting at birth | 42.1 | 49.8 | 8.1 |
| Single at birth | 45.5 | 42.3 | 12.1 |

SOURCE: Data from the Fragile Families and Child Wellbeing Study (weighted by national sampling weights).

NOTES: N = 3,562; Participants who were not in wave at year 5 or for whom information was missing were excluded. Unmarried at baseline (at the birth of their child) includes mothers who were single or cohabiting with the biological father. Mothers who were single at birth, then with the biological father at year 5 and reported one total transition were coded as having 0 transitions (n = 200).

TABLE 5.7
*Number of transitions at year 5 by parents' baseline relationship status (percent)*

| Parents' relationship | No transitions | 1–2 transitions | 3 or more transitions |
|---|---|---|---|
| Married at birth | 81.5 | 7.4 | 11.1 |
| Unmarried at birth | 28.0 | 24.6 | 47.5 |
| Cohabiting at birth | 42.1 | 23.4 | 34.6 |
| Single at birth | 15.0 | 25.6 | 59.3 |

SOURCE: Data from the Fragile Families and Child Wellbeing Study (weighted by national sampling weights).

NOTES: N = 3,562; Participants who were not in wave at year 5 or for whom information was missing were excluded. Unmarried at baseline (at the birth of their child) includes mothers who were single or cohabiting with the biological father. Mothers who were single at birth, then with the biological father at year 5 and reported one total transition were coded as having 0 transitions (n = 200).

TRAJECTORIES IN PARENTS' ECONOMIC WELL-BEING
AND HEALTH

The findings presented thus far show that unmarried parents are very disadvantaged relative to married parents at the time their child is born, both in terms of their individual capabilities and their relationships. The remaining sections of the chapter examine whether these gaps continue to grow after the child is born and whether family structure and stability are associated with changes in parents' economic well-being and health.

### Economic Resources

Figures 5.3 and 5.4 report the trajectories of parents' economic well-being following the birth of a child. Figure 5.3 reports findings for fathers' earnings. These estimates are based on latent growth curve models that distinguish between several family types, controlling for the demographic and human capital variables that existed at the child's birth. Figure 5.3 reports trajectories for four groups of fathers: those who were stably married from birth, those who entered marriage after birth, those who began cohabiting after birth, and those who remained single throughout the five years.

As expected, married fathers started out with much higher earnings than unmarried fathers, even after controlling for differences in demographic and human capital characteristics. Among unmarried fathers differences in earnings at birth were minimal. Over time, however, disparities among unmar-

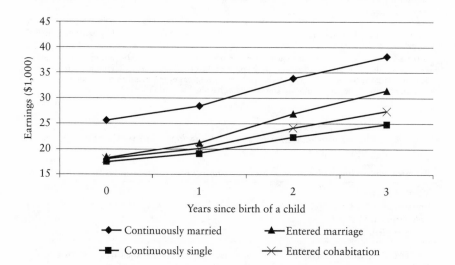

*Figure 5.3.* Trajectories in fathers' earnings by relationship status. Source: Garfinkel, McLanahan, Meadows, and Mincy. 2009; "Unmarried Fathers' Earning Trajectories: Does Partnership Status Matter?" CRCW Working Paper WP09-22-FF.

TABLE 5.8

*The association between changes in relationship status and changes in fathers'
earnings, by year of change*

|  | One year | Three years | Five years |
|---|---|---|---|
| Entered marriage |  |  |  |
| Baseline to one year | 0.29 *** | 0.44 *** | 0.66 *** |
| One year to three years | 0.19 * | 0.38 *** | 0.58 *** |
| Three years to five years | 0.14 † | 0.45 *** | 0.67 *** |
| Began cohabitation |  |  |  |
| Baseline to one year | 0.16 | 0.41 *** | 0.54 *** |
| One year to three years | 0.20 | 0.23 | 0.36 † |
| Three years to five years | 0.01 | –0.10 | 0.33 * |

S O U R C E : Garfinkel et al. 2009.

N O T E : Coefficients are based on latent growth models.

$^{†}p \leq .10; \; ^{*}p \leq .05; \; ^{**}p \leq .01; \; ^{***}p \leq .001$ (two-tailed tests).

ried fathers emerged, depending on fathers' family formation behavior. Fathers who married after birth showed the largest gains (steepest slopes) in earnings, followed by fathers who began cohabiting. Fathers who remained single over the five-year period showed the smallest gains in earnings.

The trajectories in Figure 5.3 tell us that some groups of fathers have steeper earnings trajectories than other groups, but they do not tell us anything about the timing and sequencing of changes in fathers' partnership status and changes in earnings, which is critical if we want to argue that a change in family structure has a causal effect on fathers' earnings. To investigate further, we looked at year-specific changes in fathers' partnership status and earnings. As shown in Table 5.8, there is very good evidence that both changes occur in the same year. In separate analyses (not shown here), we estimated similar models for the number of hours fathers worked and found that work hours increased markedly in the year fathers married and remained high in the subsequent period. We also estimated models that looked at within-father changes in marital status and earnings. The results from these (fixed effects) models were consistent with those from the growth curve models, suggesting that the association between marriage and increases in fathers' earnings is not due to unmeasured characteristics of the fathers that are constant. The fixed-effects results were true for marriage but not for cohabitation. Note that although our results are consistent with an argument that marriage causes men's earnings to rise, they also are consistent with the argument that improvements in fathers' work hours and earnings lead to more marriage.

Similar analyses were conducted for mothers' household income, adjusted for family size (Meadows, McLanahan, and Knab 2009). Since children typically live with their mothers after a nonmarital birth, mothers' income is a good proxy for children's economic status. Figure 5.4 compares income trajectories for five groups of mothers: those in stable married unions, those in stable cohabiting unions, those in stable single mother households, those who exit marriage, and those who enter a co-residential union with the father (marriage or cohabitation).

According to Figure 5.4, married mothers had the highest level of economic well-being at the time their children were born, followed by mothers who were married at birth and subsequently divorced, and then by all types of unmarried mothers. After birth, mothers who divorced experienced a steep decline in economic status, whereas mothers who entered a coresidential union experienced an increase in economic status. The income trajectory for mothers who entered a co-residential union after birth was similar to the trajectory for stably married mothers. Mothers who were stably single showed a smaller income gain than mothers who entered a co-residential union.

As in the case of fathers, we examined the year-specific associations between family structure change and income change to see if the change in mothers' union status occurred in the same year as the change in economic status (results not shown). For mothers who divorced or entered marriage/cohabitation after birth, we found that the increase in income occurred in the same period as the change in marital status. Again, while this finding is consistent with the argument that union formation/dissolution causes a

*Figure 5.4.* Trajectories in mothers' income by relationship status. Source: Meadows, McLanahan, and Knab. 2009. "Economic Trajectories in Non-Traditional Families with Children." CRCW Working Paper WP09-10-FF.

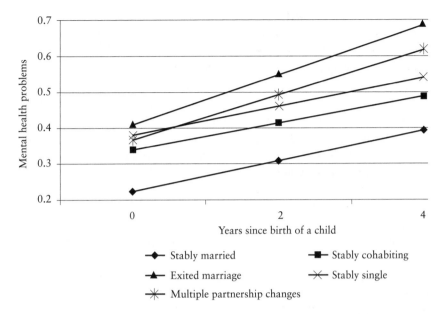

*Figure 5.5.* Trajectories in mothers' mental health problems by relationship status. Source: Meadows, McLanahan, and Knab. 2008. "Family Structure and Maternal Health Trajectories." *American Sociological Review* 73(2): 314–34.

change in family income, it is also consistent with the argument that changes in family income lead to family instability.

### Health and Mental Health

Mothers' mental health is also an important resource for children insofar as it is known to affect the quality of parenting (Kiernan and Huerta 2008). To determine whether family structure/stability led to changes in mothers' health, we estimated growth curve models similar to those described in the previous section on fathers' earnings and mothers' income. To measure mothers' physical health, we used self-reported health status. To measure mothers' mental health we used a composite score created by summing three dichotomously coded items—heavy episodic drinking (i.e., binge drinking), illicit drug use, and diagnosis of a major depressive episode. Depression was measured using the Composite International Diagnostic Interview Short Form (CIDI-SF) Version 1.0 November 1998 (see Kessler et al. 1998). Figure 5.5 reports the findings for five groups: mothers in stable unions (married, cohabiting, and single), mothers who divorced after birth, and mothers who experienced multiple partnership changes. We created a separate category for mothers who experienced multiple changes in family status because we believed that ongoing instability might be especially deleterious for mothers' health. As before, estimates are based on latent growth curve models that control for a host of demographic and human capital variables.

Whereas in the analysis of mothers' income married mothers started out much better off than unmarried mothers, in the case of mental health problems, they started out at the high and low ends of the spectrum, with stably married mothers having the fewest mental health problems and mothers who eventually divorced having the most problems. Stably cohabiting mothers started out in the middle, and stably single mothers started out about the same as mothers who subsequently divorced. The trajectories for mothers' mental health were consistent with what we would expect. Divorced mothers and mothers who experienced multiple changes in family structure had worse mental health trajectories (steeper slopes) than other mothers.

As in the previous analyses, we looked at the year-specific associations between family structure and mental health problems, which allowed us to examine the timing and sequencing of these changes (results not shown). Again, changes in family structure were associated with an increase in mental health problems *in the year in which the family change occurred* and a decline thereafter, which is consistent with the argument that family structure changes have a short-term negative effect on mothers' mental health and that most mothers recover in the absence of additional stressors. Similar analyses were conducted using mothers' self-reported health in place of mental health problems, and these yielded similar results. In other research, Meadows has examined the link between family structure and stability and fathers' health and mental health problems and has found no association between the two events (Meadows 2009).

PARENTAL CONTRIBUTIONS AND PARENTING

In the previous section I discussed our finding that family structure and instability were associated with parental resources in fragile families. In this section, I discuss whether family structure and stability are associated with parental investments in children.

### Fathers' Investments

As noted earlier, the proportion of unmarried fathers who live with their children declines markedly over time, from 51 percent at year one to 42 percent at year three and 36 percent at year five. Thus a key question is whether these fathers continue to parent their children.

Although, in principle, fathers could continue to fulfill their parenting role after they move out of the household, theory tells us that it is much more costly for them to do so (Willis 2000). According to our estimates, a large ma-

TABLE 5.9
*Unmarried fathers' involvement with their children after a*
*nonmarital birth (percent)*

| Father's involvement | Years after birth | | |
|---|---|---|---|
| | One year | Three years | Five years |
| All fathers[1] | | | |
| Lives with child | 51 | 42 | 36 |
| Nonresident fathers | | | |
| Saw child in past year | 88 | 78 | 72 |
| Saw child in past month | 63 | 55 | 51 |
| Pays formal child support[2] | 11 | 41 | 57 |
| Pays informal support | 72 | 42 | 37 |
| Provides in-kind support | 56 | 47 | 43 |

SOURCES: [1]Carlson, McLanahan, and Brooks-Gunn 2008; [2]Nepomnyaschy and Garfinkel, forthcoming.

jority of nonresident fathers continued to see their children, although contact declined over time. One year after a child's birth, 88 percent of nonresident fathers reported seeing the child at least once since the last survey, dropping to 78 percent in year three and 72 percent in year five. A similar pattern was observed for frequent contact. One year after a child's birth, about 63 percent of nonresident fathers reported seeing the child at least once in the past month (an average of twelve days a month), dropping to 55 percent and 51 percent at years three and five. In short, about two-thirds of unmarried fathers reported high levels of involvement with their children five years after birth: one-third of all fathers were living with their children, and another third were seeing their children on a regular basis (Carlson, McLanahan, and Brooks-Gunn 2008).

Several factors were associated with fathers' involvement. White fathers and immigrant fathers were less likely to maintain contact (conditional on nonresidence) than other fathers. Multi-partnered fertility and new partnerships were also associated with lower contact (Tach et al. 2010). Finally, parents' ability to cooperate was strongly associated with fathers' involvement. When the child's mother trusted the father and when she believed he shared her views about childrearing, the father was much more likely to be involved with the child on a regular basis (Carlson et al. 2008). Although one might argue that causality operates in the opposite direction—father involvement leads to better cooperation—our analyses indicate that most of the time cooperation leads to involvement, rather than the reverse.

We also looked at nonresident fathers' financial contributions to their children, measured as informal and formal financial support and in-kind contributions such as buying diapers or toys. Interestingly, informal financial contributions to children were much more common than formal contributions one year after birth; however, this pattern shifted over time, with informal contributions declining from 72 percent to 37 percent of nonresident fathers, and formal contributions increasing from 11 percent to 57 percent of fathers (Nepomnyaschy and Garfinkel, forthcoming). In-kind contributions also declined over time, from 56 percent to 43 percent of fathers. Interestingly, stronger child support enforcement did not appear to predict the amount of money a father contributed, at least not during the first five years after birth. Rather, strong enforcement simply resulted in the replacement of informal payments with formal payments. In the long run, however, analyses suggest that strong enforcement does increase payments (Freeman and Waldfogel 2001).

### Mothers' Parenting

Yet another set of papers examined the association between family structure/stability and mothers' parenting, measured as maternal stress (mothers' reports of how difficult they find the job of parenting) and parenting behaviors, such as harsh punishment, warmth, and engagement in literacy activities (Cooper et al. 2009; Beck et al. 2010). Each of these measures has been shown to affect children's cognitive and socio-emotional development. Family structure was measured according to whether the child was living with both biological parents at age 5. Family instability was measured by three indicators: total number of residential partnership changes, total number of nonresidential partnership changes and the sum of these two measures (total changes). We also distinguished between residential partnership changes that occurred between birth and age 3 (early changes) and those that occurred between age 3 and age 5 (recent changes).

As shown in Table 5.10, partnership instability was associated with maternal stress and harsh parenting but not with literacy activities. For stress,

TABLE 5.10

*The association between family structure and stability and quality of mothers' parenting*

|  | Maternal stress | Harsh parenting | Literacy-promoting behaviors |
|---|---|---|---|
| Total transitions | 0.18 *** | 0.11 * | −0.04 |
| Residential transitions | 0.13 * | 0.19 * | 0.05 |
| Dating transitions | 0.21 *** | 0.08 † | −0.02 |
| Early transitions | −0.08 | 0.06 | 0.10 † |
| Recent transitions | 0.28 * | 0.30 * | −0.03 |

SOURCE: Source: Beck et al. 2010.

NOTE: Coefficients based on OLS models.

†$p \leq .10$; *$p \leq .05$; **$p \leq .01$; ***$p \leq .001$ (two-tailed tests).

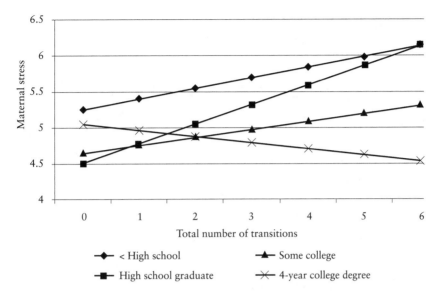

Figure 5.6.    The association between partnership instability and mothers' stress, by education. Source: Beck, Cooper, McLanahan, and Brooks-Gunn. 2010. "Partnership Transitions and Maternal Parenting." *Journal of Marriage and Family* 72(2): 219–33.

dating transitions showed the stronger association with stress, whereas for harsh parenting, residential transitions had the stronger association. An examination of the timing of partnership transitions indicated that recent transitions were more negative than distal transitions, which is consistent with prior research on divorce (Hetherington 1989).

Interestingly, in two instances—maternal stress and literacy activities— the association between family instability and parenting depended on mothers' education. As shown in Figure 5.6, each partnership transition was associated with an increase in maternal stress among mothers with less than a college degree, with the largest increases appearing for mothers with only a high school degree. Among mothers with a college degree, each transition was associated with slightly lower levels of stress.

The reverse was true for literacy activities, where the association with instability was stronger for college-educated mothers. Whereas college-educated mothers in stable families reported more engagement in literacy activities than less-educated mothers, their advantage dropped sharply with each partnership transition; by two transitions, college-educated mothers reported about the same level of engagement as mothers with a high school education (Figure 5.7). The large drop in literacy activities among college-educated mothers is likely due to the fact that these mothers typically engage in very

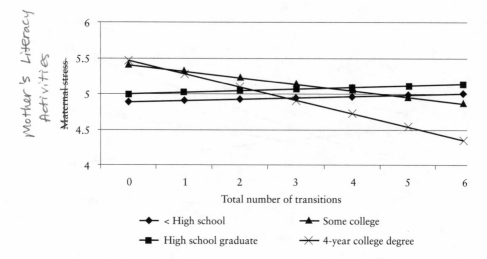

Figure 5.7.   The association between partnership instability and mothers' literacy activities, by education. Source: Beck, Cooper, McLanahan, and Brooks-Gunn. 2010. "Partnership Transitions and Maternal Parenting." *Journal of Marriage and Family*. 72(2): 219–33.

high levels of literacy activities, and thus their potential for disengagement is much greater than that of less-educated mothers.

To determine if the associations between family structure/stability and mothers' parenting were causal, we conducted several robustness checks. First, we re-estimated our models using a more extensive set of controls, including mothers' test scores, mothers' relationship history and grandparents' mental health history. Next we added a measure of mothers' parenting at year three to the model predicting parenting at year five. The logic behind this strategy (lagged dependent variable) was that parenting at year three should capture the effect of any nonchanging unobserved variables that were associated with stability and parenting. Finally, we estimated models that looked at whether mothers' future instability (between years three and five) was associated with her parenting at year three. The logic behind this "falsification test" was that the future should not predict the past; and if it did, such an association would be evidence that an unobserved variable was causing both instability and parenting. Harsh parenting and literacy activities passed all of the robustness checks. Maternal stress, however, did not pass the falsification test. Although this last finding reduces our confidence that instability has a causal effect on maternal stress, we cannot rule out the possibility that mothers' *anticipation* of a future partnership transition was responsible for stress at year three. (For more details about the analysis, see Beck et al. 2010.)

CHILD WELL-BEING

In a final set of analyses, we examined the associations between family structure/stability and child well-being at age 5 (Cooper et al. 2008). Measures of child well-being included child's cognitive ability (measured by the Peabody Picture Vocabulary Test) and the child's socio-emotional development (measured by subscales of the Behavior Problems Checklist), including externalizing behavior (aggression, rule breaking), social problems (problems getting along) and attention problems (problems focusing). These variables are frequently used to measure children's capabilities at the time they enter school, and they have been shown to be good predictors of children's future success. As before, our models controlled for a rich set of demographic and human capital variables.

As shown in Table 5.11, partnership instability was associated with lower cognitive test scores and higher levels of behavior problems, with the exception of internalizing behavior. In general, the correlations were larger for residential transitions than for dating transitions, although the differences between the two types of instability were not always statistically significant. Most interestingly, we found significant gender differences in the associations between instability and behavior problems, with the latter typically being larger for boys than for girls.

All of the results in Table 5.11 were robust to the inclusion of child well-being at age 3. Moreover, the associations between co-residential transitions and verbal ability and attention problems were robust in fixed-effects models. Although not significant, the size of the coefficient for aggression in the fixed-effects model was similar to that in the other models.

TABLE 5.11

*The association between family structure and stability and child well-being*

|  | PPVT1 | External | Internal | Attention | Social |
|---|---|---|---|---|---|
| Structure |  |  |  |  |  |
| Single at baseline | 1.37 | 0.52 | 0.39* | 0.08 | 0.36** |
| Cohabiting at baseline | 0.24 | 0.10 | 0.26 | −0.03 | 0.22 |
| Instability |  |  |  |  |  |
| Co-residential transitions | −0.79** | 0.07 | −0.03 | 0.003 | 0.03 |
| Dating transitions | −0.36* | 0.14† | −0.03 | 0.02 | 0.001 |
| Male × co-residential |  | 0.35* | 0.08 |  | 0.14* |
| Male × dating |  | 0.07 | 0.01 |  | 0.04 |
| Male |  | 0.56* | −0.09 |  | −0.32*** |

SOURCE: Cooper et al. 2008.

NOTE: Coefficients are based on latent growth models.

[1] Peabody Picture Vocabulary Test.

†$p \leq .10$; *$p \leq .05$; **$p \leq .01$; ***$p \leq .001$ (two-tailed tests).

SUMMING UP

So, what have we learned about the four questions laid out at the beginning of the chapter? And what can we say about the implication of family change for the future life chances of children from fragile families? With respect to the first question—*What is the nature of parental relationships and capabilities at birth, and what happens to relationships over time?*—unmarried parents and married parents clearly have very different capabilities. Moreover, although many unmarried parents have "high hopes" for a future together, very few follow through on their plans to marry, with nearly two-thirds ending their relationship within five years of their child's birth. Once their relationship ends, parents experience high levels of partnership instability and household complexity as mothers form new partnerships and have children with other men. These findings suggest that children born into fragile families are disadvantaged relative to other children not only in terms of their parents' capabilities but also in terms of parental social capital.

With respect to the second question—*What happens to parental resources over time?*—we find that family structure and instability operate in ways that reduce parental resources. Marriage appears to increase fathers' work hours and earnings and mothers' household income, whereas union dissolution and being single appear to reduce economic resources. Instability also increases mothers' mental health problems, at least in the short run. In turn, the reduction in parental resources along with ongoing instability and growing complexity is associated with less paternal involvement and lower-quality parenting, which speaks to our third question—*How are family structure and stability associated with parental investments in children?*

With respect to the fourth question—*How do children fare in fragile families?*—both family structure and partnership instability appear to influence child well-being. Being born to a single mother is associated with more internalizing problems and more social problems, and being born to cohabiting parents is associated with more social problems. Further, partnership instability, especially co-residential instability, is associated with lower levels of cognitive ability and higher levels of behavior problems. Of particular note, the association between instability and behavior problems appears to be more important for boys than for girls. The fact that boys are sensitive to family disruption at an early age can be consequential since problem behavior in the early grades is likely to interfere with long-term learning. Although it is much too early to say whether gender differences in children's responses to family instability might account for some of the growing gender gap in children's school achievement that has emerged during the past two decades, this issue is extremely important and must be followed carefully.

Finally, what can be said about whether the changes in family structure/ stability actually reduce the opportunities of disadvantaged children above and beyond what they would have been had their parents married before they were born? Although we cannot rule out the possibility that the observed associations between family structure and the various outcomes examined in this chapter are due to unobserved variables that affect both family stability and child well-being, the results presented here have undergone a number of robustness checks, and the evidence is consistent with the argument that being born to unmarried parents reduces children's life chances. At the same time, the findings show that being born to married parents who then divorce is also associated with lower parental resources and investments as well as poorer child outcomes. Thus it is not marital status at birth that promotes children's long-term well-being but rather the fact that marital status at birth is a pretty good proxy for children's long-term family structure.

REFERENCES

Beck, Audrey, Carey Cooper, Sara McLanahan, and Jeanne Brooks-Gunn. 2010. "Partnership Transitions and Maternal Parenting." *Journal of Marriage & Family* 72(2): 219–33.

Carlson, Marcia J., and Frank F. Furstenberg. 2006. "The Prevalence and Correlates of Multipartnered Fertility among Urban U.S. Parents." *Journal of Marriage and Families* 68(3): 718–32.

Carlson, Marcia, Sara McLanahan, and Paula England. 2004. "Union Formation in Fragile Families." *Demography* 41(2): 237–61.

Carlson, Marcia J., Sara S. McLanahan, and Jeanne Brooks–Gunn. 2008. "Coparenting and Nonresident Fathers' Involvement with Young Children after a Nonmarital Birth." *Demography* 45(2): 461–88.

Cherlin, Andrew, J. 2005. "American Marriage in the Early Twenty–First Century." *The Future of Children* 15(2): 33–55.

Coontz, Stephanie. 1998. *The Way We Really Are: Coming to Terms with America's Changing Families*. New York: Basic Books.

Cooper, Carey, Sara McLanahan, Sarah Meadows, and Jeanne Brooks-Gunn. 2009. "Family Structure, Transitions, and Maternal Stress." *Journal of Marriage and Family* 71(3):558–74.

Cooper, Carey, Cynthia Osborne, Audrey Beck, and Sara McLanahan. 2008. "Partner Instability, School Readiness and Gender Disparities." Working Paper #2008-08-FF. Princeton, NJ: Center for Research on Child Wellbeing.

DeKlyen, Michelle, Jeanne Brooks-Gunn, Jean Knab, and Sara McLanahan. 2006. "The Mental Health of Married, Cohabiting, and Non-Coresident Parents with Infants." *American Journal of Public Health* 96(10): 1836–41.

Edin, Kathryn, and Maria Kefalas. 2005. *Promises I Can Keep: Why Poor Women Put Motherhood before Marriage*. Berkeley: University of California Press.

Edin, Kathryn, and Paula England, eds. 2007. *Unmarried Couples with Children.* New York: Russell Sage.

Freeman, Richard B., and Jane Waldfogel. 2001. "Dunning Delinquent Dads: The Effects of Child Support Enforcement Policy on Child Support Receipt by Never Married Women." *Journal of Human Resources* 36(2): 207–25.

Garfinkel, Irwin, and Sara McLanahan. 1986. *Single Mothers and Their Children: A New American Dilemma.* Washington, DC: Urban Institute Press.

Garfinkel, Irwin, Sara S. McLanahan, Sarah O. Meadows, and Ronald Mincy. "Unmarried Fathers' Earnings Trajectories: Does Partnership Status Matter?" Working Paper WP09-02-FF. Princeton, NJ: Center for Research on Child Wellbeing.

Gibson-Davis, Christina, Kathryn Edin, and Sara McLanahan. 2007. "High Hopes, but Even Higher Expectations: The Retreat from Marriage among Low-Income Couples." *Journal of Marriage and Family* 67(5): 1301–12.

Harknett, Kristen, and Sara McLanahan. 2004. "Racial and Ethnic Differences in Marriage after the Birth of a Child." *American Sociological Review* 69(6): 790–811.

Hetherington, E. Mavis. 1989. "Coping with Family Transitions: Winners, Losers and Survivors." *Child Development* 60: 1–15.

Kiernan, Kathleen E., and M. Carmen Huerta. 2008. "Economic Deprivation, Maternal Depression, Parenting and Children's Cognitive and Emotional Development in Early Childhood." *British Journal of Sociology* 59(4): 783–806.

McLanahan, Sara, and Christine Percheski. 2008. "Family Structure and the Reproduction of Inequalities." *Annual Review of Sociology* 34: 257–76.

McLanahan, Sara, and Gary Sandefur. 1994. *Growing Up with a Single Parent: What Hurts, What Helps.* Cambridge, MA: Harvard University Press.

McLoyd, Vonnie. 1990. "Minority Children: Introduction to the Special Issue." *Child Development* 61(2): 263–66.

Meadows, Sarah O. 2009. "Family Structure and Fathers' Well-Being: Trajectories of Mental Health and Self-Rated Health." *Journal of Health and Social Behavior* 50(2): 115–31.

Meadows, Sarah, Sara McLanahan, and Jean Knab. 2009. "Economic Trajectories in Non-Traditional Families with Children." Working Paper #2009-10-FF. Princeton, NJ: Center for Research on Child Wellbeing.

Meadows, Sarah, Sara McLanahan, and Jeanne Brooks-Gunn. 2008. "Family Structure and Maternal Health Trajectories." *American Sociological Review* 73(2): 314–34.

Monte, Lindsay. 2007. "Blended but Not the Bradys: Navigating Unmarried Multiple Partner Fertility" In *Unmarried Couples with Children*, edited by Paula England and Kathryn Edin, pp. 183–203. New York: Russell Sage Foundation.

Nepomnyaschy, Lenna, and Irwin Garfinkel. Forthcoming. "Child Support Enforcement and Father's Contributions to their Nonmarital Children." *Social Services Review.*

Osborne, Cynthia, and Sara S. McLanahan. 2007. "Partnership Instability and Child Wellbeing." *Journal of Marriage and Family* 69(4): 1065–83.

Reichman, Nancy, Irwin Garfinkel, Sara McLanahan, and Julien Teitler. 2001. "Fragile Families Sample and Design." *Children and Youth Services Review* 23(4/5): 303–26.

Tach, Laura, Ronald Mincy, and Kathryn Edin. 2010. "Parenting as a Package Deal: Relationships, Fertility, and Nonresident Father Involvement among Unmarried Parents."

*Demography* 47(1): 181–204.

Ventura, Stephanie. 2009. "Changing Patterns of Nonmarital Childbearing in the United States." National Center for Health Statistics Data Brief #18, pp. 1–7.

Waite, Linda, and Maggie Gallagher. 2001. *The Case for Marriage: Why Married People Are Happier, Healthier and Better Off.* New York: Broadway Books.

Willis, Robert. 2000. "The Economics of Fatherhood." *American Economic Review* 90: 378–82.

Wilson, William J. 1988. *The Truly Disadvantaged.* Cambridge, MA: Harvard University Press.

# CHAPTER SIX

# Social Class and the Transition to Adulthood

## Differences in Parents' Interactions with Institutions

### *Annette Lareau and Amanda Cox*

Although the importance of social class in family life has preoccupied social scientists, it has failed to capture the attention of the general public (New York Times 2005). A body of research on social class and the family finds that middle-class individuals, defined either by education (i.e., having a college degree) or by occupation, typically have different family histories than working-class individuals (Kohn and Schooler 1983). More specifically, as Carlson and England, Cherlin, McLanahan, and others in this volume show, researchers have found class-based differences in the likelihood of marriage, divorce rates, household structures, lifespan, and health outcomes. In addition, social class has been found to be a factor in the character of childrearing (see Crosnoe and Cavanaugh 2010 for a review). While the importance of social class in family life has been documented since the classic studies by Robert and Helen Lynd (1929, 1937) in *Middletown*, Americans generally lack an awareness of social class (New York Times 2005).

As researchers have documented social-class differences in family life, increasing attention has been given to the transition to adulthood, as youth move from adolescence into the world of work (Furstenberg 2010). There are social-class differences in the timing and nature of the transition, particularly in terms of residential independence from family of origin, marriage, work, childbearing, and other signs of adulthood (Settersten, Furstenberg, and Rumbaut 2005). Many studies focus on class differences as the reason youth achieve (or don't achieve) key outcomes in adulthood. However, we have less insight into the crucial social processes through which these outcomes are produced. Indeed, social scientists have also developed a truncated understanding of how social class shapes the life chances of youth. There is a tendency among researchers to focus on the characteristics of youth. This individualistic approach discounts the degree to which youth are embedded in a social context. Notably, it fails to recognize sufficiently the role that parents play in situating their children, interacting with institutions, and transforming the circumstances that their children experience. Hence, it is

134

important to study variations in the role that parents play in facilitating their children's development, particularly in helping them deal with institutions, such as high schools and colleges. In addition, there has been disproportionate attention to the material transfer of resources. Some studies, including one by Schoeni and Ross (2005), show that middle-class parents transfer more material resources to their young adult children than do working-class parents. Others show that class differences affect savings rates for college (Conley 2001). Beyond material resources, however, there are signs of differences in class-based cultural resources, such as the amount of information that parents have about institutions (Lubrano 2004). These cultural resources, however, have received less attention from social scientists.

In this chapter we draw on a qualitative study of white and African American families to suggest that the social class of parents has an important impact on the lives of young adults by affecting how parents manage their sons' and daughters' institutional experiences. In the first part of the chapter, we highlight three key class-based resources that surfaced in the study. First, middle-class parents and youth had much deeper and more detailed knowledge of the inner workings of key institutional structures, especially those related to getting into and succeeding in college, than did working-class and poor parents and youth. Second, middle-class parents and youth had a more detailed understanding of the strengths and weaknesses of their own "cases" and unique options. Third, while all parents helped their children in many ways, middle-class parents intervened in institutions on behalf of theirs. Some of the working-class and poor parents also sought to intervene, but their efforts were less frequent and less successful. We see these three factors (i.e., global knowledge, case-specific knowledge, and a propensity to intervene) as constituting class-based cultural resources that parents drew on in their interactions with institutions such as schools. In the second part of the chapter, we suggest that parents drew on these class-based resources as they helped their children in two key ways: to *foresee and forestall problems* and to solve problems, which we refer to as *untying knots*. Thus, in addition to focusing on youths' individual characteristics and parent-child interaction within the home, we believe it is important to study the ways in which parents differ in how they work with institutions to foresee and forestall problems and to solve problems that surface.

After discussing our research methodology, we present two detailed case studies of a white middle-class young man, Garrett Tallinger, and a white working-class young woman, Wendy Driver, to show how their parents differed in their global knowledge, case-specific knowledge, and propensity to intervene in their children's institutional lives. We draw on the case studies of these two young people, as well as on the experiences of the other youth in the study, to suggest that these class-based cultural resources made a difference as the youths transitioned into adulthood. In particular, while all parents were able to foresee problems, middle-class parents were able to forestall problems much more effectively than were working-class and poor parents. In addition, all of the youth encountered problems in institutions during their transition to adulthood. However, middle-class parents had more resources for trying to solve these problems than did working-class and poor parents. In the conclusion we stress the importance of embedding the family in a broader social context, as well as the drawbacks of middle-class parents' childrearing strategies.

## METHODOLOGY

To capture the social processes that family members experience, as well as the meaning of the processes, it is essential to use qualitative methods of participant-observation and in-depth interviewing. This chapter draws on re-interviews with twelve young adults and their families approximately ten years after the young people's participation in an ethnographic study, "Unequal Childhoods," about variations in family life and children's activities (Lareau 2003). This unique data set has a number of important advantages. The original ethnographic study provided a rich portrait of the rhythm of family life. The interviews, a decade later, build on the original observations while providing a chance to assess the situation in the families a decade later as the youth were in the process of transitioning to adulthood. Figure 6.1 provides an overview of the original study. The families were white and African American and lived in a large Northeastern city or the suburbs of the city (see Table 6.1 for a breakdown of the race and class of the participants in the study, as well as the definition of social class). A more intensive observational phase was then completed with twelve of these families; there was an effort to select families that were roughly comparable across race and class (i.e., one poor girl from a deeply religious family and one middle-class girl from a similar family). (For more discussion of the criteria for selection and the methodology, see Lareau 2003.) Each family was observed for about three weeks, usually on a daily basis.

Over the years, Annette Lareau kept in touch with the families through annual holiday cards and small gifts. A decade after the original study, she located all twelve families, interviewed all of the target children, and conducted separate interviews with the youths' mothers, fathers, and siblings.[1] The interviews of the target young people took place in their parents' homes, except for one (Garrett Tallinger's), which took place in his dorm room. Family members were paid (see Figure 6.1). The interviews were tape-recorded and transcribed. For data analysis we created codes for key themes (e.g.,

**Original study**

- Classroom observations in three public schools (one predominantly white suburban school in the Northeast, one racially mixed city school in the Northeast, and there is no description of the racial makeup of the third school).

- In-depth interviews with educators and mothers and fathers of 88 children who were 9 and 10 years old.

- Most of the families came from the three observed schools; the remaining children (especially white poor and black middle class) came from social service programs or informal networks.

- Most of the data were collected in the period 1993–95, but some were collected earlier and later.

| *Observations of 12 families* | *Doing the fieldwork* |
|---|---|
| • Nine of the 12 families (but neither of the black middle-class families) came from the classrooms; response rate of people we asked was 63 percent (asked 19 to get 12) | • No question that we were disruptive, but families adjusted |
| • Usually 20 visits to each family, usually daily in the space of one month | • Yelling and cursing increased, especially on the third and tenth days |
| • Most visits lasted 2–3 hours but sometimes longer | • Children generally liked our visits, said it made them feel "special" |
| • One overnight visit per family | |
| • Families were paid, generally $350, at the end of the study | • Kept in touch with the families over the years by sending a Christmas card with monetary gift to the child |
| • Worked in racially diverse teams of 2 or 3, sharing visits to the families | |
| • Wrote field notes for 5–12 hours after each visit | |

*Follow-up study*

- Two-hour tape-recorded interviews with "target child" and mother, father, one sibling, and a spouse or serious boyfriend or girlfriend for a total of 38 interviews.

- Family members were paid an honorarium ($75 for target young person, $50 for others).

- Interviews generally took place in the homes of the families.

- Interviews 2003–05; reached all 12 families, a few family members not interviewed.

- Most children remember the study but have only a hazy memory of specific events.

*Figure 6.1.* Methodological details of study for "Unequal Childhoods" and follow-up study.

education decisions, work, perceptions of parent role, disappointments, college applications, independence) and coded the interviews accordingly. We also read and reread the interviews in order to understand the context of the coded material. Amanda Cox, who was not involved in data collection, worked on the coding with a researcher who was involved in the original research project. All names are pseudonyms, and we have substituted names of comparable colleges and have removed identifying information about the colleges attended by the youth.[2]

TABLE 6.1

*Distribution of the 12 youth in the follow-up study, by social class and race*

| Social class | White | African American |
|---|---|---|
| Middle class | Melanie Handlon<br>Garrett Tallinger | Stacey Marshall<br>Alexander Williams |
| Working class | Wendy Driver<br>Billy Yanelli | Tyrec Taylor<br>Jessica Irwin* |
| Poor | Katie Brindle<br>Karl Greeley | Tara Carroll<br>Harold McAllister |

N O T E S : In the original study, a total of 88 families were interviewed; 12 of these families were also observed. Since the 2003–05 follow-up only focused on the families that were observed, we have only included data on these 12 families. For additional information see Lareau 2003.

Middle-class children are those who live in households in which at least one parent is employed in a position that either entails substantial managerial authority or centrally draws upon highly complex, educationally certified (i.e., college-level) skills.

Working-class children are those who live in households in which neither parent is employed in a middle-class position and at least one parent is employed in a position that has little or no managerial authority and that does not require highly complex, educationally certified skills. This category includes lower-level white-collar workers.

Poor children are those who live in households in which parents receive public assistance and do not participate in the labor force on a regular, continuous basis.

* Biracial girl: black father and white mother.

Longitudinal studies using qualitative methods are rare (Burawoy 2003). It is useful that Lareau was able to reach all twelve of the youth in the intensive phase of the original study, as well as to triangulate their information with separate interviews with other family members.[3] Of course, the labor-intensive nature of qualitative research means that researchers must make hard choices. Depth of research almost always comes at the expense of breadth of the sample. The longitudinal nature of the research further compounds this problem. This study has a small sample, twelve families, and focuses on the transition to adulthood within those families. Nevertheless, the study's value is apparent in that the patterns we found are highly consistent with findings from studies using nationally representative data (Settersten, Furstenberg, and Rumbaut 2005); but the findings offer much more depth and insight into social processes than nationally representative data sets can provide. In addition, both qualitative and quantitative studies tend to focus on the actions of youth alone. Yet, since families operate in social contexts, it is important to consider how parents and youth negotiate with institutions outside the home. Also, we show that the strategies that parents adopted when their youth were in the transition to adulthood were highly consistent with strategies they followed when their children were 10 years old. This kind of longitudinal insight is rare. We see the results as helping to improve our conceptual models about the ways in which social class has an impact on family life, particularly in terms of the largely hidden advantages that many middle-class parents provide for their children by negotiating their experiences in institutions.

## CLASS AND THE TRANSITION TO ADULTHOOD: A TALE OF TWO FAMILIES

Research in the sociology of the family has largely been devoted to the life outcomes of individual youth, but there has been less attention paid to the institutions surrounding family life and the interactions between families and these institutions. In this chapter, we show that the strategies parents adopted mattered.[4] Class differences in the global and specific information possessed by parents, and how they intervened in institutions, had consequences. Working-class parents were able to foresee and forestall some key problems and untie important knots in their children's lives. However, there was a striking pattern of more aggressive intervention by middle-class parents in predicting and preventing problems and solving problems than among working-class and poor parents. In our follow-ups with these families, the middle-class youth (although over the age of 18) seemed younger, more dependent, and more child-like than working-class youth.

### Turning Points and Interventions: Garrett Tallinger

When Garrett Tallinger was in fourth grade, his family lived in a large suburban home on a leafy cul-de-sac in the predominantly white suburb of a large Northeastern city. Both of his parents had graduated from an Ivy League college (where they were both athletes). As Garrett was getting ready to enter high school, his parents, Garrett, and his two younger brothers moved to a much larger new home in an elite development to be closer to Mr. Tallinger's workplace. Their income placed them in the top 10 percent of American families. In 2003, Mr. Tallinger had a high-level managerial job; he frequently traveled for work. Ms. Tallinger worked in fundraising.

Garrett Tallinger, now a basketball player on a top-ranked basketball team at a private university, has been a talented athlete since he was a young child. When Garrett was 10 years old, his parents spent a great deal of time and effort helping him pursue his interests and skills and providing him with a wide range of activities and experiences. Garrett's schedule of activities often dictated the daily and weekly rhythm of the Tallinger family, including Garrett's two younger brothers. Backed by their own educational and work-related experiences within largely middle-class contexts, Garrett's parents possessed valuable knowledge of the ways in which "gatekeeping" institutions such as high schools and colleges work. Their understanding of these and other institutions played an important role in their ability to guide Garrett through high school and into college.

TABLE 6.2

*Selected life characteristics of intensive-study child participants, at age 20–21*

| | White | | African American | |
|---|---|---|---|---|
| | Garrett Tallinger | Melanie Handlon | Alexander Williams | Stacey Marshall |
| Middle-class families | High school graduate | High school graduate | High school graduate | High school graduate |
| | College student | Cosmetology school student | College student | College student |
| | Recruited by 2 Ivy League schools to play basketball; attends small private college on basketball scholarship; earns A's and B's | Attended community college one semester ("hated it") | Accepted early-decision to Ivy League school; has been admitted to medical school at same elite university; earns B's, some A's | Accepted at Ivy League school, but attends public university on basketball scholarship; earns mostly B's (2 C's in biology) |
| | Billy Yanelli | Wendy Driver | Tyrec Taylor | Jessica Irwin (biracial) |
| Working-class families | High school dropout | High school graduate | High school graduate | High school graduate |
| | Earned GED | Accepted at small Catholic college; chose not to attend | Started community college, did not finish 1st semester; took 1 year off; has completed 1 semester | College student |
| | Works full-time; is apprentice in painters' union | Stay-at-home mother; is pregnant, has 2-year-old; husband is in Navy | Works full-time in construction | Solicited by dozens of colleges due to PSATs in 1300s; attends small Tier 3 school on full scholarship; art major; dean's list |
| | Karl Greeley | Katie Brindle | Harold McAllister | Tara Carroll |
| Poor families | High school dropout | High school dropout | High school dropout | High school graduate |
| | Took GED classes; did not take GED test | Married, separated; has 2-year-old (father is not current husband) | Has been working at chain restaurant full-time since age 15; noon to 9 p.m. shift; 2-hour commute to work (4 buses) | Community college student, but now taking time off; wants to be a nurse; failed biology twice, C's in science courses |
| | Works full-time (nights), stocking grocery store shelves | Works full-time, cleaning houses | | Works full-time (3–11 p.m.) as caretaker for disabled people |
| | | Lives with mother and brother | Lives with brother and his family | |

When Garrett entered high school after he and his family relocated to a state nearly 1,000 miles from where Garrett had lived as a young child, Ms. Tallinger was quick to learn about the local high school and its curriculum. When she visited Garrett's future public high school, Ms. Tallinger sought detailed information about the colleges attended by the school's graduates:

> I was appalled [when I visited the local public high school]. It's ugly. It's far away. I asked how many kids go to . . . get recruited for Division I [athletic programs]. . . . they probably thought . . . they probably were wondering, "Who is this Northern hussy coming in here and asking these questions?" [laughs] But they couldn't tell me where kids went to school. . . . they all went mostly to [in-state] schools. So, [I asked], "How many would go to the Ivies, to the Stanfords or the MITs?"

As Garrett began high school, Ms. Tallinger encouraged him to take the "most rigorous" courses, and she shared her desire and her sense of her son's academic capabilities with Garrett's high school guidance counselors:

> In talking to the guidance people, I said, "I think he's capable of honors [i.e., enrolling in the honors courses]. But, obviously you-all need to decide that. . . ."

Ms. Tallinger was well informed about the global standards in higher education:

> One of the things I did know was that the more competitive colleges look at what is available in a high school, and if you're not taking the most rigorous of what's available, that's a strike against you in terms of their evaluating your transcript. And so I wanted Garrett, as is true with all my kids, I want them to take the most rigorous [course] that they're possibly capable of taking.

His junior year Garrett took Advanced Placement (AP) economics, AP calculus, and AP English literature, as well as the highest levels of physics and history offered by his high school.

Just as Ms. Tallinger oversaw and shepherded Garrett through various academic transitions and decisions, Garrett's father guided his son through the complicated (and highly strategic) process of being recruited by a top-tier collegiate basketball program. As Mr. Tallinger reports, his guidance required a complex understanding of the inner workings of what he describes as the "very political" recruiting process:

> We sent marketing packets to a lot of schools. There are a lot of recruiting websites out there. So those guys come and see kids play, and I got to know a lot of those guys, so having them write about your kid is important. Get his name out there, they do all these rankings, it's very political networking kind of deal. And then the coaches go to all of these tournaments and these camps and they watch him.

Mr. Tallinger described his understanding of the strategy involved on both sides of the recruiting process, the universities' and the athlete's:

> All these schools send you letters. So the first thing they look for: did you respond to the letter quickly, 'cause they're all trying to measure interest. So, what happens is both sides are playing the game: the schools tell you they have a priority list of kids they want. They do their best not to tell you where you are on that list. They want every kid to think he or she is number one, and we do the same thing on this end. I mean our strategy was to never [tell] a school he wasn't interested 'cause they start talking to each other. So if you tell a school of a certain kind, "I don't want to go there," they say [to other schools], "Well, don't bother to recruit him."

In addition to his quickly learned knowledge about the recruiting process, Mr. Tallinger was also knowledgeable about the likelihood of Garrett's receiving financial aid from an Ivy League university that was recruiting Garrett "very hard." Mr. Tallinger knew that Ivy League universities do not offer athletic scholarships and that his family's income of $175,000 placed them above the school's financial aid cut-off. With three children, he knew an Ivy League school was unaffordable.

The involvement of the Tallinger parents is similar to the role that they had played in Garrett's academic and athletic affairs when he was a 10-year-old. For example, when Garrett was in early elementary school, he missed the IQ cut-off for his school's gifted program by just a few points. Upon receiving the news that Garrett would not be able to join the program, the Tallingers insisted that Garrett be retested at what they felt would be a more appropriate time for him to perform at his best. Garrett was retested, but his score was again not high enough to qualify him for his school's gifted program.

Like their knowledge of how institutions work, Ms. and Mr. Tallinger's knowledge about Garrett in particular was valuable as they helped him navigate the transition from high school to college. They had a nuanced understanding of how Garrett might fare when compared with other students and athletes. Ms. Tallinger reported:

> He never cracked 1200 on the SATs. So, that was tough—familiar. 'Cause I didn't test well either, and did well in school. Obviously [I] felt for him. He didn't . . . what did he get on the ACT . . . I think he got a 27 or a 28, so that was a little bit better.

Mr. Tallinger was also aware that Garrett would not have shined at Princeton in the way that he did at Villanova:

> While I think Garrett would have done okay academically [at Princeton], I think Villanova is a better fit. Garrett is a good student, but he's not a brilliant kid. So he would have gotten by at Princeton, whereas [at] Villanova you

know he was, he got the academic award on the basketball team. He was the highest GPA on the basketball team, and he's been selected [to be on the] student athlete academic committee. . . . He was selected to represent Villanova, not just the basketball team, the whole university. So, those kinds of opportunities he wouldn't have gotten at Princeton. Now obviously Princeton's got other academic opportunities that Villanova doesn't by far, but I think it's [i.e., Villanova's] probably actually a better fit.

Mr. Tallinger also thought that after graduation the booster club networks at Villanova would help Garrett land an attractive job in business.

Garrett himself also had a sense of how his SAT scores would help or hinder his chances of acceptance into various colleges and universities and how their standards differed:

I was real worried about it [i.e., his SAT score] 'cause I was trying to get into Stanford at the time. And 1190 isn't . . . I mean, they did accept a kid with an 1140, but still it's only . . . if you're trying to get into Stanford, you need . . . that's why I wanted to get 1200 real bad. I mean, and then coming here [to Villanova], their standard's not as high.

In addition to their academic knowledge, Garrett's parents also knew their son's basketball shooting percentage ("56 percent for his career," Mr. Tallinger reported) and how he compared with other high school athletes being recruited by the same universities. For example, Mr. Tallinger saw some schools as "a stretch":

I think U. Conn. would have been a stretch ability-wise for Garrett, but they were recruiting him. And they came to see him play, and the coach called me afterwards and he goes, "You know, we know you told us he was 6'4". We were hoping he was 6'6". But we have three 6'4" kids, and we don't need another one." I had no problem with that. So you move on.

Garrett's parents had both general knowledge of how institutions worked and an ability—with a cold and critical eye—to assess the weaknesses of their son's situation. They also had detailed information about institutions not confined to college. This can be seen in how the Tallingers weighed Garrett's post-college basketball options. Although Garrett was currently playing on a basketball team that was ranked among the top twenty-five in the nation, Mr. Tallinger felt that Garrett would not be "good enough" to play professionally in the NBA upon graduation from college:

Well, realistically, if it went very well for him, he'd probably be trying to make an NBA team . . . [but] playing in Europe. [I'm] not sure if he's quite good enough to play in the NBA. I mean, hopefully he'll get better. He'll probably be one of those guys that's not drafted by the NBA, but gets him what are called "free-agent tryouts," probably ends up playing in Europe or South America for a few years or something.

Garrett also harbored doubts about his chances of making it to the NBA. When asked about his post-college plans, Garrett said, "Probably still playing basketball somewhere. In the NBA hopefully. But if not, overseas somewhere."

As Ms. and Mr. Tallinger guided Garrett through the various academic and athletic institutions that he encountered from early childhood and into college, their informal knowledge about how the institutions worked and how their son "measured up" in the face of these institutions played a key role in shaping Garrett's experiences and outcomes. Both their knowledge of the institutional workings in general and of Garrett's "case" in particular often led to the third mechanism that contributed to the transmission of advantages within the middle-class families in this study: parents' (often successful) interventions in institutions in which their children participate.

In addition to encouraging Garrett to take the "most rigorous" courses his high school had to offer and talking to Garrett's high school guidance counselors about her son being "capable of honors," Ms. Tallinger was quick to intervene when a scheduling conflict would have prevented Garrett from enrolling in both AP English literature and AP calculus:

> I did have to go fight about his schedule because they went into this new scheduling system, and if he wanted to take the AP English and AP calculus, they were given at the same time. I was like, "C'mon, this is not—you gotta figure something out. I mean, I can't believe Garrett's the only person this is impacting. You have to figure a way for these kids to maximize their opportunities, and they have to switch things around." So that I did fight for.

Similar to the way in which Ms. Tallinger intervened to maximize Garrett's chances for academic success, Mr. Tallinger played an active role in shaping Garrett's experiences on the basketball court. The summer after Garrett's junior year of high school, Mr. Tallinger negotiated to get Garrett onto a summer-league traveling team that would "give him the visibility" so he would "get the exposure" to recruiters from top-tier collegiate basketball programs. Sponsored by a well-known athletic company, Garrett's new team included a rising young star who was eventually drafted into the NBA directly after completing high school. Mr. Tallinger was grateful for the opportunity for Garrett to play on such a successful team—"I have nothing but thanks and respect for the Memphis Warriors," he said—but he felt that Garrett was not receiving enough playing time to "get the exposure" he needed. When asked if he had ever done anything to increase Garrett's playing time, he replied:

> I did, which is something I don't normally do. But I did only because . . . they were playing a lot of juniors-to-be. I was saying to [the coach], "Well, that's fine, but you have kids,"—and Garrett wasn't the only one—[where] "this is

like their last shot. If they don't get seen this summer, then it's over." . . . These juniors-to-be didn't seem remarkably better than the seniors-to-be. The whole point in the AAU [summer league] teams is to get kids seen by college coaches. . . . So that I didn't understand: why you would play these young kids when you got kids who wanted and needed scholarships sitting on the bench. . . . I guess they kind of listened. His playing time went up some.

Thus, Mr. Tallinger's intervention appeared to increase by "some" Garrett's playing time in front of college recruiters.

Later that year, when Garrett was being actively recruited to play Division I college basketball, Mr. Tallinger again used his knowledge of the inner workings of the recruiting process to intervene when he felt that the process had taken a turn that was not to Garrett's advantage:

> University of Kansas was recruiting him at one point, and then we didn't hear from them for a while. And [I] called the coach and just—I was getting bolder as the thing went on—and said, like, "What's up?" [The coach said,] "Oh, we were told that the recruiting on him was closed." I was like, "Who told you that?" . . . and Kansas—not to say they would have ultimately offered him a scholarship—they stopped recruiting [Garrett] because someone told them that they didn't have a shot.

The Tallingers' parental interventions did not end when Garrett was accepted to play basketball for a highly ranked collegiate team. His parents both continued to offer him valuable guidance as they shepherded him through the process of choosing a college major. Ms. Tallinger reported one such instance:

> I guess it was some point in freshman year, [Garrett] wasn't sure he wanted to continue to major in business or stay in the business school. He's thinking he wanted to be a math teacher and wanted to . . . major in education. We said, "Okay, that's fine." Don, of course, again being the more pragmatic, said, "If that's all you want to earn for the rest of your life . . . as a teacher. . . . But give yourself the most options when you come out of school." . . . Anyway, so on his own he came to the decision that he's gonna stay in the business school and sort of shift emphasis to marketing.

In the end Garrett Tallinger did not miss the opportunity to be recruited by several top-ranked college basketball programs, nor did he fail to "give himself the most options" a few years later when choosing a college major and a potential career path. His parents' knowledge and understanding of institutions and of their son's strengths and weaknesses in relation to the standards and expectations of these institutions eased Garrett's negotiations and transitions at school, within his elite basketball club, and throughout the college recruiting process. When they felt that Garrett's experience within an institution was not what it should be, Ms. and Mr. Tallinger did not hesitate to intervene on their son's behalf. As we explain below after discussing the case of Wendy Driver, these three factors constituted class-based cultural resources that helped the Tallingers foresee and forestall problems and untie knots in their son's life.

### *"Awesome" Parents: Wendy Driver*

Wendy Driver, a cheerful and friendly 10-year-old, grew up in a white working-class family where her daily life centered on visiting with family, playing with her cousins, and attending family events. After Wendy's parents separated, she lived with her maternal grandparents, her mother, and her older brother. By the time Wendy was in fourth grade, her father had died and her mother and Mack moved in together before the birth of their daughter, Valerie. Ms. Driver and Mack married, and Wendy grew up living in a small rented townhouse in a large Northeastern city. Ms. Driver worked as an administrative assistant while Mack worked in a unionized position. Wendy was involved in a few organized activities, but unlike Garrett Tallinger's, Wendy's activities did not dominate family life, and Wendy's mother and Mack saw her activities not as a way for Wendy to develop skills but as things to "give her something to do" and "keep her off the street."

A decade later Wendy is a tall, thin, fresh-faced young wife who, at the age of 20, has an 18-month-old daughter and another child on the way. When Wendy's older brother went into the Navy, he introduced her to Ryan, who is also in the Navy and is out on a submarine six months at a time. Wendy had learned in November after her high school graduation that she was pregnant, just before Ryan's (already planned) marriage proposal. Her parents were supportive. Wendy had had her heart set on a big wedding, but Wendy and Ryan "wanted to get married for the baby." Her parents helped her work out a plan for two weddings: a small wedding took place when Wendy was three months pregnant, and then there was a large, formal, and elaborate wedding when the baby, Clara, was 1 year old. Wendy lives about four hours away from her parents, but when Ryan is out at sea, Wendy and Clara visit Wendy's parents for long stretches of time.

Throughout Wendy's life, Mr. and Ms. Driver have intervened in her life. Wendy sees her mother as having been particularly helpful in "fighting" for her in school-related matters and in giving her a model she hopes to emulate with her own children:

> I have to go to school and fight for my child. If my mom can do it, then I can do it. I remember my mom going to school and fighting for me all the time. They told me I had to go to a special school and my Mom is like, "No, she's fine."

As they are today, Mr. and Ms. Driver were devoted parents when Wendy was a child. They assessed the specifics of their daughter's situation, and they frequently intervened to help her. For example, at the end of eighth grade Wendy was not admitted to the magnet high school of her choice. She was redirected to the neighborhood school which, with metal detectors, a high dropout rate, and occasional fights, was widely characterized as a "bad" school. Ms. Driver was extremely concerned. Wendy's "Pop Pop" (i.e., her paternal grandfather) paid the $3,000 annual tuition to send her to the Catholic high school that Wendy's mother and sisters had attended. Wendy reported that her eighth-grade counselors were not supportive of the idea:

> The eighth-grade counselor told my mom that they would be wasting their money. Because I wouldn't make it. And when I got down there I struggled freshman year. That's when the counselor started coming . . . and I had different people coming and giving me tests and talking about it, telling the school, "This is what you have to do to cope with my disability." And it just like made it *so* much easier. But even my freshman year in high school, I had teachers tell me to quit now, just to drop out and to try to get my GED by myself. And that just made me and my mom push even harder.

The high school arranged for tests to be read to Wendy and allowed her to provide verbal answers. With this system in place, Wendy earned a place on the honor roll. Later in her high school years, when multiple knee surgeries kept Wendy out of school, Ms. Driver coordinated with the school to have tutors work with Wendy so she would not fall behind in her studies. Wendy graduated.

Wendy's parents also helped her in her personal life. When Wendy and Ryan began dating during her senior year in high school, after she and Ryan became close, Ms. Driver sent Wendy to the doctor to get birth control. In November after she graduated from high school, Wendy (unexpectedly) became pregnant. Wendy did not believe in abortion. Her mother was firm on this point as well: "We don't believe in abortion, and there's no issue about giving the baby up for adoption. If it came down to it, me and Mack would have taken it," Ms. Driver said definitively.

Ms. Driver intervened and had a frank conversation with her future son-in-law before he married Wendy to determine if he was willing to accept the responsibility of being a father:

> I'm not one to hide my feelings. And I said to Ryan—we were sitting on the couch—and I said, "I want to ask you something. . . . The first thing a lot of young guys say is, 'It's not mine, and they take off, and you never see them again.'" I said, "Don't." I said, "If you have any doubt in your mind [and if you think that] this child is not yours, there's the door. You can walk out now, and you do not have to come back."

Ms. Driver's intervention was an effort to avert a disaster in the future. She spoke to Ryan directly:

> I said, "I do not want two months from now, five months from now, six months from now you [to] say to her [that] this is not your child. If there is any doubt in your mind at all, or if you have second thoughts that you don't want this child. . . ."

Contributing $5,000 (more than Wendy had wanted them to contribute) to the big wedding, Ms. and Mr. Driver also assisted in the planning and preparations for it. Both parents like their son-in-law. Ryan's troubled past, which includes heavy drinking and arrests for possession of a pipe bomb, as well as Wendy's difficult relations with Ryan's mother (who refused to attend either of the weddings) do not seem to trouble Mr. and Ms. Driver. They are very optimistic about the future. When asked directly what would happen if Wendy and Ryan separated or divorced, they are quick to indicate that Wendy always has a home with them. As Mack, Wendy's stepfather, says:

> Oh, she's more than welcome to come home. . . . We'd just have to make arrangements and make the house bigger probably. [Laughs] But we'd discuss it, and everything would be fine.

Since Wendy moved away from home, Mack has been an invaluable source of transportation. Like her mother, Wendy does not drive. Wendy lives four hours from her childhood home, and although public transportation between the two cities exists, it is not convenient and, with the baby, not ideal. At least once a month, and sometimes more often, Mack makes the eight-hour roundtrip drive to fetch Wendy and Clara. Thus, Ms. Driver and Mack continue to help Wendy and Ryan by providing child care, transportation, and emotional support. All in all, Wendy characterizes her family as "awesome." She says, "They are what I would want. If I need anything, I can call them."

Wendy has warm relations with her parents and, like Garrett, sees her parents as very helpful to her. However, we found differences in the kind of help provided by middle-class parents in relation to institutions and that provided by working-class and poor parents. We found that working-class and poor parents possessed important kinds of information about institutions, but middle-class parents had even more, including information that was often highly specialized and customized to the specific case of their child. This pattern also was present, in a different fashion, among the young adults themselves. Specifically, compared to Garrett, Wendy had limited global information about key matters involving institutions, and her information was much more general. For example, throughout high school and then during the college admission process, there were many moments when

Wendy's learning disability was discussed. Wendy was admitted to a college that offered a program for students with learning disabilities and included the provision of a note taker, additional time on tests, and other learning supports. There are many different types of learning disabilities, but Wendy had only a vague understanding of the nature of her own:

> AL: Did you learn the name of what your disability was?
> Wendy: No, they call it LD.
> AL: Do you know what LD stands for?
> Wendy: Learning Disability.

In high school Wendy's learning disability made it difficult for her to complete her school work. She reported, "And then finally I got the nerve up to tell my good friends, 'Look, I am retarded. I can't do this.'" The term "retarded" is rarely, if ever, used by professionals today to describe a learning disability. While on the one hand Wendy understood that she had a learning disability, she was not fluent in the categories and terms used by educators.

A similar pattern existed for Wendy's parents. Unlike the Tallingers, who possessed deeper and more detailed global knowledge of institutional structures and specific knowledge of their son's relative place and options within those structures, Ms. Driver often had incomplete information about the inner workings of key institutions, and her knowledge about the specifics of Wendy's educational trajectory was vague and partial. Therefore the Drivers relied on professionals who had specialized training in such areas. The Drivers' lack of detailed knowledge about key institutional structures and their reliance on school personnel were evident when Wendy applied to colleges. With the assistance of her friends and an accommodation for her learning disability, Wendy had been able to graduate from high school. Her mother very much wanted her to go to college, and the high school counselor guided the family through the college application process:

> Ms. Driver: She had to go to a particular college that would help her with her disability. Because she couldn't get into another college. They [the high school] want[ed] a college that would have other children with disabilities who need help. She went up to . . . where'd she go? Brockport maybe?
> AL: Brockport?
> Ms. Driver: Yeah. She didn't get accepted there.

Ms. Driver passionately wanted her daughter to go to college. Her global knowledge of higher education systems was limited; for her, a wide variety of institutions were included under the term "college." The differences among colleges that preoccupied the Tallingers did not preoccupy her. Nor did she fixate on Wendy's relative chances of acceptance at various schools or in relation to other students. The Drivers were guided by Wendy's high school counselor, who selected the schools to which Wendy would apply and then helped Wendy with the applications. Wendy's parents were powerful emotional supports for her, but since she was being guided by the counselor, they did not become involved with the application process. Hence it is not surprising that Ms. Driver did not know Wendy's SAT scores or her high school grade-point average.

Other steps in the college application process that were extremely important to middle-class parents such as the Tallingers were less salient to the Driver parents. For example, neither Mr. nor Ms. Driver could recall the names of the colleges to which Wendy had applied. They could only remember the names of the towns in which the colleges were located. Similarly, although Ms. Driver and Mack had driven Wendy to the college she planned to attend, had filled out a financial aid form for the school, and had had numerous conversations about the school, Ms. Driver could remember the name of the town (Reading) but not the name of the college (Alvernia) to which Wendy had been admitted:

> Ms. Driver: She got accepted up in West . . . West Reading. I can't think of the name of [the college]. It had an "A" like that.
> AL: West Reading?
> Ms. Driver: Up in West Reading. And they accepted her there.

Unlike the Tallingers, who memorized a great deal of ancillary information, including exact tuition costs, financial aid awards, and the gap between the two at the various colleges to which Garrett had applied, what the Drivers focused on was what they would be required to pay, which amounted to $1,000 per month (i.e., $12,000 per year).

Neither Ms. Driver nor Mack had ever been to college, nor had anyone in their immediate families. Thus it is reasonable that their understanding of the general structure of the college application process would be minimal. For example, Mack had been surprised to learn that colleges do not return application fees, and Ms. Driver misunderstood a key communication during a fall visit to the college to which Wendy was later admitted:

> It was really shocking because of the interview. The person we met with was very nice and looked at her grades and SATs and all that stuff . . . and when we left they said, "Well, we will see you in a couple months for [the] reception." And we were ecstatic!

Having thought that Wendy had been accepted, Ms. Driver continued:

> When we left we had to go down to the front desk. And they said, "We'll be calling you." And I said, "What do you mean you'll be calling me?" [They said,] "Well, we'll give you a call or a letter to let you know if you're accepted."

And I'm like, "She's accepted." They're like, "What?!" I said, "They said she was accepted." They said, "You know that's not a promise."

Ms. Driver and Wendy had not known that there is a "season" to the college application process, wherein students apply in the fall and are notified of acceptances and rejections in the spring.

In the end, however, Wendy did not go to college. She reported being very "stressed" during the summer following her high school graduation, and in June she told her parents that she was "not going":

> I couldn't see myself. . . . I applied to make my mom happy. I did everything to make her happy. . . . I had a scholarship. That made it into a bigger deal because I had a scholarship. . . . I said, "I am not going." [My mom] said, "What?" [I said,] "I do not want to go."

Wendy was concerned that she did not have the academic skills to succeed in college:

> Every day I would tell her, "Mom, it is not that [i.e., that Wendy did not want to leave her boyfriend Ryan]. I don't want to go away." I tried to explain to her I wasn't going because I didn't want to fail. Because if I failed, I didn't know how I would personally take it. . . . My friends were in honors classes in high school, and they were having problems [in college]. My friend went to [SUNY Geneseo] and she dropped out, and then she went to community college in January and dropped out of there, and now she is supposed to go to Rutgers. . . . I didn't want to fail, which I knew would happen.

Wendy had worked in two different part-time jobs all the way through high school. After she decided not to go to Alvernia, she continued working. She explored the option of attending the local community college in January. She reported speaking with someone in a learning disability program:

> I even applied to community. I was going to community in January. I had applied. I went down. They wanted me to go to night school: it was a whole free [learning disability] program, and I had to go for six months.

When Wendy ran into some difficulties with the program, she saw these complications as her own to overcome. Unlike many of the middle-class youth when faced with similar issues, Wendy did not involve her parents; nor did she request their help in solving her problem. Wendy's placement test did not put her in a class for which she would receive college credit. Instead she was told that she had to take remedial (non-credit) courses. This decision seemed unreasonable to her given her honors in high school:

> I want to go to a class to get credit first. They said, "No." They wouldn't do it. If I paid for the [learning disability] program then I could do it. . . . I tried to talk to the guy . . . and they didn't want to hear it!

Wendy felt that the program did not understand the nature of her disability:

> They wanted me to live with a bunch of kids with ADHD or [who were] bad. I'm not bad—I'm a good student. I have a learning disability. I can't read or write. I can write. I can't spell. I can write a word down and he doesn't understand it, but I do. Basically he told me "No, this is what [you] have to do." I just got upset.[5]

Wendy wanted to enroll in a program at the community college similar to the one that she had been offered at Alvernia:

> [At Alvernia] I would have been in a regular class. [There would have been a] note taker and testing accommodation: [for a] three-hour test I would have six hours. The teacher could read the test to me. [I would] have chances to retake the test to get a better grade. Alvernia was going to have that plan.

The lack of flexibility at the community college bothered Wendy. She did not go back. Unlike Garrett Tallinger, she did not even consider involving her parents in her interactions with the community college. When asked if she had considered having her parents go to the community college to help her, Wendy visibly bristled at the idea, noting that she has adult status and these institutional interactions are her responsibility:

> Because I was old enough to make my own decisions. I knew what was wrong with me. My parents could have come down, and they [i.e., the program officers] basically would have told them the same thing. I didn't want that. I am 18. I am old enough to make my own decisions!

Wendy hopes, at some point, to go back to school, to get "my degree," to "take night classes," and to get a degree in "early childhood education" so that she can run a day care center in her own house.

Although Wendy did not, in the end, go to college, it is striking how much the Drivers depended on the high school counselor and other professionals throughout the college application process. Moreover, there is a clear parallel between the approach of the Drivers to educational institutions when Wendy was in high school and when she was in fourth grade. For example, when Wendy was not reading by the time she had reached the fourth grade, Ms. Driver welcomed the efforts of educators at Lower Richmond School to determine the reasons underlying Wendy's difficulties with language-based activities. Taking Wendy to the eye doctor, listening to her read, and helping her with her homework, Ms. Driver promptly and precisely followed each recommendation by Wendy's teachers and the reading specialist at Lower Richmond. However, when these efforts led to only minimal improvements in Wendy's reading skills, Ms. Driver was hesitant to pursue any course of action beyond those suggested by school personnel: "I don't want to jump into anything and find out that it's the wrong thing," Ms. Driver reported at the time.

In sum, Wendy (correctly) sees her parents as being very proactive in her life. In many different ways they gathered knowledge and they intervened to improve her situation. However, there were key differences in the institutional involvement of the Tallingers and the Drivers, as well as between the actions of the two young adults. For example, Garrett lives in a dorm and goes out with his friends; Wendy is married and is responsible for running a household and caring for a toddler. In key ways, Wendy seems older, more experienced, and more mature than Garrett, who in comparison with Wendy and many of the other working-class and poor youth in the study, seems younger, less exposed to the world, and more dependent.

PARENTS' USE OF CLASS-BASED RESOURCES:
FORESEEING AND FORESTALLING PROBLEMS AND
UNTYING KNOTS

All of the parents in the study wanted the best for their children, but social class made a difference in the resources parents were able to draw on and the strategies they adopted as their children entered adulthood. We see global information about institutions, specific information about their child's particular "case" within an institution, and the propensity to intervene in institutions as constituting class-based cultural resources that parents drew on in their interactions with institutions such as schools. We find that parents drew on these resources as they helped their children in two key ways: to *foresee and forestall problems* and to *untie knots* (i.e., to solve problems that arose). In this section, we draw on the case studies of Garrett Tallinger and Wendy Driver, as well as on the experiences among the other youth in the study, to suggest that these class-based cultural resources made a difference as the youths transitioned into adulthood. In particular, while all parents were able to foresee problems, middle-class parents were able to forestall problems much more effectively than were working-class and poor parents. In addition, all of the youth encountered problems, what we refer to as "knots," in institutions during their transition to adulthood; however, middle-class parents had more resources for solving these problems.

### Foreseeing and Forestalling Potential Problems

Familiar with educational institutions themselves, middle-class parents in our study proactively tried to alter the conditions under which their children functioned. They were often able to anticipate potential problems before they arose and to redirect their children or intervene strategically to prevent the potential problem from altering a child's trajectory. For example, Garrett's mother had a clear understanding of academic tracking.

When she told the counselor that she wanted her son to be in "the most rigorous courses," she was hoping to forestall a potential problem: that Garrett (who had never tested extremely well) would not have the strongest possible profile in his college applications. Similarly, Garrett's father strategically managed the college basketball recruitment process; he negotiated for Garrett to play on a summer-league team to "give him the visibility" he needed, arranged for Garrett to attend tournaments where he would be seen by college recruiters, and spoke with coaches on the phone to convey Garrett's interest. Mr. Tallinger did not focus only on one or two schools; instead he systematically conveyed interest to coaches in a wide variety of schools to make sure that Garrett would have options. Similarly, Garrett's parents' knowledge of the academic demands of institutions, of the specific strengths of their son, and of the potential catastrophic problems that could emerge if their son was "over his head" at a school allowed them to critically assess Garrett's weaknesses and his strengths. They sought a situation that would be a good "fit" for him, both academically and athletically, even if it was not the most highly ranked college.

The pattern of foreseeing and forestalling problems that we observed with Garrett also appeared among the other middle-class youth in our study. For example, in the African American middle-class Marshall family, when Stacey Marshall was in high school, in order to ensure that Stacey was well positioned for acceptance at selective colleges, her mother spoke regularly with Stacey's high school counselor regarding Stacey's course selection, and she enrolled Stacey in an expensive ($1,500) ten-day summer science program at a local university. When Stacey entered college, Ms. Marshall corresponded directly with Stacey's college basketball coach about her exercise-induced asthma, which was diagnosed during the summer before Stacey departed for college. In addition, Ms. Marshall instructed her daughter in how to use institutional supports, such as arranging for a consultation with her academic adviser before selecting her courses. At other times Ms. Marshall advised Stacey on course selection herself so as to prevent potential problems. Since Stacey aspired to attend medical school after completing college, when Stacey received a C in biology during her first semester in college, Ms. Marshall counseled her to "get out of calculus" because "you don't want your GPA to get too low, because then you can never dig yourself out of it." Ms. Marshall also counseled Stacey to avoid taking a class that Ms. Marshall thought was not in Stacey's best interest:

> She emailed me first and then she called me one night at eleven o'clock. And it was like, "Well, I can take the cinema course." I said, "*Stacey.*" [Laughs] I said, "Do you know anything about this? Do they even give you a description?" [She said,] "Wellllll, no, not really." But she . . . was on the computer;

she could see that there were seats in this class; the time was right. I said, "Sometimes you can be jumping out of the frying pan into the fire. This course may have an interesting name but, one, it sounds like yeah, you'd be watching movies, but, two, you'll probably be writing about [them]. You have these other courses where you will be writing. You are telling me that you don't like to write."

Other middle-class parents reported similar patterns of frequent intervention aimed at preventing potential problems from arising. National reports also echo this pattern. Indeed, some colleges are working to develop formal programs to "push parents out" of their children's college lives in order to facilitate the development of independence in college-aged youth (Gabriel 2010).

Working-class and poor parents also foresaw and forestalled problems in key areas of their children's lives. For example, at the end of eighth grade, when Wendy was not admitted to the magnet high school of her choice, Ms. Driver anticipated the educational disadvantages that Wendy might face by attending her neighborhood public school, which had a high dropout rate and frequent fights, and she arranged instead for Wendy's grandfather to pay the tuition for Wendy to attend the Catholic high school. When Wendy became sexually active, Ms. Driver sought to forestall an unplanned pregnancy by seeing that her daughter used birth control, and when Wendy became pregnant, Ms. Driver proactively sat her future son-in-law down for a frank discussion about his willingness to accept the responsibility of being a father and husband.

Like the Drivers, the other working-class and poor parents in the study anticipated and helped their children avoid potential problems. For example, Mr. Yanelli, a white working-class father, helped his son Billy buy a car when he needed transportation in order to work as a house painter in the painters' union. The mother of Katie Brindle, who grew up in a poor family, gave Katie work cleaning houses so Katie would be able to pay her bills when her husband went back to jail. However, working-class and poor parents appeared to be heavily dependent on professionals in their institutional interactions (e.g., with educational institutions, health care institutions, and criminal justice institutions).

Despite the Drivers' attempts to foresee and forestall problems in Wendy's life, they did not possess information about colleges or about Wendy's potential "fit" with them that would allow them to intervene effectively to help Wendy navigate key turning points. For example, the Drivers lacked the nuanced knowledge of the higher education system that might have helped them assess and augment the advice that Wendy was receiving from her high school guidance counselor. Without this knowledge, Wendy's parents were dependent on the guidance counselor's selection of possible schools for

Wendy and were not prepared to help customize the college fit in ways that the Tallingers and other middle-class parents in the study did.

Unfamiliar with the inner workings of these institutions, working-class and poor parents found it difficult to forestall difficulties by intervening. For example, Mr. and Ms. Yanelli could tell in sixth grade that Billy's schooling was not going well. They were sick with worry. Ms. Yanelli wanted to move Billy to a private school, but the tuition would be difficult for the Yanellis to afford, and Ms. Yanelli was convinced that Billy would not be admitted. She wasn't able to resolve the problems that Billy faced at school, and her efforts to encourage Billy to stay in school were not effective. Eventually Billy dropped out of high school in the tenth grade. Thus, although the Yanellis foresaw problems, they were unable to prevent them.

### Untying Knots

As youth moved through institutions, they inevitably became entangled in "knots." Some of these knots were small, and others were large. Youth injured themselves and needed surgery, encountered conflicts in the scheduling of high school courses, had unplanned pregnancies, or dropped out of high school or college. Put differently, some knots were relatively inconsequential, and others had the potential to knock a child off of a life trajectory. Although the parents of all of the young adults in the study attempted to help their children untie knots as they transitioned into adulthood, untying knots in their children's education often required that parents possess detailed information about how institutions worked, specific information about their young adult's "case" within the institution, and the belief that intervention was appropriate. As we have discussed above, these resources were unequally distributed among the families by social class.

As the middle-class youth transitioned into adulthood, their knots tended to be smaller than those of their working-class and poor counterparts, but their parents tried vigorously to help their children untie them. When a scheduling conflict threatened to prevent Garrett from taking both AP English and AP calculus, Ms. Tallinger pressured Garrett's high school to reschedule the courses; and as Garrett's interest in playing college basketball developed, his father spoke to Garrett's coach about increasing his playing time and later initiated contacts with college coaches to generate interest in Garrett. Alexander Williams' mother, a middle-class African American woman, also helped untie a knot for her son: when Alexander was in college and his summer internship fell through at the last minute, Ms. Williams helped him develop a new plan for the summer that would allow him to develop his pre-med interests and skills as well as his résumé.

There were some problems that middle-class parents could not fix. After Stacey Marshall got a C in a pre-med course, her mother wasn't able to untie the knot that was Stacey's low GPA. Similarly, despite daily reminders at home from her mother, Melanie Handlon, a young white woman from a middle-class family, stopped attending community college courses, did not officially withdraw, and failed the semester. In these situations parents could only let their children find their way, provide emotional support when asked, and hope for the best. Thus being middle-class did not prevent young adults from facing important challenges. Still, as middle-class parents supervised their children's institutional lives, the parents were often ready, willing, and able to intervene with officials in institutions. In some cases, when the youth ran into significant problems, middle-class parents' interventions could help to untie knots and facilitate their children's progress.

Like the middle-class parents, the working-class and poor parents also attempted to untie knots for their children. When Wendy Driver could not attend school after knee surgery, her mother helped arrange for a tutor so Wendy could graduate from high school. However, when Wendy had difficulty enrolling in the classes she wanted at her local community college, she did not look to her parents for guidance. Nor did her parents take it upon themselves to get involved. It is easy to imagine that a middle-class parent such as Garrett Tallinger's mother would have called the program administrator, submitted documentation of her daughter's disability, hired a private psychologist to test her, or paid privately for the learning-disabled program for one semester. However, Wendy, who was only 17 years old, did not think of those options. Since she was "grown," she believed it was unacceptable to rely on her parents for help; and in any case, Wendy did not think that her parents would do anything different than what she had already done. So, having failed to untie that knot, Wendy never attended college. As a result, she entered the labor market as a high school graduate and never earned the college credits that might have helped increase her future earnings (Settersten, Furstenberg, and Rumbaut 2005).

In some instances working-class and poor parents were quite effective at untying knots for their children. For example, Billy Yanelli enjoyed recreational use of marijuana, but during his apprenticeship in the union as a house painter, he was subjected to random drug tests. After one of Billy's drug tests turned up "hot," Billy was warned by the union. Billy's mother was extremely anxious about these developments, but his father used his own union membership to smooth the situation over for his son. After three violations, Billy should have been dismissed (per union policy), but he was not kicked out.

Like Billy, Tyrec Taylor, a young African American man from a working-class family, benefited from his parents' help in untying knots as he transitioned into adulthood. Tyrec, a talented basketball player, was in a public middle school where he excelled. He then enrolled in a charter high school without a basketball team. Although he was doing well academically, Tyrec pleaded with his mother to allow him to leave the charter school to go to Lower Richmond High, which had a basketball team. His sophomore year his mother relented. Tyrec's grades immediately plummeted, and he did not qualify academically to play. Tyrec started hanging around with friends that his parents did not approve of, and he was arrested in a juvenile offense. His father, using a credit card, hired a lawyer and Tyrec was released without charges. Tyrec's mother tried to send him back to the charter school he had been attending, but the school was full. An application to another charter school was also turned down because it was too late in the academic year, and this second school was also full. (Tyrec's low grades were also a concern.) Tyrec's mother pleaded with Tyrec's father to put him in a private school. In the end, Mr. Taylor took out a loan to cover the private school tuition of approximately $4,000. Tyrec graduated, but in his junior and senior years, although colleges visited his school, he never ended up taking the SAT or applying to college. As Tyrec explains, his mother wanted him to go to college, but it did not work out:

> AL: And when you finished that, did anyone talk to you about the possibility of going to college?
> Tyrec: Yeah they came to our school. Colleges came to our school. I could have went to SUNY Geneseo, but I never really like took no SATs. I wasn't really thinking about going away to no university. I could have. My mom and them probably wanted me to, but I was like . . . after high school I really wanted to do what I wanted to do.

Tyrec reports, "My mom and them kept trying to get me to go to school." However, Tyrec's mom's approach differed in key ways from that of the Marshall and Tallinger families. She felt that in crucial ways the decision was fundamentally up to Tyrec; her actions were less interventionist than those of the middle-class families. In short, although Tyrec's parents were able to untie some knots in their son's educational trajectory, they were unable to untie others.

Although the interventions of working-class and poor parents such as the Drivers, Yanellis, and Taylors were consequential in helping their youth transition to adulthood, when faced with knots related to educational institutions the parents of the working-class and poor youth in the study were often less equipped than their middle-class counterparts to untie them.

Harold McAllister, a young African American man who grew up in a poor family, failed to untie a knot in high school that contributed to his leaving school without a diploma. Like Tyrec, Harold's passion in life was basketball. He desperately wanted to play on his high school's basketball team but wasn't selected. Harold's own efforts to resolve the situation—by talking to the coach and by seeking help from the principal—did not lead to his being put on the team. (Without interviewing the coach, it is hard to know exactly why Harold wasn't allowed to play. But the key point here is that he was not chosen for the team.) The basketball decision ended up being hugely consequential for Harold. Raised by parents who generally deferred to educators to resolve situations at school, Harold did not have the benefit of interventionist parents such as the Tallingers or other middle-class parents. Harold began working full-time to "take his mind off" of basketball. He got off work late, got home late, and began missing school. In the end, he dropped out of school. While Harold's close friend, who was ranked below Harold in the city-wide basketball rankings, is playing college ball, Harold is not playing anywhere. This life event was traumatic for him.

It is possible, of course, that Harold exaggerated his basketball prowess and that he wasn't as skilled as the players who made the team. Nevertheless, when institutional conflicts occurred, the parents of middle-class youth were more likely to understand the "system" and their own children's particular circumstances and could more easily intervene to resolve problems. The parents of working-class and poor youth provided them with emotional and material support, but most did not or could not intervene on their children's behalf with institutions.[6]

## CONCLUSION

As the children moved from fourth grade through middle school, into high school, and beyond, they experienced numerous challenges. Dropping out of high school, not considering college, selecting a college, choosing a major, getting pregnant, and marrying were each crucial moments in these young people's lives. Some were more consequential than others.

As McLanahan and others in this volume show, studies of the family have documented important social class differences in key aspects of family life. In contrast, social scientists have frequently focused on the individual behaviors of youth, such as time spent on homework and talking to parents about school (see Walpole 2003 for a review). Other models have sought to introduce "intervening variables" in predicting youth outcomes (Warren and Hauser, 1997). Nonetheless, most of this work has focused on aspirations rather than on parents' detailed, site-specific knowledge of how institutions function or the highly idiosyncratic interventions made by parents on behalf of their young adults. These studies have taught us a great deal. Yet in crucial ways the research has disconnected youth from their family settings. The ways that parents shape and intervene in youths' life paths are not fully conceptualized. There are signs that there is more between-class variability in the strategies that parents bring to bear when negotiating their children's institutional lives than studies acknowledge.

In addition, we do not fully understand the kinds of informational resources that parents bring to the table. In analyzing the transition to adulthood, researchers have focused more often on the key outcomes—college graduation, employment, marriage, birth of the first child—than on the process (Settersten, Furstenberg, and Rumbaut 2005). Such research does not necessarily reveal how parents are able to transmit advantages across generations.

In our longitudinal interviews it was clear that the parents in all social classes loved their children and wanted the best for them. Most of the working-class and poor parents aspired to college for their children. Although not the focus of this paper, there is ample evidence of devotion and sacrifice on the part of the working-class and poor parents for their children as they scraped together scarce resources for food, shelter, and transportation, encouraged their children to do their best, activated their networks to find employment, and generally sought to offer advantages to them. Thus, within the limitations of this sample, we did not see striking differences—at least in terms of what we learned through interviews—in the kinds of devotion parents showed to their youth or the level of material sacrifice they made for them.

Where we did see differences, however, was in parents' interactions with institutions. Although all of the parents loved their children deeply, middle-class parents' interactions with institutions were linked to their more *global information* about how educational institutions worked, more *specific information* about the strengths (and weaknesses) of their child's situation, and a greater *belief in and history of intervening* in educational matters than working-class and poor parents. Since all of the youth faced challenges, turning points, and dilemmas as they aged, the class differences in parents' actions affected how they confronted those challenges. All of the parents wanted to foresee and forestall problems. All of the parents also wanted to help their children untie knots in their children's lives. But to do that, parents needed very detailed "insider" information about how educational institutions work. Parents could not plan for or prevent a problem if they did not know it might arise. Similarly, untying knots in children's educational careers required that parents had detailed information about how institutions worked, an understanding of their child's particular case in relation to the institution, and the belief that parental intervention was appropriate.

What is striking from these interviews is the degree to which middle-class parents consistently and aggressively gathered information, were preoccupied (in some cases almost obsessed) with the college application process, intervened in little and big ways, and were a constant resource for their young adults. And their interventions were not exclusively in the realm of education. Garrett Tallinger's father learned about the athletic recruiting system, contacted coaches, and intervened to get his son more playing time. In contrast, Harold McAllister, who also had a passion for basketball, hit a snag in his basketball career in high school and was unable to overcome it. It is hard to know for certain, but it seems likely that if Harold had had parents who approached institutions in the way that Garrett Tallinger's parents did, there might have been a different outcome for Harold.

We found class differences in parents' institutional knowledge at a general level as well as class differences in parents' knowledge of and ability to evaluate the specific "fit" between their children and institutions. We also found class differences in the kinds of interventions parents made for their young adult children. Middle-class parents were more likely to anticipate problems and to work successfully to untie knots along their youths' trajectories. In some instances, the interventions that middle-class parents made seemed to be more effective than the interventions attempted by working-class and poor families.

Researchers make a mistake when they treat the standards of institutions as neutral and parents' compliance with these institutional standards as an indication of the value parents place on their children's success. A better approach would be to try to unpack the forms of cultural knowledge and expertise that facilitate parents' ability to understand, "decode," and comply with institutional standards. When Ms. Driver told an Alvernia College employee that Wendy had been "accepted," she misunderstood a fundamental aspect of the college admission process. When Harold's father told him to stay at his current high school, he was depending on the school to manage his son's academic and athletic trajectory. In contrast, in Garrett's family, his parents took charge of such matters, not relying on the school to guide their son in the right direction.

At the same time, we should not ignore the drawbacks of the strategies adopted by middle-class parents. College administrators sometimes complain that middle-class parents' efforts to help their children can thwart the development of their independence. Indeed, the working-class and poor children in the study seemed older and more mature than the middle-class youth (see Lareau 2011).

By definition, the professionals who work in institutions are middle class. Policymakers are also college graduates and are employed in professional occupations. As such, many aspects of the sorting mechanisms in the stratification system are "taken for granted" and are hard for individuals to articulate. But the invisible nature of these standards should not blind us to the somewhat arbitrary and historically specific nature of the standards. Nor should it lead us to ignore the ways in which parents' social class facilitates compliance with these standards. By unpacking the ways in which parents guide, hover over, and transform the "choices" that their children face, social scientists stand to improve our knowledge of one of the most important dynamics in the reproduction of inequality in American family life.

REFERENCES

Burawoy, Michael. 2003. "Revisits: An Outline of a Theory of Reflexive Ethnography." *American Sociological Review* 68 (October): 645–79.

Conley, Dalton. 2001. "Capital for College: Parental Assets and Educational Attainment." *Sociology of Education* 74 (January): 59–73.

Crosnoe, Robert, and Shannon E. Cavanaugh. 2010. "Families with Children and Adolescents: A Review, Critique, and Future Agenda." *Journal of Marriage and Family* 72 (3): 594–611.

Furstenberg, Frank F. 2010. "On a New Schedule: Transitions to Adulthood and Family Change." *The Future of Children* 20(1): 68–87.

Gabriel, Trip. 2010 (August 22). "Students, Welcome to College; Parents, Go Home." *New York Times*.

Kohn, Melvin L., and Carmi Schooler. 1983. *Work and Personality: An Inquiry into the Impact of Social Stratification*. Norwood, NJ: Ablex Publishing Corporation.

Lareau, Annette. 2003. *Unequal Childhoods: Class, Race, and Family Life*. Berkeley: University of California Press.

———. 2011. *Unequal Childhoods: Class, Race, and Family Life*. 2nd ed. Berkeley: University of California Press.

Lareau, Annette, and Elliot B. Weininger. 2008. "Class and the Transition to Adulthood." in *Social Class: How Does it Work?* edited by Annette Lareau and Dalton Conley, pp. 118–51. New York: Russell Sage.

Lubrano, Alfred. 2005. *Limbo: Blue-Collar Roots, White-Collar Dreams*. New York: Wiley.

Lynd, Robert S., and Helen Merrell Lynd. 1929. *Middletown: A Study in American Culture*. New York: Harcourt, Brace.

———. 1937. *Middletown in Transition: A Study in Cultural Conflicts*. New York: Constable.

New York Times. 2005. *Class Matters*. New York: Times Books.

Schoeni, Robert F., and Karen E. Ross. 2005. "Material Assistance from Families during the Transition to Adulthood." In *On the Frontier of Adulthood: Theory, Research, and Public Policy*, edited by Richard A. Settersten, Jr., Frank F. Furstenberg, Jr., and Ruben G. Rumbaut, pp. 396–416. Chicago: University of Chicago Press.

Settersten, Richard A., Jr., Frank F. Furstenberg, Jr., and Ruben G. Rumbaut, eds. 2005. *On the Frontier of Adulthood: Theory, Research, and Public Policy*. Chicago: University of Chicago Press.

Walpole, MaryBeth. 2003. "Socioeconomic Status and College: How SES Affects College Experiences and Outcomes." *The Review of Higher Education* 27: 45–73.

Warren, John Robert, and Robert M. Hauser. 1997. "Social Stratification across Three Generations: New Evidence from the Wisconsin Longitudinal Study." *American Sociological Review* 62: 561–72.

NOTES

We gratefully acknowledge the generous financial support of the Spencer Foundation. Additional support was provided by the University of Pennsylvania and Temple University. We have benefited from feedback on earlier versions of this work, including at the conference "Thinking about the Family in an Unequal Society," the American Educational Research Association Annual Meetings (2010), the colloquia at the University of Pennsylvania, the University of California San Diego, Northwestern University, the University of Southern California, George Mason University, Indiana University, and the University of California, Los Angeles. We appreciate the comments of a number of readers, including Kevin Roy, Erin McNamara Horvat, Demie Kurz, and especially Elliot Weininger. Any errors are the sole responsibility of the authors.

1. One set of parents, Mr. and Ms. Williams, declined; one father, Mr. McAllister, was in poor health; and one husband, Katie Brindle's husband, was hard to schedule and then was in jail. In some families Lareau interviewed additional people: in the McAllister family, for example, a cousin who had lived with the family at the time of the study.

2. In the presentation of quoted material, we have in some instances eliminated false starts and filler words including "um," "so," "uh," and "mmmm." In a few instances we have reordered speech for clarity if we felt the meaning would not be changed.

3. Yet the data set has important and difficult limitations: there is no observational data; there are no interviews with critical educators; there is no independent confirmation of the reports of the family members by the institution; and the reports are retrospective. Still, a key point of this chapter is to analyze class differences in this small, non-random sample. There are not any signs that the methodological limitations of the study were more prominent with some families than others.

4. The selection of the two cases presented in this section was guided by the following factors. We began by considering possible working-class or poor families. In order to make a comparison with middle-class families, we wanted a working-class or poor family in which there was as much institutional contact as possible. The Drivers, Carrolls, and Taylors had more contact with institutions than other working-class and poor families, in part because their youth had made some contact with colleges. We also wanted, if possible, a youth who was reasonably typical of our sample (and national patterns). Ideally we wanted to compare youth of the same racial and ethnic backgrounds and for whom we had interviews with all of the parents. Once we took into account these factors, the Wendy Driver/Garrett Tallinger comparison was our best option. For a comparison of Tara Carroll and Stacey Marshall, see Lareau and Weininger 2008.

5. Wendy also said: "I had to go to community and take a test. You had to go back down and they put you up into a different section. Of course I was the only little white girl there. I was the only white girl." Later in the interview, however, she insisted that the key factor was not that she was the only white girl (which "didn't bother me," she said) but that she could not move into classes where she would receive college credit.

6. Put differently, working-class and poor youth did not have the cultural resources that had the potential to produce "profits" in a particular sector.

# CHAPTER SEVEN

# Family Change, Public Response
## Social Policy in an Era of Complex Families

*Timothy M. Smeeding and Marcia J. Carlson*

As summarized in the introductory chapter to this volume, the latter half of the twentieth century witnessed dramatic changes in family demography that have served to increase the complexity of U.S. families. The longstanding link between marriage and childbearing that once prevailed throughout the Western world has been notably weakened. Today adults are likely to spend time living in one or more marital or cohabiting unions with different partners, and children often experience one or more changes in their family of origin by the time they reach age 18. Many children will spend significant time living apart from at least one of their biological parents—typically their father. And those with low or moderate educational attainment will suffer in labor markets hungry for college graduates (see Cherlin, this volume).

These family changes are of great interest to social scientists who are concerned about the family, particularly with respect to the role that families are expected to play in the care and socialization of children. Marriage is one of the oldest institutions in Western society, and previous studies have documented strong associations between stable marriage and a range of positive outcomes for adults and children (McLanahan and Sandefur 1994; Nock 1998; Waite and Gallagher 2000). While it is unclear the extent to which marriage and family stability have a causal effect on well-being—or are merely associated with other individual and couple characteristics that promote positive outcomes—emerging patterns of unstable and complex families which are associated with worse outcomes suggest that major and ongoing changes in family behavior be taken seriously.

The growing complexity and instability within families is also of interest to researchers and policymakers who care about inequality and stratification. Racial and ethnic minorities are much less likely to have children within marriage—and to have all of their children with the same partner (Carlson and Furstenberg 2006), and they are disproportionately affected by family change and instability. For example, whereas 29 percent of white children in 2009 were born to unmarried parents, the numbers for African

165

TABLE 7.1

Birth patterns of women and men by level of education

| Level of education | Percent of women with first birth by age 25[1] | Percent of women with first birth by age 40[1] | Average number of children born to women by age 40[1] | Median age at first birth[2] | | Completed fertility: percent of all children born[1] |
| | | | | Women | Men | |
|---|---|---|---|---|---|---|
| Dropouts | 78 | 86 | 2.6 | 19 | 22 | 16 |
| High school graduates* | 64 | 83 | 1.9 | 21 | 23 | 32 |
| Some college | 49 | 81 | 1.8 | 23 | 24 | 28 |
| College graduates | 20 | 74 | 1.6 | 28 | 29 | 24 |

SOURCES: [1]Ellwood, Wilde, and Batchelder 2009, using annual CPS files 1960–2004; for total children born to women in 1960–64 cohort observed in 2004, see Wilde 2009.

[2]Berger and Langton, forthcoming, using 2002 NSFG.

*Includes GED holders.

American and Hispanic children are 73 percent and 53 percent, respectively (Hamilton, Martin, and Ventura 2010). Being born to unmarried parents is also tied to social class: women in the bottom two-thirds of the educational distribution have experienced large increases in nonmarital childbearing since 1970, while women in the top third of the distribution have experienced virtually no increase (Ellwood and Jencks 2004).

Table 7.1 summarizes the differences in fertility patterns by education. Mothers with a high school education or less typically have their first child in their late teens or early-twenties (and outside of marriage), whereas mothers with some college education or higher typically have their first child sometime in their mid- to late twenties (and within marriage). On average, high school dropouts have 2.6 children per woman by the time they are age 40, compared to 1.6 children for college graduates. Fully 48 percent of all children in the 1960–64 birth cohort were born to mothers with a high school degree or less. Further, the typical father of one of these children is in his twenties and earns less than $20,000 per year (Smeeding, Garfinkel, and Mincy 2011. These differences in family formation and family structure are an important factor in the growing inequality among Americans over the past forty years (Martin 2006; McLanahan 2004; McLanahan and Percheski 2008).

Public policy toward families is an "infant industry" by historical standards (Bogenschneider and Corbett 2010), and there has been disagreement about the extent to which government should be involved with or influence family life. For example, Daniel Patrick Moynihan, the author of the famous Moynihan Report on family life (Moynihan 1965), often remarked that family policy efforts such as "marriage policy" belonged to churches and synagogues, not to elected bodies (Moynihan, Smeeding, and Rainwater 2004). In fact, public policy toward the family can be thought of in at least two ways: as providing support to all types of families, especially the unstable ones; or, as attempting to change the family into a more acceptable and effective social force; also, both could be pursued together.

The first approach is to accept the family more or less as it is and to try to support vulnerable parents and children by providing jobs, cash welfare or in-kind benefits (such as health care and health promotion, education, and food). The U.S. tax and transfer system has been designed to support disadvantaged families (as opposed to a more general social insurance model) primarily via means-tested programs. It has also undergone significant changes in both goals and structure since the mid-twentieth century. As attitudes, behaviors, and mores have changed in society more generally, policy has attempted to respond. Polices are much more oriented toward work and work supports (refundable tax credits, food assistance, child care, and health care provision for working poor families and their children) than toward unlimited cash welfare support. Taken together, the greater variability in family life today, and the fact that instability and complexity are most concentrated among disadvantaged groups, present challenges for policymakers as they attempt to devise policies that effectively support low-income families with children. And, as we noted above, almost half of all children live in families where children are born early and where instability is common.

The second approach to family policy—attempting to change the nature of what constitutes family—is more difficult. Efforts by the George W. Bush administration to promote marriage among unmarried couples with children have faced significant challenges, and early results suggest that their success has been limited (Wood et al. 2010). The nonmarital birth ratio (the proportion of all births that occur outside marriage) continues its steady climb since the mid-twentieth century and is now at 41 percent of all live births (Hamilton, Martin, and Ventura 2010). Teen pregnancy and birth rates notably declined from the early 1990s to 2009 (except for a brief rise in 2005–07), but still remain a central component of *first* nonmarital births. And finally, efforts to change the family and the home into a more nurturing place for young children to grow up in is most difficult (Furstenberg 2010 and this volume); there is limited evidence that parenting programs have a positive influence on parenting skills (Magnuson and Duncan 2004; Waldfogel 2006), although we highlight below several new programs that have achieved some limited success. Overall, changing the structure, balance, and tenor of families is not something that policy has shown much capacity to effectively accomplish. Moreover, stopping nonmarital pregnancy is liable to dramatically reduce fertility in America—to below replacement rates—and lead to other policy challenges (See Table 7.1 and Preston 2004).

Finally, there may be good reason to follow both lines of policy response. That is to pursue ameliorative and preventive strategies at the same time.

In this chapter, we describe the key social and economic programs and policies that are designed to support disadvantaged families (particularly economically), as well as policy efforts to strengthen families or to change/prevent their demographic structure. We also discuss key challenges and conundrums that emerge from family complexity and rising inequality.

## PUBLIC POLICIES AND PROGRAMS FOR FAMILIES AND CHILDREN

As U.S. family life has changed, along with attitudes, values, and expectations about family roles and responsibilities, public policy has sometimes tried to support families and sometimes to change families. These policies also come in the context of—and likely contribute to—rising inequality. In effect, we face two contemporary worlds of children's and families' futures:

in one world, early childbearing and temporary coupling before school completion (or after finishing secondary school only) result in poor job and career choices, often failed or no marriages, and bleak life chances for children; these patterns are also correlated with high rates of multi-partnered fertility (MPF) outside of marriage. As mentioned above, about half of all children are in such risky circumstances (see McLanahan, this volume).

We can compare this world with that of college-educated parents, who have fewer kids, are less likely to divorce, and have their children later in their lives and only after completing their education, establishing a career, getting married, and planning to have children (McLanahan 2004). Multi-partnered fertility in this second world is more likely to be encountered under conditions of divorce and remarriage rather than outside marriage. In all cases, parents will do all they can to promote their children's future well-being—but with about $50,000 of annual income per child in the second world compared to $9,000 in the first world (Haveman and Smeeding 2006), opportunities to privately support children vary immensely by socioeconomic status (SES). Therefore, it is toward the first world of disadvantaged children that compensatory income and other support policy is targeted.

In this chapter we address three key policy domains, including policies designed to: (1) provide economic support and improve material well-being; (2) strengthen family relationships and improve parenting; and (3) prevent unstable families from forming. Since economic resources and parental time and investment are the two key domains that families provide and that are shown to be important for children's well-being (Duncan, Kalil, and Ziol-Guest 2008; Morris, Duncan, and Rodrigues 2004; Sayer, Bianchi, and Robinson 2004), we describe these separately. Then we discuss policies that have been designed to directly affect family choices and demography with respect to union formation or fertility and schooling. In other words, as linked to our two-category classification of (1) policies designed to support families and (2) policies designed to change families, our first domain is about primarily about *supporting* families (economically) as they are, the third domain is about *changing* family structure or individual behavior, and the second falls somewhere in between. We summarize U.S. policies and contemporary challenges in each of these areas, and we compare U.S. policies with those of other countries where relevant.

Unfortunately, we are not able to discuss all polices targeted at low-income families in the United States. For instance, underlying some specific policies are larger dilemmas over whether, when, and how to separate children from nonsupportive parents (i.e., through child welfare and custody decisions) and how to help children directly in the absence of strong parental involvement (through early childhood education, comprehensive programs such as the Harlem Children's Zone, and independent living programs). Nor is there space to discuss new policy options such as conditional cash transfers (CCTs), which might provide income support in return for parental and child behaviors related to improved health care and education. In addition, we limit our discussions of public housing, health care provision, and education (see Garfinkel, Rainwater, and Smeeding 2010 on health and education). Finally, we do not focus on asset-building polices for the disadvantaged, which present substantial conundrums and contradictions when they are carried out in the face of asset-tested income maintenance programs, thus providing yet another dilemma for targeted programs. Appropriately, some programs such as "food stamps," now formally the Supplemental Nutrition Assistance Program (SNAP), have begun to target clients based only on income and not on savings or possessions such as an automobile (Smeeding, Garfinkel, and Mincy 2011).

The discussion that follows is aligned with models of support for children and families that reflect widely held American values upon which current policies are based and which, when taken together, produce many of the conundrums and contradictions that we now face as a nation (Ellwood 1988). We also discuss these efforts in the context of the great recession that began in 2007 (and has been particularly unkind to younger undereducated adults) and the American Recovery and Relief Act of 2009 (ARRA) which has offered a great deal of aid to many low-income families with children, and is now extended through 2011. For instance, there were more than 42 million people receiving SNAP benefits in November 2010, an increase of 44 percent from 2007; the SNAP program now serves one in every eight persons and one in four children nationwide. Indeed, SNAP expenditures for 2010 are expected to be in the neighborhood of $65 billion, making it the most recession-responsive program in the nation (U.S. Department of Agriculture [USDA] 2011). The number of individuals receiving extended unemployment benefits also more than doubled in the first year of the recession, to about 9.1 million persons by October 2009 (Burtless 2009). The 2009 official poverty rate of 14.5 percent is expected to exceed 15 percent in 2010 (Monea and Sawhill 2010; Smeeding et al. 2011).

*Policy Set #1:*
*Policies to Increase and Maintain Family Economic Resources*
Targeted and "means-tested" income transfer policies are largely designed to deal with what *is*—meaning that they take family form and complexity as is and try to mitigate the economic downside. While these polices may affect fertility or marriage behavior, we discuss them here as if such policies have no effect on fertility or marriage, leaving this topic to the other sections below. (Those interested in such effects, which are small in any case, can start with Baughman and Dickert-Conlin 2009 and Lopoo and Deleire 2006.)

*Temporary Assistance to Needy Families and the earned-income tax credit.* Perhaps the oldest debate about (and longest-held source of support for) poor children and their mothers has been cash welfare policies—Aid to Families with Dependent Children (AFDC) and its successor, Temporary Assistance to Needy Families (TANF). From cash grants designed to support mothers' staying home to raise their children, these polices have evolved to now include strict work tests and time limits for cash aid to single parents. This approach has significantly increased employment among single mothers but has done little to reduce their poverty status. Indeed, almost 60 percent of TANF benefits are now in the form of child care subsidies, transportation subsidies, and worker preparation, and not in cash (Pear 2003); hence, many TANF benefits are not included in the calculation of official poverty rates. The federal outlays for TANF have been fixed at about $24 billion in nominal dollars since 1996. Child care subsidies related to work have increased since 1996, but not enough to ensure complete coverage for working single parents and again, often at the expense of cash support. And in the face of the ongoing recession, states have been hard-pressed to maintain these levels of support. TANF, which once helped more than 14 million people in the early 1990s (as AFDC), enrolled an average of only 4 million in the 2009 fiscal year, a slight increase from the 3.8 million served in fiscal 2008 (Wolf 2010; Bitler and Hoynes 2010).

In order to make work pay for working single parents, policymakers have also developed and expanded the earned-income tax credit (EITC) to the point where at about $50 billion per year in federal assistance alone, it is our second largest income transfer program after SNAP, though delivered in the form of a year-end, one-time tax refund. At least twenty-four states have supplemented the EITC with additional state tax refunds (Levitas and Koulish 2008). In fact, the Obama administration's American Recovery and Reinvestment Act (ARRA) of 2009 expanded the EITC and refundable child tax credits, such that in Wisconsin (for example), a family with two children earning $14,000–16,000 in 2009 could receive combined tax credit relief plus a federal EITC refund and state EITC of over $8,000. A similar family with three or more children at this level of earnings could receive benefits that are even higher.

These policies have resulted in several dilemmas and conundrums. Work encourages self-reliance but may diminish parental time with kids, especially younger ones, and may even endanger some older kids (Gennetian et al. 2002). But some evidence suggests that children are not harmed when mothers transition from welfare to work (Chase-Lansdale et al. 2003), and we know that the general rise in women's employment since the 1970s has *not*, in fact, been accompanied by a decline in mothers' time with children (Bianchi, Robinson, and Milkie 2006; Sayer, Bianchi, and Robinson 2004).

Yet the unrelenting U.S. policy of "work first" may have fulfilled Daniel Patrick Moynihan's prediction that TANF would "punish children by making their parents' lives as miserable as possible" (Moynihan and Smeeding 2004). Employment rates have risen for lone parents, but child poverty has also risen since 2000. Indeed, the British have embarked on their own version of welfare reform, which allows low-income parents to combine income support (their TANF) with work and their own EITC (the Working Family Tax Credit). As in the United States, these programs also reward work over welfare. But by contrast, they are not time-limited and hence allow mothers with younger children to forgo market work while their children are still infants, providing a cushion for recessions that TANF does not (Hills and Waldfogel 2004; Waldfogel 2006; Waldfogel 2010).

Because U.S. policy is attuned to our uniquely high societal preference for market work by all adults and parents, we are left with a safety net built on work, which produced more earnings and market work in the booming economy of the late 1990s but that leaves people to struggle during a deep recession, when little work is available. So far, food stamps (now called SNAP, as noted above) and public housing beneficiaries are not subject to work requirements, although some policy makers say that they should be (Haskins 2006; Mead 2004).

Finally, the rise in multi-partnered fertility among low-income unmarried families has led to an unresolved policy dilemma surrounding the EITC, whereby fathers who pay their child support are not allowed to claim their children as an expense in qualifying for the EITC unless they are living with them. There is growing evidence that mothers of co-resident children are willing to bargain with absent fathers who support their children to allow for many patterns of claiming the EITC (see Mendenhall et al. 2010). And the ARRA recession spending has done very little for these men, as we will see below.

*Unemployment insurance.* At this writing in late 2010, unemployment was still above 9.4 percent, but the federal extension of unemployment insurance (UI) benefits has protected some of the unemployed from the most severe hardship. The UI extension under ARRA includes tax breaks, employer health insurance subsidies, and an increase in weekly benefits (Burtless 2009). But what about those who do not qualify for UI and other federal programs, especially those with long-term barriers to employment that only worsen during a downturn? Large numbers of low-income young men fall into this category. Their jobless rate is very high: over 40 percent of black teens and over 30 percent of young black men ages 16 to 24 are unemployed (and those figures do not count those who have given up on finding work and dropped out of the labor force; see Sum 2010). Unemployment is highest among the young (especially among men ages 18–29), among the less-educated (those with a high school degree or less), and among minorities (Engemann and Wall 2010). Yet with very limited work histories, the vast majority of jobless young men do not qualify for UI. In fact, unemployed men under age 30 constitute 39 percent of all men who are unemployed, but only 20 percent of all male UI recipients. Therefore, two-thirds of all young unemployed men missed out on over $120 billion in UI aid in 2009–10. Indeed, the only income support program generally available to help younger single men is SNAP (Smeeding, Garfinkel, and Mincy 2011; U.S. Department of Labor 2010).

This pattern is of concern because, by age 30, nearly three-fourths of men with a high school education or less have children to support (Berger and Langton 2011). Most of these young men already suffer from poor schooling, deficiencies in basic skills, and (often) discrimination. If today's unusually high jobless rate continues, more low-skilled men may turn to crime, and most will find meeting current child support obligations nearly impossible. Additional employment barriers will hinder those with criminal records forever (Pager 2007), while the high taxes and withholding on their wages due to unpaid child support debts will drive many poor fathers out of the workforce or into the underground economy. And, without custody of their children, low-income men are much less likely than poor mothers to receive welfare or food stamps.

*Supplemental Nutritional Assistance Program.* The Supplemental Nutritional Assistance Program (SNAP), since 2008 the new name for the food stamp program, is the only targeted, universal negative income tax-like program that requires only that families be in need. The SNAP program added 4.8 million households in the period 2008–09, to reach 42 million people in December 2010; indeed, it has responded to the 2007 recession in the form of an automatic stabilizer of great importance (USDA 2011). And much of this growth took place before the ARRA-driven, 14 percent benefit increase that took effect in April 2009. SNAP outlays are liable to be close to $65 billion in 2010 and in 2011.

Programs like SNAP are not conditioned on family status (including the presence of children) and can be collected according to household size and structure alone. Changes in SNAP regulations since 2001, including allowing on-line applications in many states, debit card payments, increasing the allowable value of a car (or omitting the car value test altogether), and special treatment of the EITC benefit for liquid asset-testing all led to greater participation even before the recession (Ratcliffe, McKernan, and Finegold 2007). Twenty-eight states currently have no liquid asset test for SNAP (USDA 2010). Indeed, the SNAP program is one well-functioning, universally accessible program where eligibility and benefits are more or less immune to the complexities of changing family structure.

But still, there are conundrums. In some states (e.g., California and Texas), SNAP rolls have increased only modestly because fingerprinting and in-person application are required (to prevent illegal immigrants from benefiting from the program), and there are insufficient numbers of state eligibility certification personnel. Thus the safety net is less responsive to economic need than it could be. But in generous SNAP states that allow easy enrollment, changes in income that reduce benefits or would eliminate them are often not reported to the SNAP vendors, creating overpayment issues and prompting cries for benefit reduction or benefit garnishment by the EITC.

*Child support enforcement.* Child support enforcement (CSE) has grown in recent years along with various state-specific policy experiments (Cancian, Meyer, and Caspar 2008). In the United States, child support payments are the primary way that absent parents support their children financially. Indeed, for several decades, AFDC and TANF benefits were reduced almost dollar for dollar (after a $50 per month disregard) for child support received by a parent in either program. In the case of married parents who have divorced, a monthly payment by the absent parent is well established and increasingly functions as the preferred mechanism for providing children's support, as long as the absent divorced parent has adequate earnings.

When the custodial parent is unmarried, and when the absent parent (usually the father) cannot or will not pay because of low earnings, incarceration, or other reason, the mother and the child are often left helpless (other than the safety net programs mentioned above). Guaranteed child support or Child Support Assurance (CSA) is not provided in the United States. In most European nations, this back-up guarantee is available to all caretakers, even if they do not file child support claims. In these cases, if a father cannot or will not pay, CSA provides support to the custodial parent.

In the case of unmarried parents with little or no earnings, and even more so in the case of multi-partnered fertility, we face a major policy conundrum. Although parents should be obligated to support their children regardless of living arrangements, public support of children (in lieu of child support enforcement), such as was the case in the pre-TANF AFDC program and possibly also SNAP and public housing discourages fathers from paying child support and may alienate them from their role as fathers. Indeed, low-income fathers seem to provide informal child support (i.e., cash or in-kind support outside of the formal child support system) when they can, at least in the early years after a nonmarital birth (Edin and Kefalas 2005; Nepomnyaschy and Garfinkel 2008). And many mothers feel that enforcement of formal child support obligations on fathers who cannot pay creates animosity and drives fathers away from their children (Waller and Plotnick 2001).

Strong child support enforcement may produce even worse results in complex families, where fathers are reluctant to support other men's children (i.e., the mother's children from other partners) despite their responsibilities to their own biological children, who are typically living with mothers and hence also with their half-siblings from mothers' other partners. Indeed, there is strong evidence that absent fathers are reluctant to have their money used to support other nonbiological children in their former partner's household (Cancian and Meyer 2010). In addition, when fathers have children with a new partner, they provide less economic support to nonresident children from a previous union (Manning and Smock 2000). Also, we know that the determination of child support orders is complicated by MPF, since current guidelines typically assume that fathers' children are all by the same partner. That is, for each subsequent child, fathers have to pay a smaller fraction of their earnings based on the assumed economies of scale from their children living together—which is obviously not the case in paternal MPF. Meyer, Cancian, and Cook (2005) find that a substantial fraction of mothers on welfare—and the fathers with whom they have been involved—have children by more than one partner, and the effective collection of child support from fathers is hindered in the context of MPF. Further, for fathers who are incarcerated, child support obligations build up as debts; upon release from prison, these fathers face inordinately high marginal tax rates on their market work, driving many into the underground economy and even further from their children. Pilot programs to forgive such fathers their child support debts in return for beginning and continuing child support payments are being implemented in the state of Wisconsin (Cancian, Heinrich, and Chung 2009).

A refundable child tax credit for custodial parents who have some earnings can be seen as a halfway solution in this country, which has no Child Support Assurance like the United Kingdom's. A tax credit would support kids regardless of family relationships, but would not likely make up for the loss of income from nonpayment of child support by low-income fathers. Indeed the lack of earnings amongst young, undereducated men is a topic to which we now turn.

*Employment and training.* Employment and training programs, called "active labor market policies" (ALMPs) in the rest of the world, intend to enhance earnings in lieu of unemployment, loss of skills, or inadequate schooling. Such programs are taking on increasing importance in the face of declining opportunities and pay for unskilled labor. In the face of rapid changes in technology and slowing college graduation rates, ALMPs are a key to helping non-college-bound men (Haskins, Holzer, and Lerman 2009; Peck 2010). Indeed, Furstenberg (e.g., see 2002) often suggested that the Wilson hypothesis of unmarriageable males (Wilson 1987) was important, and that even the most well-intentioned couplings and marriages foundered when men especially could not support their families. Disconnected men who are neither in school nor in the formal labor market can be seen as the least marriageable, even if they have fathered a child outside of marriage. Qualitative interviews among unmarried women with children point to men's low economic status as a fundamental barrier to marriage (Edin and Kefalas 2005; Gibson-Davis, Edin, and McLanahan 2005).

Some programs attempt to connect secondary school to technical training and jobs. Career Academies, for example, link young men and women directly with employment after they have completed technical school job and career preparation (Kemple and Willner 2008; Heinrich and Holzer 2010). But the track record for ALMPs in the United States is weak. Not much money is spent on such programs, certainly less than 0.5 percent of GDP, compared to about 3 percent of GDP in major European countries (Grubb and Puymoyen 2008). Moreover, wages of the unskilled are so low in the United States that even impressive returns, such as earnings increases of 15–20 percent, still leave workers with hourly wages of $10–11.

Career Academies have been shown to boost both earnings and marriage among low-skilled men, but they are only effective for the tenth to fortieth percentiles of secondary school students—i.e., those who will finish high school but not go on to a four-year college. Those who have already dropped out or who barely achieve a GED by the age of 18 or 19 are not much affected by Career Academies or other ALMP programs (Kemple and Willner 2008).

Finally, the United States has recently begun to experiment with "second chance" programs designed to help, especially, incarcerated men who are released from prison and who are trying to enter the job market. Recidivism rates of 50–65 percent among these men pose a huge challenge to economic self-sufficiency, especially for jobs in the recession economy of 2009, where teen and unskilled unemployment rates are near 25 percent (Sum 2010).

### Summary

The poor need help to maintain and strengthen their families and raise their incomes above the poverty level, especially in the face of joblessness and low pay. Young undereducated men (and women) and their children need several kinds of public aid in the face of rising poverty. Some recent suggestions for policy, including a new set of programs designed to meet this need and some to extend the ARRA to 2011 or beyond, are discussed below (see also Cancian, Meyer, and Reed 2010).

Many poor children live with just one parent, usually their mother, and single-parent families are more vulnerable to economic downturns than two-parent families. We need polices designed to reduce poverty in the context of the current work-based safety net, in which low-income families with children rely increasingly on mothers' and cohabitors' incomes. Such polices ought to support resident and nonresident parents' efforts to balance work and parenting. These include making high-quality, affordable child care and preschool more readily available. The Obama administration's 2010 education bill provided new monies to support education and for technical college degrees and certificates (Lichtblau 2010). The bill was made possible by a $10 billion reduction in SNAP, as well as the cancellation of government-insured college loans in favor of increased Pell grants. Unfortunately, the portion of the bill that would have added federal subsidies for more early childhood education in the state school systems was eliminated, largely because of states' inability to match federal dollars during the recession. The recession sheds light on the urgent need for many of these programs, but the family needs we identify here are chronic and structural, not purely cyclical.

A major part of any new federal jobs initiative should link low-wage workers with jobs, while reaping the maximum job creation per dollar (Heinrich and Holzer 2010). Federally funded jobs (paying roughly $8–10 per hour) could include, for example, work doing home repairs and weatherization for low-income housing, building parks and recreational facilities, and providing child care or home care assistance for elderly and disabled Americans. Workers in these new jobs who have family responsibilities could qualify for work supplements, such as the earned-income tax credit, SNAP, and other benefits. Noncustodial fathers would be better able to pay their child support, which would in turn reduce federal welfare costs for mothers and bring fathers closer to their children. And finely targeted job creation would cost far less per job created than the government's original stimulus bill or other recent job-creation proposals.

Third, we believe there should be more training on and off the job. The federal government could direct additional money into youth and young adult employment and training programs like AmeriCorps, YouthBuild, and the Youth Service and Conservation Corps. It could provide fiscal relief to state governments with earmarks for community colleges and training programs. And it could require any new federally funded infrastructure projects to set aside limited funds for apprenticeships and other training. A double-pronged effort that helps young adults earn enough to support their children while improving their work skills is badly needed.

The best remedy for many of these ills is a strong economy with low unemployment (Blank 2009). But the economy may not recover fully for five years or more. At this writing, over 8.5 million jobs have been lost in the recession, and, while there were weak signs of recovery in private employment as of November 2010, to reduce unemployment to under 5 percent by 2015 the economy would need to create 11 million jobs (Rampell 2010;

Monea and Sawhill 2009; Smeeding et al. 2010). Thus, unless policies are enacted to directly help low-skilled workers with family responsibilities, we expect that unemployment for low-skilled young men will remain extremely high for a very long time and will scar many for life (Bell and Blanchflower 2010; Peck 2010).

*Policy Set #2:*
*Policies to Strengthen Family Relationships*

While the majority of policy initiatives targeted toward low-income families have been intended to increase economic security, some have also been focused on encouraging parental responsibility and strengthening family ties. These policies are contingent on the presence of children, in contrast to the third category of policies discussed below, which are intended to deter—or defer—early (or nonmarital) childbearing in the first place. Two of the main focuses are fathers' involvement with children and mother-father relationships (including co-parenting).

*Father involvement.* Whereas the primary mission of the child support enforcement system has been collecting money from nonresident parents, several smaller fatherhood programs have aimed to improve fathers' labor market outcomes (with the hope of increasing child support paid) and to strengthen fathers' relationships with their children. The first major demonstration in this area, the Parents' Fair Share (PFS) program, was a random-assignment program administered in seven U.S. cities in the mid-1990s and evaluated by MDRC. Program clientele were fathers who were divorced and unemployed, had fallen behind in their child support payments, and were disconnected from their children.

Evaluation of the program highlighted the difficulty and complexity of improving labor market outcomes for low-income men and the fact that child support and welfare programs are not adequately equipped to meet the needs of poor fathers (Johnson, Levine, and Doolittle 1999). The PFS program had limited impact on increasing fathers' employment and earnings and did not, on average, increase the frequency of noncustodial fathers' visits with their children (Knox and Redcross 2000). However, the program did increase employment and earnings for the most disadvantaged men and did increase fathers' involvement with children for those who had been least involved at the start (Miller and Knox 2001). The overall disappointing results from the PFS program may have been due to the fact that the intervention occurred too late. The program participants were men who had *already* fallen behind in their child support obligations, who were no longer involved with the mother, and who had limited contact with their children; recent research confirms the "package deal" of partner and parent relationships for unwed couples (Tach, Mincy, and Edin 2010), suggesting that earlier intervention—when mothers and fathers are still romantically involved—may hold greater promise.

More recently, numerous small-scale programs have been developed to serve divorced fathers as well as unmarried fathers; these programs have different emphases but are intended to improve both fathers' parenting skills and their employment capabilities and to increase their connection to their children (see Mincy and Pouncy 2002 for an overview of fatherhood programs). In March 2000, the Department of Health and Human Services (DHHS) approved ten state demonstration projects designed to increase unmarried fathers' support for their children, both financial and emotional (DHHS 2000). These demonstration programs, which evolved from the Partners for Fragile Families (PFF) programs sponsored by the Ford Foundation in the 1990s, focused exclusively on low-income fathers and families. Their stated objective was to encourage "team parenting" among unwed parents and increase the earnings capacity of low-skilled fathers. These HHS-sponsored demonstrations represented the first national effort to develop programs specifically to meet the needs of unmarried fathers with children. The evaluation by the Urban Institute pointed to modest gains in child support outcomes—though little effect on employment and earnings—and suggested that support services to low-income men in the form of peer support and parenting education might help strengthen fathers' ties to children (Martinson et al. 2007).

One program, developed in 2009 by Philip and Carolyn Cowan and colleagues, has shown promise for increasing fathers' engagement with their children. The Supporting Father Involvement program is a sixteen-week intervention designed for low-income fathers that includes weekly sessions on topics such as parenting and co-parenting, couple communication, sources of stress and support, and participants' self-conception and goals. In a randomized trial ($n$ = 289), fathers who participated in the program remained more engaged with their children—and their children had better behavioral outcomes—eighteen months later than the control group; the results were even stronger for fathers who participated as part of a couple rather than alone (Cowan et al. 2009). These results are encouraging about the prospect of designing interventions to strengthen disadvantaged fathers' involvement with children.

A major challenge for fathers' programs, given high rates of multipartnered fertility, is to recognize that fathers are often coordinating parental responsibilities with multiple mothers, a situation that makes creating consistent rules and contexts for children extremely difficult (Jayakody and Seefeldt 2006). Further, in addition to being the biological father of some children, men may be simultaneously acting as social fathers to other children (Edin, Tach, and Mincy 2009). Thus, programs to strengthen father-child ties must consider the whole array of potentially complex family relationships and the potentially diverging commitments of fathers and mothers in light of their other commitments to children (and partners).

*Couple relationships and marriage.* Under the George W. Bush administration, a new policy effort was designed to promote "healthy marriage" among low-income couples with children in order to foster family stability and improve child well-being (Dion 2005). The Deficit Reduction Act of 2005 (P.L. 109-362) allocated $150 million per year for research and demonstration programs related to healthy marriage promotion and responsible fatherhood. From the start, this was a controversial policy, and support has been far from universal (Lichter, Graefe, and Brown 2003). Proponents cited the large volume of research showing that married families fare better on a number of economic, health, and well-being outcomes than unmarried families (Korenman and Neumark 1991; McLanahan and Sandefur 1994; Waite and Gallagher 2000). Critics said that government should not interfere in the family lives of its citizens and raised concerns about encouraging single mothers to marry men who might be physically or emotionally abusive (Coltrane 2001; Coontz and Folbre 2002).

While designed to promote marriage, the actual intervention typically consists of relationship skills and parenting programs that follow several models: improving couples' communications skills; improving awareness of and remedies for issues related to the transition to parenthood; and providing new parents with older couples as role models (Garfinkel and McLanahan 2003). Although some experimental data suggest that these programs can improve outcomes, the vast majority involved middle-class couples (Karney and Bradbury 1995; Ooms and Wilson 2004). Indeed, until recently, there has been little information available about whether relationship programs would increase marriage probabilities for parents in fragile families, but that is changing.

The Building Strong Families (BSF) project (sponsored by DHHS and operated and evaluated by Mathematica Policy Research, Inc.) was designed to strengthen the relationships of unmarried couples who were expecting a child or had just had a baby (Dion et al. 2008). Over 5,000 couples were randomly assigned to eight program models in eight urban and rural locations around the country. Unfortunately, the early impact evaluation of the BSF program (about fifteen months after couples had applied to the program) showed that, across all programs, BSF did not increase the quality of couple relationships, the stability of relationships, or the likelihood of marriage (Wood et al. 2010). Indeed, it did not do as much for marriage as the Career Academies program (Kemple and Willner 2008), suggesting that decent jobs are a precursor to marriage and partnership.

A second project, the Strengthening Healthy Marriage project (sponsored by DHHS and operated by MDRC), is currently working to enhance the stability of marriages among low-income couples in eight locations (MDRC 2005); early impact results are expected in 2012. For a summary of studies in progress designed to strengthen parental roles and couple relationships, see Knox et al. 2010.

Some researchers have questioned whether marriage is a viable option for many parents and whether these programmatic approaches can promote marriage among this population (McLanahan 2005), particularly since a large proportion of unwed parents have had children by other partners. Indeed, more than half the births in the Fragile Families study were to couples with children from other relationships. In these families, the question arises, "who should marry whom?" (Mincy 2002). Data from the Fragile Families study suggest that programs targeted toward fathers or couples may have a positive effect *if* they are targeted on the right parents and *if* they are timed correctly (McLanahan 2005). However, policies that strengthen couple relationship skills without also improving men's human capital and family income will likely have little impact on helping unmarried couples with children establish long-term stable relationships (Furstenberg 2002).

*Co-parenting by mothers and fathers.* Given the high rates of break-up among low-income and unmarried couples with children, new attention has been focused on the co-parenting relationship, defined as parents working together to rear their common child. Co-parenting has been identified as a construct that is distinct from both couple relationship quality and parenting behavior (Hayden et al. 1998; McHale 1995; McHale et al. 2000). For parents living apart—the majority of unmarried parents only a few years after a focal child's birth (Osborne and McLanahan 2007)—co-parenting may represent the primary (or only) regular interaction they have with each other, as they (in the best case) endeavor to coordinate their parental investments in their common child across households (Margolin, Gordis, and John 2001).

A growing evaluation literature is providing evidence about how intervention programs can enhance co-parenting among fragile families and consequently improve other family relationships and individual outcomes. While, as noted above, most couple relationship and parenting programs have been designed for and tested on middle-class couples (Ooms and Wilson 2004), there is emerging evidence from several small interventions targeting couples that are low-income, unmarried, or expecting their first child (regardless of marital status). Among low-income couples with children, interventions to improve parental education and relationship skills are shown to positively affect couple relationships, to reduce parenting stress, and to encourage fathers' involvement with children—all of which are related to positive co-parenting (Knox et al. 2010). There is growing recognition that targeting the co-parenting relationship directly and engaging mothers in a "whole-family" approach is important, even in interventions focused on encouraging fathers' involvement with children (Belotti 2004; Pruett et al. 2009).

Several interventions to improve co-parenting provide optimism that this construct can be strengthened. In a recent randomized experiment among 169 expectant couples (including one-fifth cohabitors), Feinberg and Kan (2008) found that an eight-session psychosocial intervention significantly improved co-parental support among the treatment group. Fagan (2008) found that a five-session intervention improved adolescent fathers' perceptions of their co-parenting capabilities. The results of the demonstration programs developed as part of the Healthy Marriage Initiative may also shed light on how to strengthen co-parental relationships (particularly for couples who remain together), since they use a range of program models, are implemented in an array of geographic locations, and are targeted toward a diverse clientele (Knox et al. 2010).

*Policy Set #3:*
*Policies to Affect Family Demographic Behaviors Directly*

The third set of policy alternatives takes the long view and tries to prevent the situations of complex families described above before they occur. The particular goals of the programs are important, but efforts to sustain and persist in these policies are also needed, since human behavior is not easily changed. Polices designed to affect family behaviors take two primary forms: (1) those aimed at avoiding nonmarital births by young women, and (2) those aimed at keeping both women and men in school and, hence, on a path toward both economic self-sufficiency and positive family behaviors. In both cases, we believe that education is the key to offering better alternatives to premature motherhood for young women—and better options than gang behavior, dropping out of school, crime, and incarceration for young men.

Perhaps the most promising policy actions are concentrated on preventing pregnancy among young unmarried women. After almost a decade of "abstinence only" policy that often didn't have its intended effects (Brückner and Bearman 2007), and with nonmarital births reaching 41 percent in 2009 (Hamilton, Martin, and Ventura 2010) and likely higher still in 2010, the change in policy comes not soon enough. Since 2000, there are new and better options for birth control and "morning after" treatments for young women to avoid childbearing. And now there is some evidence that abstinence programs delivered outside of religious institutions can help prevent early pregnancy (Jemmott, Jemmott, and Fong 2010). Further, several promising programs for comprehensive sex education are now available (Ball and Moore 2008), and a number of programs have been shown to be effective in reducing teen pregnancy using varying approaches, such as school curricula, service learning programs, youth development programs, parent programs, and community-wide programs (National Campaign 2010).

However, it is clear that abstinence counseling and birth control alone will not be enough to reduce nonmarital childbearing. Indeed, there is evidence that out-of-wedlock childbirth is seen by some younger women as a way to "straighten out their lives" and avoid crime and imprisonment (Kreager, Matsueda, and Erosheva 2010). More and better experiences with parents, schools, religious organizations, nonprofits, and mentors may result in more college-educated young women and higher returns to schooling (Jemmott, Jemmott, and Fong 2010). One must ask: if the "marriage bar" is so high for young women who have children (Edin and Kefalas 2005; Gibson-Davis, Edin, and McLanahan 2005), why do they fail to recognize that the price of unmarried motherhood before school completion and partnering is even higher?

Similarly, young men need to understand that success in school can lead to other alternatives. They need exposure to programs designed to improve their chances of success in college (particularly for the upper half of the high school student body), as well as job and career training programs like Career Academies (Kemple and Willner 2008). Moreover, high school may not be early enough for such policies to have their best effects. They must be started in middle school or even earlier. Effective pre-school education can help prevent children from being retained in grade school and disillusioned in middle school, and from never completing secondary school (Heckman 2006). The major problem with this approach is that—even in a nonrecessionary environment—it will take a generation or longer to overcome the schooling gaps between rich and poor children, which are even larger than those between racial and ethnic groups (Furstenberg 2010).

CONCLUSION

This chapter has discussed public policies designed to influence economic well-being and family life in an age of growing inequality across the income distribution, but especially between children who come from disadvantaged families—and in an era when it takes longer to exit adolescence, complete schooling, and enter adulthood. Childbirth by young mothers in such a world, as well as the disadvantaged circumstances that lead up to it, severely and increasingly handicaps their children and their families and reduces their economic and social mobility. Further, the increasing tendency for young unmarried persons to have children with multiple partners creates complex and unstable family forms that also penalize children. These underlying factors present both conundrums and challenges. Policy must confront contemporary family complexity and consider the tradeoffs between providing public support for mothers and children and encouraging private support in the form of child support and increased earnings.

It is well known that the American welfare state is underdeveloped and unfriendly to young unmarried parents and children, especially men. In the face of an economic recession and increasingly complex families, polices often fail to deliver much in the way of support or hope for low-SES parents. Indeed, American-style public policy raises many conundrums even as it confronts family complexity, despite its nature, aims, and motivation.

In our view, polices aimed at maintaining economic resources and changing family structure "after the fact" (i.e., after unstable families with children have formed) will face serious challenges given the U.S. focus on targeting and our ever-growing family complexity. Families' best hope for a better long-term future lies in avoiding parenthood while young and increasing educational attainment in the coming generations. Developing policies that promote those goals will require large efforts by parents, schools, and communities, but they are the best options for improving social and economic mobility and success for younger generations in the long run. Low-skilled younger men and women who are jobless and cannot support their children need our help in the mean time, regardless of their family circumstances. The way out of poverty is employment at wage levels that can support a family, not income transfers alone.

REFERENCES

Ball, Victoria, and Kristin A. Moore. 2008. "What Works for Adolescent Reproductive Health: Lessons from Experimental Evaluations of Programs and Interventions." Publication #2008-20. Washington, DC: Child Trends.

Baughman, Reagan, and Stacy Dickert-Conlin. 2009. "The Earned Income Tax Credit and Fertility." *Population Economics* 22: 1432–75.

Bell, David, and David G. Blanchflower. 2010. "Youth Unemployment: Déjà Vu?" Working Paper #4705. Bonn, Germany: Institute for the Study of Labor (IZA).

Belotti, J. 2004. "Lessons Learned from the Early Head Start Fatherhood Project." *Head Start Bulletin* 77: 1–6.

Berger, Lawrence, and Callie Langton. 2011. "Young Disadvantaged Men as Fathers." *Annals of the American Academy of Political and Social Science* 635.

Bianchi, Suzanne M., John P. Robinson, and Melissa A. Milkie. 2006. *Changing Rhythms of American Family Life*. New York: Russell Sage Foundation.

Bitler, Marianne, and Hilary W. Hoynes. 2010. "The State of the Safety Net in the Post–Welfare Reform Era." Working Paper 16504. Cambridge, MA: National Bureau of Economic Research (October).

Blank, Rebecca M. 2009. "Economic Change and the Structure of Opportunity for Less-Skilled Workers." In *Changing Poverty, Changing Policies*, edited by M. Cancian and S. Danziger, pp. 63–91. New York: Russell Sage Foundation.

Bogenschneider, Karen, and Thomas Corbett. 2010. "Family Policy: Becoming a Field of Inquiry and Subfield of Social Policy." *Journal of Marriage and Family* 72(3): 783–803.

Brückner, Hannah, and Peter Bearman. 2007. "After the Promise: The STD Consequences of Adolescent Virginity Pledges." *Journal of Adolescent Health* 36: 271–78.

Burtless, Gary. 2009. "The 'Great Recession' and Redistribution: Federal Antipoverty Policies." Fast Focus #4. Madison: Institute for Research on Poverty, University of Wisconsin-Madison.

Cancian, Maria, and Daniel R. Meyer. 2010. "I'm Not Paying for His Kid." Presented to the Population Association of America, Dallas Texas, April.

Cancian, Maria, Carolyn Heinrich, and Yiyoon Chung. 2009. "Does Debt Discourage Employment and Payment of Child Support? Evidence from a Natural Experiment." Discussion Paper no. 1366-09. Madison: Institute for Research on Poverty, University of Wisconsin-Madison.

Cancian, Maria, Daniel R. Meyer, and Emma Caspar. 2008. "Welfare and Child Support: Complements, Not Substitutes." *Journal of Policy Analysis and Management* 27: 354–75.

Cancian, Maria, Daniel R. Meyer and Deborah Reed. 2010. "Promising Antipoverty Strategies for Families." Madison: Institute for Research on Poverty, University of Wisconsin-Madison.

Carlson, Marcia J., and Frank F. Furstenberg, Jr. 2006. "The Prevalence and Correlates of Multipartnered Fertility among Urban U.S. Parents." *Journal of Marriage and Family* 68: 718–32.

Chase-Lansdale, P. Lindsay, Robert A. Moffitt, Brenda J. Lohman, Andrew J. Cherlin, Rebekah Levine Coley, Laura D. Pittman, Jennifer Roff, and Elizabeth Votruba-Drzal. 2003. "Mothers' Transitions from Welfare to Work and the Well-Being of Preschoolers and Adolescents." *Science* 299: 1548–52.

Coltrane, Scott. 2001. "Marketing the Marriage "Solution": Misplaced Simplicity in the Politics of Fatherhood." *Sociological Perspectives* 44: 387–418.

Coontz, Stephanie, and Nancy Folbre. 2002. "Marriage, Poverty, and Public Policy." Discussion Paper. Chicago: Council on Contemporary Families.

Cowan, Philip A., Carolyn Pape Cowan, Marsha Kline Pruett, Kyle Pruett, and Jessie J. Wong. 2009. "Promoting Fathers' Engagement with Children: Preventive Interventions for Low-Income Families." *Journal of Marriage and Family* 71: 663–79.

DHHS (Department of Health and Human Services). 2000 (June 17). "HHS' Fatherhood Initiative" Press Release. Washington: U.S. Department of Health and Human Services.

Dion, M. Robin. 2005. "Healthy Marriage Programs: Learning What Works." *The Future of Children* 15: 137–256.

Dion, Robin M., Alan M. Hershey, Heather H. Zaveri, Sarah A. Avellar, Debra A. Strong, Timothy Silman, and Ravaris Moore. 2008. "Implementation of the

Building Strong Families Program." Washington, DC: Mathematica Policy Research for the Office of Planning, Research, and Evaluation at the Administration for Children and Families, U.S. Department of Health and Human Services.

Duncan, Greg J., Ariel Kalil, and Kathleen Ziol-Guest. 2008. "Economic Costs of Early Child Poverty." Washington, DC: Pew Foundation, Partnership for America's Economic Success, Issue paper #4.

Edin, Kathryn, and Maria Kefalas. 2005. *Promises I Can Keep: Why Poor Women Put Motherhood before Marriage.* Berkeley: University of California Press.

Edin, Kathryn, Laura Tach, and Ronald Mincy. 2009. "Claiming Fatherhood: Race and the Dynamics of Paternal Involvement among Unmarried Men." *Annals of the American Academy of Political and Social Science* 621: 149–77.

Ellwood, David T. 1988. *Poor Support: Poverty in the American Family.* New York: Basic Books.

Ellwood, David T., and Christopher Jencks. 2004. "The Uneven Spread of Single-Parent Families: What Do We Know?" In *Social Inequality*, edited by K. M. Neckerman, pp. 3–78. New York: Russell Sage Foundation.

Ellwood, David, Ty Wilde, and Lily Batchelder. 2009. "The Mommy Track Divides: The Impact of Childbearing on Wages of Women of Differing Skill Levels." Working Paper series. New York: Russell Sage Foundation.

Engemann, Kristie M., and H. J. Wall. 2010. "The Effects of Recessions across Demographic Groups." *Federal Reserve Bank of St. Louis Review* 92: 1–26.

Fagan, Jay. 2008. "Randomized Study of a Prebirth Coparenting Intervention with Adolescent Young Fathers." *Family Relations* 57: 309–23.

Feinberg, Mark E., and Marni L. Kan. 2008. "Establishing Family Foundations: Intervention Effects on Coparenting, Parent/Infant Well-Being, and Parent-Child Relations." *Journal of Family Psychology* 22: 253–63.

Furstenberg, Frank F. 2002 (August 13). "What a Good Marriage Can't Do." *New York Times.*

———. 2003. "Teenage Childbearing as a Public Issue and Private Concern." *Annual Review of Sociology* 29: 23–39.

———. 2007. *Destinies of the Disadvantaged: The Politics of Teen Childbearing.* New York: Russell Sage Foundation.

———. 2010. "The Challenges of Finding Causal Links between Family Characteristics and Educational Outcomes." In *Social Inequality and Educational Disadvantage*, edited by G. Duncan and R. Murnane. New York: Russell Sage Foundation.

Garfinkel, Irwin, and Sara McLanahan. 2003. "Strengthening Fragile Families." In *One Percent for the Kids: New Policies, Brighter Futures for America's Children*, edited by I. Sawhill. Washington, DC: Brookings Institution.

Garfinkel, Irvin, Lee Rainwater, and Timothy M. Smeeding. 2010. *The American Welfare State: Laggard or Leader.* Oxford, UK: Oxford University Press.

Gennetian, Lisa A., Greg J. Duncan, Virginia W. Knox, Wanda G. Vargas, Elizabeth Clark-Kauffman, and Andrew S. London. 2002. "How Welfare and Work Policies for Parents Affect Adolescents: A Synthesis of Research." New York: MDRC (Manpower Demonstration Research Program).

Gibson-Davis, Christina, Kathryn Edin, and Sara McLanahan. 2005. "High Hopes but Even Higher Expectations: The Retreat from Marriage among Low-Income Couples." *Journal of Marriage and Family* 67: 1301–12.

Grubb, David, and Agnes Puymoyen. 2008. "Long Time-Series for Public Expenditure on Labour Market Programmes." *OECD Social, Employment and Migration Papers*, No. 73. DELSA/ELSA/WD/SEM(2008)10.

Hamilton, Brady E., Joyce A. Martin, and Stephanie J. Ventura. "Births: Preliminary Data for 2009," *National Vital Statistics Reports* 59(3). Hyattsville, MD: National Center for Health Statistics.

Haskins, Ron. 2006. *Work over Welfare: The Inside Story of the 1996 Welfare Reform*. Washington, DC: Brookings Institution.

Haskins, Ron, Harry Holzer, and Robert Lerman. 2009. "Promoting Economic Mobility By Increasing Postsecondary Education." Washington, DC: Pew Charitable Trusts Economic Mobility Project.

Haveman, Robert, and Timothy Smeeding. 2006. "The Role of Higher Education in Social Mobility." *The Future of Children* 16: 125–50.

Hayden, Lisa C., Masha Schiller, Susan Dickstein, Ronald Seifer, Steven Sameroff, Ivan Miller, Gabor Keitner, and Steven Rasmussen. 1998. "Levels of Family Assessment: I. Family, Marital, and Parent-Child Interaction." *Journal of Family Psychology* 12: 7–22.

Heckman, James J. 2006. "Skill Formation and the Economics of Investing in Disadvantaged Children." *Science* 312 (June 30): 1900–02.

Heinrich, Carolyn, and Harry Holzer. 2010. "Improving Education and Employment for Disadvantaged Young Men: Proven and Promising Strategies." In *Young Disadvantaged Men: Fathers, Families, Poverty, and Policy, Annals of the American Academy of Political and Social Science* 635, edited by T. M. Smeeding, I. Garfinkel, and R. B. Mincy.

Hills, John, and Jane Waldfogel. 2004. "A "Third Way" in Welfare Reform? Evidence from the United Kingdom." *Journal of Policy Analysis and Management* 23: 765–88.

Jayakody, Rukmalie, and Kristin S. Seefeldt. 2006. "Complex Families, Multiple Partner Fertility, and Families across Households: Implications for Marriage Promotion Efforts." Paper presented at the IRP Working Conference on Multiple-Partner Fertility, September 14–15, 2006, Madison, WI.

Jemmott, John B., Loretta Sweet Jemmott, and Geoffrey T. Fong. 2010. "Efficacy of a Theory-Based Abstinence-Only Intervention over 24 Months: A Randomized Controlled Trial with Young Adolescents." *Archives of Pediatric & Adolescent Medicine* 164: 152–59.

Johnson, E., A. Levine, and F. Doolittle. 1999. *Fathers' Fair Share: Helping Poor Men Manage Child Support and Fatherhood*. New York: Russell Sage Foundation.

Karney, Benjamin R., and Thomas N. Bradbury. 1995. "The Longitudinal Course of Marital Quality and Stability: A Review of Theory, Method, and Research." *Psychological Bulletin* 118: 3–34.

Kemple, James J., and Cynthia J. Willner. 2008. "Career Academies: Long-Term

Impacts on Labor Market Outcomes, Educational Attainment, and Transitions to Adulthood." New York: MDRC.

Knox, V., and C. Redcross. 2000. "Parenting and Providing: The Impact of Parents' Fair Share on Paternal Involvement." New York: MDRC.

Knox, Virginia, Philip A. Cowan, Carolyn Pape Cowan, and Elana Bildner. 2011. "Policies to Strengthen Fatherhood and Family Relationships: What Do We Know and What Do We Need to Know? An Introduction to the Issues." In *Young Disadvantaged Men: Fathers, Families, Poverty, and Policy, Annals of the American Academy of Political and Social Science* 635 (May), edited by T. M. Smeeding, I. Garfinkel, and R. B. Mincy.

Korenman, Sanders, and David Neumark. 1991. "Does Marriage Really Make Men More Productive?" *Journal of Human Resources* 26: 282–307.

Kreager, Derek A., Ross L. Matsueda, and Elena A. Erosheva. 2010. "Motherhood and Criminal Desistance in Disadvantaged Neighborhoods." *Criminology* 48(1): 221–58.

Levitas, Jason, and Jeremy Koulish. 2008. "State Earned Income Tax Credits: 2008 Legislative Update." Washington, DC: Center for Budget and Policy Priorities.

Lichtblau, Eric. 2010 (February 4). "Lobbying Imperils Overhaul of Student Loans." *New York Times.*

Lichter, Daniel T., Deborah Roempke Graefe, and J. Brian Brown. 2003. "Is Marriage a Panacea? Union Formation among Economically Disadvantaged Unwed Mothers." *Social Problems* 50: 60–86.

Lopoo, Leonard M., and Thomas DeLeire. 2006. "Did Welfare Reform Influence the Fertility of Young Teens?" *Journal of Public Policy Analysis and Management* 25: 275–98.

Magnuson, Katherine, and Greg Duncan. 2004. "Parent- vs. Child-Based Intervention Strategies for Promoting Children's Well-Being." In *Family Investments in Children: Resources and Behaviors that Promote Success*, edited by A. Kalil and T. DeLeire. Mahwah, NJ: Lawrence Erlbaum.

Manning, Wendy D., and Pamela J. Smock. 2000. "'Swapping' Families: Serial Parenting and Economic Support for Children." *Journal of Marriage and the Family* 62: 111–22.

Martin, Molly A. 2006. "Family Structure and Income Inequality in Families with Children, 1976 to 2000." *Demography* 43: 421–45.

Martinson, Karin, Demetra Smith Nightingale, Pamela A. Holcomb, Burt S. Barnow, and John Trutko. 2007. "Partners for Fragile Families Demonstration Projects: Employment and Child Support Outcomes and Trends." Washington, DC: Urban Institute.

McHale, James P. 1995. "Coparenting and Triadic Interactions during Infancy: The Roles of Marital Distress and Child Gender." *Developmental Psychology* 31: 985–96.

McHale, James P., Regina Kuersten-Hogan, Allison Lauretti, and Jeffrey L. Rasmussen. 2000. "Parental Reports of Coparenting and Observed Coparenting Behavior during the Toddler Period." *Journal of Family Psychology* 14: 220–36.

McLanahan, Sara. 2004. "Diverging Destinies: How Children Are Faring under the Second Demographic Transition." *Demography* 41: 607–27.

———. 2005. "Fragile Families and the Marriage Agenda." In *Fragile Families and the Marriage Agenda*, edited by L. Kowaleski-Jones and N. Wolfinger. New York: Springer.

McLanahan, Sara, and Christine Percheski. 2008. "Family Structure and the Reproduction of Inequalities." *Annual Review of Sociology* 34: 257–76.

McLanahan, Sara, and Gary Sandefur. 1994. *Growing Up with a Single Parent: What Hurts? What Helps?* Cambridge, MA: Harvard University Press.

MDRC (Manpower Demonstration Research Corporation). 2005. "Guidelines for Supporting Healthy Marriage Demonstration Programs." New York: MDRC.

Mead, Lawrence M. 2004. *Government Matters: Welfare Reform in Wisconsin.* Princeton, NJ: Princeton University Press.

Mendenhall, Ruby, Kathryn Edin, Susan Crowley, Jennifer Sykes, Laura Tach, Katrin Kriz, and Jeffrey R. Kling. 2010. "The Role of the Earned Income Tax Credit in the Budgets of Low-Income Families." Working Paper #10-05. Ann Arbor: National Poverty Center, University of Michigan.

Meyer, Daniel R., Maria Cancian, and Steven T. Cook. 2005. "Multiple-Partner Fertility: Incidence and Implications for Child Support Policy." *Social Service Review* 79: 577–601.

Miller, Cynthia, and Virginia Knox. 2001. "The Challenge of Helping Low-Income Fathers Support Their Children." New York: MDRC.

Mincy, Ronald B. 2002. "Who Should Marry Whom?: Multiple Partner Fertility among New Parents." Working Paper #2002-03-FF. Princeton, NJ: Center for Research on Child Wellbeing, Princeton University.

Mincy, Ronald B.. and Hillard Pouncy. 2002. "The Responsible Fatherhood Field: Evolution and Goals." In *Handbook of Father Involvement: Multidisciplinary Perspectives*, edited by C. Tamis-LeMonda and N. Cabrera. Mahwah, NJ: Lawrence Erlbaum.

Monea, Emily, and Isabel Sawhill. 2010. "Simulating the Effect of the 'Great Recession' on Poverty, an Update." Washington, DC: Brookings Institution, Center on Children and Families.

Morris, Pamela, Greg J. Duncan, and Christopher Rodrigues. 2004. "Does Money Really Matter? Estimating Impacts of Family Income on Children's Achievement with Data from Random-Assignment Experiments." New York: MDRC.

Moynihan, Donald P. 1965. "The Negro Family: The Case For National Action." Washington: Office of Policy Planning and Research, United States Department of Labor.

Moynihan, Daniel P., and Timothy M. Smeeding. 2004. "A Dahrendorf Inversion and the Twilight of the Family: The Challenge to the Conference." In *The Future of the Family*, edited by D. P. Moynihan, T. M. Smeeding, and L. Rainwater. New York: Russell Sage Foundation.

Moynihan, Donald P., Timothy M. Smeeding, and Lee Rainwater. 2004. "The Future of the Family." New York: Russell Sage Foundation.

National Campaign. 2010. "What Works: Curriculum-Based Programs that Help

Prevent Teen Pregnancy." Washington, DC: National Campaign to Prevent Teen and Unplanned Pregnancy.

Nepomnyaschy, Lenna, and Irwin Garfinkel. 2008. "Child Support, Fatherhood, and Marriage: Findings from the First Five Years of the Fragile Families and Child Well-being Study." *Asian Social Work and Policy Review* 1: 1–20.

Nock, Steven L. 1998. *Marriage in Men's Lives.* New York: Oxford University Press.

Ooms, Theodora, and Pamela Wilson. 2004. "The Challenges of Offering Relationship and Marriage Education to Low-Income Populations." *Family Relations* 53: 440–47.

Osborne, Cynthia, and Sara McLanahan. 2007. "Partnership Instability and Child Well-Being." *Journal of Marriage and Family* 69: 1065–83.

Pager, Devah. 2007. *Marked: Race, Crime, and Finding Work in an Era of Mass Incarceration.* Chicago: University of Chicago Press.

Pear, Robert. 2003 (October 13). "Welfare Spending Shows Huge Shift." *New York Times.*

Peck, Don. 2010. "How a New Jobless Era Will Transform America." *Atlantic Monthly* (March).

Preston, Samuel H. 2004. "The Value of Children." In *The Future of the Family,* edited by D. P. Moynihan, T. M. Smeeding, and L. Rainwater, pp. 263–66. New York: Russell Sage Foundation.

Pruett, Marsha Kline, Carolyn Pape Cowan, Philip A. Cowan, and Kyle Pruett. 2009. "Lessons Learned from the Supporting Father Involvement Study: A Cross-Cultural Preventive Intervention for Low-Income Families with Young Children." *Journal of Social Service Research* 35: 163–79.

Rampell, Catherine. 2010 (August 6). "Comparing This Recession to Previous Ones: Job Changes." *New York Times.* http://economix.blogs.nytimes.com /2010/08/06/comparing-this-recession-to-previous-ones-job-changes-5/.

Ratcliffe, Caroline, Signe-Mary McKernan, and Kenneth Finegold. 2007. "The Effect of State Food Stamp and TANF Policies on Food Stamp Program Participation." Washington, DC: Urban Institute.

Sayer, Liana C., Suzanne M. Bianchi, and John M. Robinson. 2004. "Are Parents Investing Less in Children? Trends in Mothers' and Fathers' Time with Children." *American Journal of Sociology* 110: 1–43.

Smeeding, Timothy, Irwin Garfinkel, and Ronald Mincy, eds. 2011. "Young Disadvantaged Men: Fathers, Families, Poverty, and Policy; An Introduction to the Issues." In *Young Disadvantaged Men: Fathers, Families, Poverty, and Policy, Annals of the American Academy of Political and Social Science* 635 (May), edited by T. M. Smeeding, I. Garfinkel, and R. B. Mincy.

Smeeding, Timothy M., Jeff E. Thompson, E. A. Levanon, and E. Burak. 2011. "The Changing Dynamics of Work, Poverty, Income from Capital and Income from Earnings during the Great Recession." Working paper. Presented at the Stanford Poverty Center, Stanford University, February 13.

Sum, Andrew. 2011. "No Country for Young Men." In *Young Disadvantaged Men: Fathers, Families, Poverty, and Policy, Annals of the American Academy of Political and Social Science* 635 (May), edited by T. M. Smeeding, I. Garfinkel, and R. B. Mincy.

Tach, Laura, Ronald Mincy, and Kathryn Edin. 2010. "Parenting as a Package Deal: Relationships, Fertility, and Nonresident Father Involvement among Unmarried Parents." *Demography* 47: 181–204.

U.S. Department of Agriculture (USDA). 2011. "SNAP Monthly Data." Washington, DC: USDA. http://www.fns.usda.gov/pd/34SNAPmonthly.htm.

U.S. Department of Labor. 2010. "Characteristics of the Insured Unemployed." Washington, DC: U.S. Department of Labor.

Waite, Linda J., and Maggie Gallagher. 2000. *The Case for Marriage: Why Married People Are Happier, Healthier, and Better Off Financially*. New York: Doubleday.

Waldfogel, Jane. 2006. *What Children Need*. Cambridge, MA: Harvard University Press.

———. 2010. *Britain's War on Poverty*. New York: Russell Sage Foundation.

Waller, Maureen R., and Robert Plotnick. 2001. "Effective Child Support Policy for Low-Income Families: Evidence from Street Level Research." *Journal of Policy Analysis and Management* 20: 89–110.

Wilde, Ty. 2009. Personal communication.

Wilson, William J. 1987. *The Truly Disadvantaged: The Inner City, the Underclass, and Public Policy*. Chicago: University of Chicago Press.

Wolf, Richard. 2010 (January 28). "Welfare Rolls Up in '09; More Enroll in Assistance Programs." *USA Today*.

Wood, Robert G., Sheena McConnell, Quinn Moore, Andrew Clarkwest, and JoAnn Hsueh. 2010. "Strengthening Unmarried Parents' Relationships: The Early Impacts of Building Strong Families." Princeton, NJ: Mathematica Policy Research.

# CHAPTER EIGHT

# The Recent Transformation of the American Family

## Witnessing and Exploring Social Change

*Frank F. Furstenberg, Jr.*

I entered sociology a half-century ago, initially as a major at Haverford College in the late 1950s and then as a graduate student at Columbia from 1961 to 1967. Little did I know that I would witness a transformation in the institution of marriage and kinship, the likes of which were simply unimaginable when I began my academic career. It is no exaggeration to say that the American, and more broadly the Western, family changed more dramatically in the latter half of the twentieth century than in any comparable span of time in our history.

Explaining why and how family change occurs has been the consuming passion of my professional life. And I continue to puzzle over what is happening to the institution of marriage and kinship after five decades of watching the "the second demographic transition," as demographers call it, in the West (Lesthaeghe 1995). This transition has seen many family practices revised, and some reversed or abandoned. Family historians and scholars of contemporary family life have contributed substantially to our understanding of this transformation: why the Western family followed this unexpected course from a seemingly stable and nearly ubiquitous arrangement to a far more complex form that many regard as "deinstitutionalized," with rules dissolved, time-honored practices eschewed, and seemingly "rational" bargains reneged on (Cherlin 2004).

As has always occurred in times of family revolution or evolution, critics and defenders of these changes describe them in starkly different terms. Social scientists are committed to understanding or explaining change, not condemning or valorizing it, but as I develop my account here, it will become clear enough how the costs and benefits of this transformation have been borne by different segments of American society.

My initial task is to weave together a prospective and ongoing narrative of the key elements of change in marriage and kinship, trying first to portray the world of the family as it appeared to Americans a half-century ago. I trace the path of change from the period when the nuclear family was dominant to its present "postmodern" form, as some social scientists characterize the contemporary family (Beck-Gernsheim 2002). The changes that have taken place involve some cultural and normative continuities as well as many discontinuities. Observers tend to focus far more on the latter than the former, but I attempt to give both their proper due. In providing this account of change, I apply a theoretical lens that helps us to understand how and why such monumental changes occurred in the institution of marriage and the family, and why they have been so pervasive in the Western world.

My interpretation alternates between the macro-level and the micro-level. I show how and why changes create tensions for individuals and couples, making it difficult, if not impossible, to conform to prevailing ideals of marriage, parenthood, and kinship (Mills 1959). The tensions are not always initiated by exogenous shocks or pressures at the macro-level; they often emerge at the micro-level when customary ways of doing things no longer appear to make sense. These contradictions or incompatibilities may affect one part of the population and, under certain conditions, diffuse beyond the group that initially experiences the tensions.

Social historians of the family have always recognized that changes in family and kinship practices occur unevenly and sometimes spread more broadly when new behaviors become common or even legitimized by common practice (Ozmet 2001; Shorter 1977; Stone 1977). This analytic frame is hardly a "theory" of family change, but it helps one avoid the untenable assumption that change in family systems occurs for a single reason or even a common set of reasons that play out similarly in all societies or within all parts of a single society. Clearly we must separate the initial sources of change from the way that change is diffused within a given society if we are to reach a satisfactory understanding of how change actually takes place (Watkins 1991). To do so inevitably requires blending observations produced by qualitative and quantitative studies on family demography, beliefs, and practices.

## THE ISOLATED NUCLEAR FAMILY IN THE POSTWAR ERA: FACT AND FICTION

There are now many good histories of the postwar American family that prevailed in the wake of the Great Depression and the Second World War (Cherlin 1992; Coontz 2005; May 1988; Mintz 2004; Modell 1989). When I took my first sociology courses in the late 1950s, I was immediately immersed in contemporary accounts of what had happened to the family in the *first half* of the twentieth century, such as Burgess and Locke's famous treatise on marriage, the work on the Polish peasant by Thomas and Znaniecki (1996), and, of course, Parsons's (1964) writings on American kinship. All of these were enormously influential in the middle of the previous century.

Virtually all accounts at the time viewed the contemporary, mid-century family as a form that emerged after a lengthy period of emancipation (for better and worse) from a more patriarchal and extended kinship system that had prevailed before industrialization. A year after I entered graduate school, I took a course with William J. Goode, who at that time was putting the final touches on his monumental study of family change. I quickly became steeped in the debates over grand theories of social change and the family. Goode used to say that sociologists lacked a convincing, empirically testable theory of family change. He was right. The reigning paradigm, which he largely embraced, was "functional analysis." The form and functions of the family were biologically based and universal. The institution of marriage and kinship created ways of avoiding inbreeding (rules against incest), and established social exchange by defining property rights and paternal connections (Bell and Vogel 1968; Coser 1964; Davis 1985). Kinship fostered social integration, reducing conflict within and between many agrarian-based, feudal societies. There was, in short, a kind of inevitability in the "triumph" of the "modern family" over outdated and antiquated systems, as seen through the eyes of historians and family sociologists. This triumph, however, was bringing the family to the verge of disintegration (Shorter 1977; Stone 1977).

As economies became less agrarian and more industrialized, kinship ceded its pervasive influence as the institution of the family shed its patriarchal practices and more complex household forms. Throughout the West, the introduction of a job-based economy eroded the power of elders, males in particular. In its place emerged the "isolated nuclear family," a form that was largely detached from the influence of kinship lines of authority (Parsons 1964). The nuclear family was believed to be far more compatible with the demand for a flexible and geographically mobile labor supply. It offered a more efficient gender-based division of labor, allowing men and women to specialize in work and domestic duties, respectively. With the growth of education and training, the family ceded responsibility to other institutions. Goode (1963) argued in *World Revolution and Family Change* that this conjugal form privileging marital bonds over lineage ties would emerge in a growing swath of economically developing nations.

I entered the discipline when grand theory was largely a separate enterprise from empirical research, though my graduate training occurred just at the point when historical research based on population records was in its infancy. The advent of the computer was about to revolutionize the field of family studies. Sociologists and anthropologists were beginning to make use of the Human Relations Area Files, a project begun by social anthropologists who were attempting to catalogue properties of kinship systems, marriage patterns, and family organization from nonliterate and modern societies (Davis 1985; Murdock 1957; Whiting and Whiting 1975). In about the same period, historical demographers were beginning to reconstitute household change using church registries and census records to understand how families arrange themselves in space and over time (Laslett 1972; Smith 1972). For the first time, researchers were beginning to conduct empirical work on the broad class of modernization theories that largely viewed family change as evolutionary, growing out of technological, economic, and cultural changes (Berger and Berger 1983; Lasch 1977; Nisbet 1953). It is difficult to remember without consulting the literature of the time just how ahistorical and culturally limited most writings on the family were before the mid-1960s. There was a contingent of mostly senior scholars whose writings lamented the presumed waning of the extended family (Zimmerman 1947). However, most scholars, following Parsons, applauded features of the so-called modern family, with its emphasis on companionate marriages and more intimate relations across the generations. It was as if the American family stood as the beacon of the future. The optimism of the postwar era made it seem inevitable that other nations would follow the same path of development. To be sure, there was a murmur of discontent about the nature of contemporary family life. Conservative scholars noted that the family's functions had been usurped; others complained about the emotional intensity of the new family form (overprotection of children by their mothers) or the disappearance of fathers as a source of authority (Berger and Berger 1983; Lasch 1977).

There was a small but lively empirical literature among American sociologists of the family in the 1960s and 1970s that attempted to test some of these critiques. Scholars sought to demonstrate that kinship was still alive and well in the United States and England, particularly among the working class (Gans 1962; Young and Willmott 1957). And there was an almost obsessive interest in courtship and marriage practices. A high proportion of publications in the leading journals examined in detail how young couples moved into marriage, why marriages failed, and how individuals repaired the damage by contracting new and more secure remarriages. The field of scholarly research largely embraced functional theory that held that the contemporary family had successfully adapted to the new economic realities (Hill 1971; Litwak and Szelenyi 1969; Sussman 1959; Winch 1958).

My first published paper, "Industrialization and the American Family: A Look Backward," was based on my own small effort to test the impact of early industrialization on the family (Furstenberg 1966). I examined foreign travelers' observations on the American family in the first half of the nineteenth century to create a small data set (all the accounts that I could find in the Columbia library stacks) on courtship, marriage, family formation, and childrearing practices among Americans before industrialization.

Surprisingly, the data revealed that the main features of the so-called modern family were entirely evident to foreign observers well before the advent of industrialization in this country. Americans lived in nuclear families, marriages were seen as egalitarian, and the relations between parents and children were more democratic than was customarily the case in Europe, so most of the travelers (regardless of political view) reported. The family "then and now" was far less different than any current theory on the link between industrialization and the family predicted.

That paper ultimately helped to secure my first job at the University of Pennsylvania and began the next stage of my professional involvement in the study of family change.

### ENTERING ACADEMIA ON THE PRECIPICE OF CHANGE

I was hired in an era when many students entered academia without yet completing their Ph.D., much less publishing. I came with Ph.D. in hand, but only the vaguest idea of what academic issues I would explore. My thesis on the transmission of values in the family was a micro-level study of socialization. It produced a single article that has largely been forgotten, no doubt deservedly so. Having studied deviant behavior under Richard Cloward, I arrived at Penn with as much interest in criminological as in family studies. My pre-tenure years could be best described as shaky and unpromising. My early publications counted as many articles on the topic of crime as on the family. I lacked professional direction.

By a quirk of fate, in 1965, without recognizing what I was undertaking, I began a lifelong longitudinal study of teenage mothers in Baltimore. As I have recounted elsewhere, it took me almost a decade to understand what I was doing, and longer than that before I recognized that this study could become an important project in the study of individual and family change (Furstenberg 2002). At the outset, I was still largely unschooled in the emerging literature in sociology and demography on the life course.

Shortly after arriving at Penn, I had the good fortune to meet Glen Elder at a conference. Elder was just beginning to synthesize different strands of current theory and research based on the ideas of Mannheim and Mills into a life-course framework. His work would synthesize historical, sociological, and psychological elements (Elder 1974). It was under his informal mentorship that I began to read widely in the emerging historical, demographic, and sociological literature on aging. The Social Science Research Council published its monumental review of the field, *Aging and Society*, edited by Matilda Riley and Norman Ryder in 1968, and this three-volume set contributed incalculably to the development of family demography and life-course sociology.

During the same period, the first sprouts of feminist research in family sociology were beginning to appear. The study of gender was not yet an explicit subfield of family sociology, but it was to become so in short order after the publication of Betty Friedan's *The Feminine Mystique* in 1963. The fields of social history, feminist writings, and life-course demography were beginning to infuse the intellectual backwater area of sociology of the family with new ideas. Eventually, I began to appreciate the possibilities of examining the unfolding lives of teenage mothers and their offspring as a far more ambitious enterprise than I had previously imagined. These families, I can now say in retrospect, provided a window to understanding why marriage began to lose its grip on low-income couples in the final third of the twentieth century.

RECONSIDERING MARRIAGE: THE ORIGINS OF CHANGE

Beginning in the mid-1960s, the meaning and practice of teenage marriage and childbearing was testing the limits of marriage, or at least the form that was known then. The near hegemonic practice of early marriage and parenthood during the marriage rush after World War II and the ensuing baby-boom era of the 1950s and early 1960s was suddenly proving unworkable for one segment of the population—lower income blacks. The single-family wage earner, never practicable in the black community, was rapidly becoming an unaffordable luxury to a growing number of American families as well. Less-affluent young women and their parents were beginning to recognize the importance of education for gaining a secure foothold in the economy. Moreover, the high levels of marital dissolution following early marriage and parenthood created a negative feedback loop, especially, in low- and moderate-income black communities, which were beginning to cast a skeptical eye on the benefits of "shotgun weddings." (See, for example, Weeks 1976.)

Until the 1960s, premarital pregnancy had been part of the American courtship system. Romantic love or what passed for it in the 1940s and 1950s propelled many teenage couples who barely knew each other into "committed relationships" where sexual relations were tolerated. The median length of courtship—the time between meeting and marriage—in the 1950s was only six months (Rapoport 1964). Marriage provided a safety net for sexual risk taking among youth who, increasingly, were unwilling to maintain the lofty standard of premarital chastity. Indeed, in the 1950s nearly half of all teen marriages were preceded by a pregnancy. Arnold Green (1941), a shrewd student of family life, observed in a study of Polish-American couples that women relaxed their strict sexual standards, believing that their partners would consent to marry in the event of pregnancy.

Clark Vincent (1957), another leading family researcher, in his widely read book *Unmarried Mothers*, noted that a shadow system of adoption had provided a backup to white women whose partners were unwilling or unable to wed.

In interviews with a sample of predominately black women in the Baltimore study in the mid-1960s, I discovered a strong note of skepticism about the payoff of early marriage (Furstenberg 1976). This was particularly evident in interviews with mothers of pregnant teens, whose own lives had often worked out poorly because so many had married precipitously after becoming pregnant at an early age. A number of these women counseled their daughters to defer marriage and continue their education. More generally, rates of nonmarital childbearing were rapidly rising among low- and moderate-income blacks, a pattern that was attributed to the cultural legacy of slavery rather than to their current economic circumstances (Moynihan 1965; Rainwater and Yancey 1967). Although I did not recognize it at the time, this shift away from early marriage among pregnant black teens was a harbinger of things to come—the future unraveling of "marriage as we knew it" in mid-century America.

## PRESSURES ON THE NUCLEAR FAMILY

In hindsight, it is far easier now to see the building tensions in the nuclear family under way after the war. The postwar family—now ironically regarded as the "traditional family"—was, it would turn out, merely a passing phase in a continuously changing family system. It was also the culmination of a set of ideals that had developed over several centuries.

Marriage in the early Christian era was never as pervasive as is popularly believed (Coontz 2005; Glendon 1989). The modern form of the family began to take root during the Renaissance when privacy, intimacy, and individual expression were first given greater cultural currency (Aries 1962; Ozmet 2001; Stone 1977). Historians still disagree on the precise package of influences that produced the modern family. Patriarchy largely survived until the twentieth century, but the institutionalization of women and children's rights through legal statutes and social conventions was a gradual process, evolving over several centuries in the West (Therborn 2004).

Edward Shorter (1977) wrote that the family was "born modern" in colonial America, but if this was true, it was surely because many early settlers were extending religious and political freedoms that had met with enormous conflict in Europe. No doubt the availability of land, the isolation of the New World, the diversity of peoples, and the emergence of a distinctive American culture contributed to a range of marriage and family practices that helped to speed the decline of patriarchy (Hawke 1988). That is not to say that patriarchy did not exist in early America, but the ability of males to control their wives and their offspring ran up against the democratic ethos of the postcolonial period, a point that I discovered in my paper on the accounts of foreign travelers in the first half of the nineteenth century (see also De Tocqueville 1945).

The innovative scholarship beginning in the late 1960s by social historians and historical demographers began to reconstruct family histories, revealing sharp changes in family formation patterns in relatively short periods of time, and huge variability by geographic region, social class, and religious affiliation (Carter and Glick 1976; Smith 1972). Clearly, historical research in North America and Europe indicates a great deal more cultural and individual diversity than is commonly acknowledged even today. Evidence seems to go only so far in altering our image of what Goode referred to as "the classical family of Western nostalgia."

Even as the nuclear or companionate family type reached its apogee in the middle of the twentieth century, it exposed a set of contradictions and paradoxes that would lead to its undoing, although at the time, few social scientists seemed even dimly aware of these incipient tensions. The companionate marriage form (in which a man and wife join together and form one indissoluble union) was built upon a gender-based division of labor that appeared to be as "natural" as the birds and the bees. The fact that teenagers—half of all women were married by age 20 in the late 1950s—were establishing "lifelong" unions with partners they often barely knew (often with a child on the way) only began to trouble experts when it became abundantly clear that many marriages were not surviving beyond the first few years.

As noted above, the end of the postwar economy in the 1960s, during which American workers had enjoyed a period of unprecedented economic gains, had begun to erode the prevailing single-earner model. The loss of manufacturing jobs paying union wages, as William J. Wilson (1987) noted two decades ago, imperiled the black family, but it also later helped to undermine the gender-based division of labor among low- and middle-income white families.

More affluent couples were reexamining the institution of marriage and the family for another set of reasons. First, women's rising levels of education resulted in greater aspirations among college-educated women, who no longer were content to invest their human capital solely in childrearing (Komarovsky 1973). Second, mounting divorce rates began to give women pause about whether they would be able to support themselves if their marriage dissolved. Third, the advent of the pill in the 1960s provided women a means to regulate their fertility to better suit their personal desires and childbearing intentions. Fourth, the growth of mass marketing no doubt stimulated consumption desires that could only be satisfied by two earners in a middle-income household. Finally, there was a growing emphasis on the quality of children rather than the quantity, which began to spread from the affluent and better-educated downward. Even poor families like those I was studying in Baltimore wanted to control their family size. (Only one-third of the teen mothers ultimately had more than two children.)

This constellation of economic, social, and demographic conditions combined with the ideology of civil rights and equal rights in the early 1970s was a heady mixture for changing marriage practices and the form of the family. Among the well-off, the pressures for change were slightly different and perhaps more ideologically influenced. Men like me were learning that they had to take a greater hand in domestic life as women entered the labor force in ever larger numbers. I can attest to the power of social pressure in the early 1970s. Between the birth of my first child in 1967 and my second in 1970, I somehow managed to learn how to change diapers and boil an egg.

Initially, the changes resulted in a rising age of marriage and, at least among young black women, a sharp increase in nonmarital childbearing. But gradually, as I recount later on, the shift in marriage practices became more widespread and dramatic.

## MARRIAGE AND THE CHANGING LIFE COURSE OF YOUNG ADULTS

As I was completing my first book on the Baltimore study in the mid-1970s, I returned to my interest in the social history of the American family. With my friend and collaborator John Modell, I delved into historical census records on the black family and became involved in the contentious debate over the Moynihan Report, a controversial document describing the plight of the black family in the United States. During the course of our collaboration, Modell and I began to examine the organization of the life course in the twentieth century, showing how the timing of leaving home, completing school, entering the labor force, and embarking on marriage and parenthood became tightly scheduled and highly coordinated during the middle part of 1900s (Modell, Furstenberg, and Strong 1978). Marriage had been the mainspring of the transition, particularly for females, who often completed their education, got married, left home, and became parents (usually in that order) in their late teens and early twenties. Our analysis ended with the 1970 census, but the data hinted at an emerging pattern of delay and diversity that would quickly and dramatically reverse the prevailing pattern of early adulthood, extending this passage and making it more complex and less linear. It was another two decades before I would come to appreciate just how much the change in family formation was affecting the timing of adult transitions in ways that would alter the meaning of marriage and parenthood.

## THE GROWTH OF FAMILY DIVERSITY

My growing interest in the social organization of the life course led me to think more searchingly about the changing institution of marriage and how rising levels of divorce and remarriage were complicating family forms and practices. In the late 1970s, I undertook a review of the sparse literature on remarriage and concluded that the exclusive attention on the nuclear family was diverting our attention away from the fact that a growing number of children were being reared in alternative family systems. Divorce and remarriage were not an aberration but an intrinsic feature of our family system. I characterized this pattern as "conjugal succession," an ungraceful term that I coined to signify that remarriage after divorce was becoming a more prevalent option in the Western kinship system. Rather than recreating the nuclear family, remarriage instead represented a widespread and largely unexamined alternative family form.

*Recycling the Family*, the book I coauthored with Graham Spanier (1984), described how parents and children moved through divorce and remarriage, how grandparents adapted to these changes, and how children adapted to the complexities of living in a kinship system created by chains of relationships spanning divorce and remarriage. In a chapter in the book, I contended that the family form that was so widely assumed to be universal was, in fact, undergoing fundamental change:

> [T]here is reason to suspect that the rise of conjugal succession is related to a general shift in the pattern of family formation which has unraveled marriage from what was once a common strand of status transitions. As marriage has become independent of other events in the life course, it is seen as a more voluntary and less permanent arrangement. This does not necessarily mean that individuals today expect less of marriage. Indeed, it is entirely possible that as marriage has become less binding and inviolable, standards of what constitutes a gratifying and satisfying marriage have risen. (Furstenberg 1982, p. 110)

These ideas closely paralleled speculations that Andrew J. Cherlin (1978) had advanced in his important piece "Remarriage as an Incomplete Institution." Our similar views on what was happening to the American family led to a lifelong personal and intellectual collaboration, including writings on grandparenthood and the effects of divorce on children, stepfamilies, and the broader American kinship system.

Andy and I also attempted in the 1980s to project what the family might look like at the beginning of the twenty-first century, given changing economic conditions and new technology. Needless to say, our projections came up short in many respects. However, we did argue that the family would never return to its early postwar form. The growing freedom from control of parental authority due in part to the extension of education and the economic opportunities afforded young adults, the availability of contraception that permitted couples to postpone marriage and parenthood, the cultural and economic changes allowing women to escape the extreme form of interdependence, among other conditions, were permitting and, one could argue, requiring a greater level of individual discretion and personal control in making family choices (see also Rosenfeld 2007). Cohabitation, we believed, would become more common; we did not believe it would replace marriage but rather fill in periods when marriage was premature (in early adulthood) or spans after divorce and before remarriage.

Our speculations, it turns out, were not bold enough. Even in the early 1980s, we failed to see just how profound were the changes taking place in the institution of marriage or to appreciate fully the growing impact on family of economic inequality that became more evident over the past quarter of a century. The growing gaps by education, occupation, and income have profoundly altered the conditions under which family formation, childbearing, and parenting now occur. In hindsight, we also missed how technological change would influence childbearing and childrearing, a topic that I will come to later. And we could not have foreseen the huge effect of the wave of immigration that began in the 1980s and its contribution to more culturally varied family practices.

By contemporary standards, Americans lived in far more homogeneous family forms in the middle of the past century. Even so, we are now inclined to exaggerate the uniformity of family arrangements that existed in the first half of the twentieth century. Important differences in household form and family practice have always existed by race and social class, and especially the combination of the two. Indeed, a great deal of attention was devoted to social class differences during the first half of the twentieth century. It was not until the beginning of the 1960s that scholars began to move away from the class-based analysis of family patterns that had been so much a part of the stock and trade of our research on family life when I started my academic career (Furstenberg 2007, 2009).

In part this shift happened because of a growing attention to gender and ethnic differences, for quite legitimate reasons. The lens of gender, often absent in earlier analyses of family life, provided powerful insights into cleavages within the household. Building on the writings of early feminist sociologists such as Mirra Komarovsky, Jessie Bernard, Rose Coser, and Alice Rossi, many sociologists of the family began to view gender as the bedrock for understanding how and why marriage was under challenge. Similarly, later in the twentieth century, we began to recognize anew the important differences among new immigrant groups who introduced to the United States different models of how families operate. The attention to gender and ethnicity need not have diverted our gaze from social class, but I suspect it did.

An important reason for the waning class analyses during this period was the consuming interest in racial differences in the family that was sparked by the publication of the Moynihan Report in 1965 (Furstenberg, 2007, 2009). Although Moynihan was certainly aware of the long tradition of social class differences in the black family, his almost exclusive focus on poor black families and communities ignited an intellectual debate and an outpouring of studies on low-income black families. In doing so, his powerful contribution to analysis of the conditions that produce unstable family life among low-income blacks was widely misinterpreted, in part because he failed to recognize that the same set of conditions might produce similar effects on whites (and Asians or Hispanics in more recent times).

Moynihan was not wrong in seeing the crushing pressures on the low- and moderate-income black families arising from a changed labor market, but he did not foresee that many of the same economic and cultural forces that were making marriage problematic for blacks would begin to create similar dilemmas for other low-income populations in the United States. The cultural legacy of slavery may have been far less potent than the economic legacy of slavery and racial discrimination, which persisted throughout the twentieth century. The Moynihan Report created the false notion that low-income blacks (re)created a distinctly different family form owing to their special history. In fact, lower-income blacks had long exhibited family patterns at variance with many practices observed in the middle class—patterns that in recent decades low-income whites have begun to mimic (Margolis and Furstenberg 2010).

That patterns of family life have always varied across economic class is hardly news to students of the family. However, the nuanced analysis of how socioeconomic position shapes and constrains family practices in ways that recreate family forms over generations is still understudied despite the vast outpouring of work on the poor that occurred in the last third of the past century. We continue to act as if the poor and nonpoor create different family worlds, without recognizing that patterns of family life have always varied both across and within social strata, including the broad middle class. Differences both in priorities and in the means to realize them have long existed among the different social strata. As inequality has grown in American society over the past several decades, it is likely that the differentiation has grown greater. The greater variability in marriage patterns and family practices may be widening the gap in outcomes for children and their long-term prospects for escaping poverty (McLanahan 2004; Furstenberg 2007).

It also remains to be seen how the new and increasing streams of different immigrant populations may be interacting with economic opportunities. In the study of immigrant families we focus a lot on the differences by generation, assuming a high level of assimilation over time. However, we focus less on how such differences may play out for different nationalities over time. The dynamic of differential assimilation by social class will be especially important to follow both in the United States and in other advanced economies. Understanding the interplay between ethnicity, social class, and national policy has become one of the most urgent and attractive items on the growing agenda of comparative research (Rumbaut and Portes 2001).

## NEW MARRIAGE PATTERNS AND THEIR CONSEQUENCES

As I mentioned earlier, the information- and knowledge-based economy that emerged in the final third of the previous century exerted a different set of pressures on moderate- and higher-income couples to delay marriage, also linked to economic prospects. As the economy began to shift from manufacturing to service-, information-, and knowledge-based industries, the premium placed on educational attainment increased. This premium first appeared during the 1970s, as jobs declined and a huge baby-boom population began to enter the labor market. The recession of 1972 and the waning of the Vietnam War initiated a period of low economic growth that was only interrupted for brief spells over the past several decades (Danziger and Gottschalk 1997; Levy 1998). This created an incentive for those who could to remain in school for longer periods of time, putting off home leaving for many and marriage for nearly all. The median age of marriage began its seemingly relentless climb upward, from 20 for women in 1957 to 26 in 2007 (and still rising).

Later marriage was accompanied by widespread adoption of patterns that historically had been practiced by a relatively small number of outliers: sexual intercourse *without* the intention to marry (among females) and cohabitation before marriage.

Beginning in the 1960s and picking up pace in the 1970s, women largely abandoned the practice of delaying sex until marriage (or almost until marriage), and the long-held double standard that permitted men to have sex while encouraging women to remain virgins collapsed (Zelnik, Kantner, and Ford 1981). Youth from educated and affluent families started to have sex too, albeit slightly later, without the pretense that marriage would ensue. The combination of the extension of higher education, marriage ages, and availability of new and more reliable methods of contraception all contributed to severing the link between marriage and sexual initiation.

Along with the change in sexual standards, larger numbers of young college-goers began to cohabit, first clandestinely and then openly. The *New York Times* heralded this change when it profiled an undergraduate couple from Columbia and Barnard who were cohabiting in the late 1960s, questioning the traditional role of the college as an institution that served *in loco parentus* (Silverman 1977). It was not long afterward that social scientists began to take notice of this "new practice." Of course, cohabitation had always existed as an alternative to formal marriage, but it operated, as do many family practices, in the shadows. Public notice of underground practices can propel normative change by providing quasi-legitimacy for those who might otherwise be unwilling to buck prevailing norms.

Floyd Allport (1924), the social psychologist, referred to this process as "pluralistic ignorance," a collective recognition that private behavior is more widely shared than ever imagined. Normative shifts of this type occur as individuals find they are unable to adhere to standard practices. As they stray from the fold, they experience or engage in what Hyman Rodman (1963) once labeled "value stretch." Much like the teenage mothers in the Baltimore sample (but for somewhat different reasons), a growing number of youth in their late teens and early twenties began to regard early marriage as economically and psychologically impractical. When the link between sexual initiation and marriage was decoupled, arguably it also reduced, in turn, the incentive to wed as early as possible.

In the decades to follow, cohabitation proved to be an attractive way of managing premarital sexual relationships for growing legions of young adults who were finding it increasingly difficult or hazardous to form permanent commitments while still in school or while they were testing the waters in the labor market. Cohabitation also permitted young couples to practice marriage or a marriage-like relationship without the long-term obligations that wedlock entailed. Of course, initially many parents were unhappy (or offended and outraged) when their children cohabited rather than wed. By now this is ancient history in most parts of the country as the practice of cohabitation has become commonplace.

The creation of this hybrid form of union had profound implications for the institution of marriage itself. It began a long-term shift away from marriage as an *advance pledge* of a lifelong commitment to marriage as a *celebration* of a commitment that develops in the course of living together. Cohabitation has become a common stage in the process of family formation—neither courtship nor engagement—that can lead to a more binding commitment over time if circumstances permit. Parenthood, it seems, is one of those circumstances, propelling some couples into marriage or, alternatively, testing the relationship and finding it cannot bear the weight of new demands (Carlson and McLanahan, 2004; England and Edin 2007; Gibson-Davis, 2007; McLanahan, 2009).

The decoupling of sex and marriage and the emergence of cohabitation are prime examples of what might be called the "unpackaging" of elements of the family and kinship system, a more general process that has become characteristic of the contemporary Western family. We can refer to this change as the "deinstitutionalization" of marriage, as Cherlin and others have described it, but it also could be seen as a process of reinstitutionalization of family formation that allows for greater flexibility to fit with a changing life course. Whether this flexibility improves the life chances of children now born into unions is a separate and critical question that I will return to later. However, I see this process of uncoupling and recoupling of discrete elements of marriage, family, and kinship as inevitable as the family system in different social strata adapts to changing economic, cultural, and social conditions. Whether this means that the institution of marriage and family is "declining" in importance or becoming permanently "deinstitutionalized" is in my view still an open and unsettled question.

Undoubtedly, Americans are "doing" marriage quite differently than they did at the middle of the twentieth century. Let us not forget, however, that Americans in the 1950s certainly did marriage quite differently from those in 1900 or 1850 (Cherlin 2009; Coontz 1992). We may be prone to exaggerating the significance of recent changes while diminishing the significance of changes in the more distant past after they have become normalized.

Almost all young Americans hope to marry, most will eventually wed or enter civil or marriage-like unions, and they will continue to have children, largely in unions. Still, the process of family formation has become less uniform, predictable, and stable than it once was. At the same time, it is more flexible and adaptable to the circumstances of couples, allowing greater choice and discretion in union formation.

The legalization of same-sex marriages is also a part of the reinstitutionalization of marriage and parenthood. The notion that marriage was exclusively a heterosexual institution is giving way to a more inclusive standard of eligibility. The legal contract has less to do with the management of sex or the regulation of parenthood than with certifying the rights and obligations of partnership and parenthood. Accordingly, a series of court decisions revised the legal meaning of marriage. Fathers no longer can refuse child support because they were unmarried when their children were born and, accordingly, will be given access to their children whether they live with them or not. Stepparents who invest in children over time inevitably will be accorded a greater share of access and control over the children in whom they invest and help to rear. More recently, courts have begun to recognize the rights of same-sex couples to legal marriage, broadening access to a still culturally valued institution that affords rights and requires responsibilities.

## THE CHANGING MEANING OF LOVE AND
## ITS PLACE IN MARRIAGE

Over time and across societies, kinship systems have regarded romantic love as a threat to family control over marriage, a desirable precondition for marriage, or, alternatively, the sine qua non for entering marriage (Goode 1962). Two centuries ago, even in America, parents viewed romantic love as a basis for marriage with circumspection (Rothman 1984). A half-century ago, love in its most passionate form became a compelling motivation or justification for marriage (Coser 1974). (It might be that sexual desire and love were less easily distinguishable then than they are now.) Today, I would venture to say that being in love has become a necessary but insufficient reason for marriage, if only because it can comfortably exist outside of marriage in a system where marriage has become more optional.

Understanding how love and marriage co-exist has been insufficiently examined in the recent literature on the family (Beck-Gernsheim 2002; Swidler 2001). I cannot hope to do so here, but I must observe that my collaborators and I were amazed to discover in analyzing open-ended interviews of nearly five hundred young adults that we rarely heard "talk of love" as individuals reported on the marriage process (Kefalas et al. forthcoming). Wedlock these days is more about becoming and being committed, less about promises, and more about demonstrations of commitment that develop over time.

It seems that the test of commitment is exercised quite differently across social strata. Among the poor and the near-poor, who often now bear children long before they wed, the test of paternal commitment involves showing support in the form of affection, time, and material aid. Men may come and go, but they stay only if they prove to be reliable parents and partners (Edin and Kefalas 2005; Liebow 1967; Waller 2002). This pattern, it seems, is extending upward as women in the middle strata are becoming more skeptical about the benefits of marriage. In part, this is both because men's economic position has eroded and also because the standard of what constitutes a "good man" has extended beyond just being a good provider to also being a good parent and a good partner.

Years ago, when I was interviewing the young adult offspring of the teen mothers in Baltimore, I was impressed by how much "feminist" concerns infused their language (Furstenberg 1995). Increasingly, women were looking for and expected a greater range of socio-emotional skills than most men were able to demonstrate. Increasingly, couples are waiting to see that the relationship works before they enter marriage. Young couples with limited education and income are embedded in a social world that is populated by adults who have had failed marriages. Increasingly, they want proof before making what they see as a "permanent" commitment even when children enter the picture (Edin and Kefalas 2005).

It is probably also the case that the definition of a suitable partner is changing. More is expected of men than before because women have the option of opting out. Of course, men do too, and the "shotgun" strategy of pressuring (or even persuading, as was the policy of the George W. Bush administration) young couples into marriage is simply no longer viable because neither partner is willing to stay together merely for the sake of the child, even if they believe that it is better to live together if at all possible. This is because young people have grown up in an era when marriage standards have been climbing to new and daunting levels. Men and women must now collaborate around economic and domestic support in ways their parents and grandparents never faced.

This requires a new "vocabulary of motives," as Gerth and Mills (1993) described the way that social structure insinuates itself into the realm of cultural standards and personal needs. Women want men to perform a new repertoire of roles for which they are often ill-prepared. Men, as Goode (1980) perceptively noted decades ago, may resist, feeling that the expectations for them are too high and require behaviors that they regard as inappropriate. In turn, men find women far less passive and accepting of their foibles and limitations than they did in an era when the choice of living alone was less acceptable. So as the standards of what constitutes a "good marriage or partnership" have risen, couples, particularly those with less education and income, have struggled to make a good match.

A generation ago, educated men like me went through the process of revising the marriage contract with similar doubts and reluctance. Divorce rates among the well-educated were significantly higher in the late 1970s than they are today (Carter and Glick 1976). They have dropped for several reasons. First, the longer young adults stay in school, the longer they take to find a partner, mostly to good effect. Second, the educational process itself has had a salutatory impact on acquiring the "soft skills of marriage." By that I mean that a growing number of men and women who progress through college and beyond are learning to acquire the habits of a more egalitarian relationship in word and deed. In part, young people acquire these habits inside families by watching their parents cope with their relationships, but they also acquire them through everyday dealings in educational and work settings. This process of cultural realignment has been gradual and is surely incomplete. But there is no doubt that in the United States and throughout the Western world, marriage or its equivalent has been revised. This revision ultimately is producing a more symmetrical marriage form that is replacing the patriarchal model that prevailed until the middle of the twentieth century.

Another feature of contemporary marriage is a shift away from the classic model of the previous era often characterized as a "companionate" marriage system (Burgess and Locke 1960). I like to describe that form with the formula "one plus one equals one" (he and she become one). Two individuals coming together, it was believed a generation ago, should merge into a single entity defined by common interests. (Of course, in actuality it was frequently expected that women would subordinate their own interests to their husbands'). It seems now that the model is shifting to a different formula: "one plus one equals three" (he and she now become he, she, and us). Far more space is permitted and even encouraged for individuals to keep their distinct needs and desires. This new form of marriage is most conspicuous among highly educated couples.

Why has the change disproportionately been concentrated at the top? There are many overlapping reasons. Women are in a better position to bargain for more separation and enforce the bargain. More-educated men, who have many arenas in which to fulfill their status, may be more accepting of the changes. Both men and women have also had greater opportunity to acquire the necessary skills to meet the new demands of successful relationships through education and work. And of course, couples spend much more time practicing living together than they once did.

Our information on what is happening in families where one or both partners have had some higher education but have not completed college or entered a well-paying occupation is very limited. My own current research is on families in the middle, but unfortunately it is still too early for me to say much about the topic. If I had to guess, I suspect that my collaborators and I will find a mixed picture that reflects a blend of the old and new (as is still true for privileged couples), but the blend may differ from that among the highly educated. In fact, it is remarkable how much of our research concentrates on either the top (people like us) or the bottom of the social structure. Too few researchers examine the full range of family formation practices, particularly what goes on inside marriages and cohabitational unions. Oddly, for all the attention given to the sociology of culture in recent decades, research on how couples go about living together is still fairly sparse.

## THE CHANGING PASSAGE TO PARENTHOOD

Between the 1950s and the late 1970s, our cultural understanding of what it meant to be a parent began to change, and so too the passage to becoming a parent. Through the postwar period, the link between marriage and parenthood remained virtually indissoluble, though the signs of change were evident by 1970 (Cutright 1972). Nonmarital childbearing, even in the black community, where rates were modestly high by standards of the time, received near universal opprobrium until a half-century ago. However, disapproval of single parenthood began to soften in the 1960s, first among blacks and in subsequent decades among less-well-off whites and Hispanics. As marriage became more problematic, and with the sharp rise of divorce rates in the 1970s, fewer couples felt compelled to wed, at least immediately, when premarital pregnancy occurred.

It is difficult to know just why this shift occurred so rapidly in the United States and indeed in almost all Western nations. The change took place along with, and in part in response to, shifting legal doctrines about the status of "illegitimate" children. However, the legal doctrines themselves reflected a disintegration of long-held understandings about the role of marriage in designating ownership and inheritance rights. Children were no longer seen as property, a significant departure from longstanding patriarchal practice in the West (Therborn 2004).

Marriage and parenthood were delinked in another way: for the first time, significant proportions of married women elected not to have children. In the 1950s, childlessness within marriage was viewed as a personal tragedy. By the 1970s, people were beginning to view parenthood within marriage as voluntary (Thornton and Freedman 1982; Koropeckyj-Cox and Pendell 2007). By the end of the century, the rate of childlessness among women had risen to one in five. A 2004 General Social Survey poll indicated that nearly half of all Americans thought parenthood was not necessarily part of the transition to adulthood. Those who did were less educated and more religious (Furstenberg et al. 2004).

The decoupling of marriage and parenthood reconfigures kinship in a profound way that shapes family and intergenerational ties. The West has long been characterized by bilateral kinship ties that equally emphasize both maternal and paternal lines—although the significance of maintaining paternal last names hints at the enduring elevation of men's rights over women's. (It was not until the beginning of the twentieth century that women began to retain custody over children in the event of a divorce.) As divorce and nonmarital childbearing have become more prevalent, the kinship system has been tilted in a distinctly matrilineal direction, at least for the time being.

Cherlin and I (1991) first noted this trend when we wrote on the effects of divorce on intergenerational contact between children and their grandparents. It seemed that nonresidential fathers frequently withdrew from biological children after they established a new partnership, particularly one with children. Stated indelicately, many of these men engaged in a pattern of "child swapping" as child care obligations in their "new" families replaced those with their first set of biological children. Fathers do not always willingly withdraw; sometimes they are pushed out by mothers, who become gatekeepers by discouraging contact and influence in an effort to promote the relationships with their current partners. This pattern within non-nuclear households has profound consequences for maintaining intergenerational bonds. Many children lose contact with their paternal kin over time, diminishing the level of available support and resources. Thus the matrilineal tilt, most evident among lower-income families, can and often does diminish the network of effective kin who sponsor, mentor, and monitor children and young adults.

My impression, backed up by all too little data, is that over the past several decades nonresidential fathers have gradually become committed and been permitted to retain ties with biological offspring from a prior relationship. However, the psychological, social, and economic complexities of multi-partnered fertility constitute considerable structural barriers to maintaining the equitable balance of kinship ties from paternal and maternal lines. Of course, remarriage, or at least recoupling, introduces new potential kin on the father's side, but there is every reason to believe that step- and quasi-stepkin are not as reliable or constant a source of support to offspring whose biological parents live apart (Johnson 1988).

We know relatively little about how kinship operates among same-sex couples and their offspring (for a conspicuous exception, see Weston 1997). However, there is every reason to suspect that these kinship patterns operate relatively similarly to those among heterosexual couples. It would be useful to examine the impact of formal marriage on the workings of the kinship system for both heterosexual and same-sex couples.

One other structural feature of kinship deserves greater attention than it has received to date. Earlier I alluded to the dramatic change that has taken place in the transition to adulthood. Since the turn of the twenty-first century, I have devoted my time to understanding these changes. The lengthening of education and the difficulty of early entrance to the labor market has changed the timetable for growing up or extended parents' responsibilities well into the third decade of life (Furstenberg 2010). Parents are increasingly called on to support their children during the transition, although many less-educated and less-affluent families are in a poor position to provide the material and cultural capital necessary to support children in college and beyond.

The structural fissures that I have just discussed are quite evident during this new stage of life. Divided families and multi-partnered parenthood often compromise the available assistance to young adults. Less-advantaged parents must place more of the burden on young adults to support themselves during their late teens and early twenties. To the extent that they help out, they are potentially depleting their retirement savings. Thus the extension of early adulthood puts an almost impossible squeeze on less-affluent families, and in all likelihood it reduces the prospects of educational attainment for young adults from low- and moderate-income families and/or depletes the limited resources of their parents. Or, to put it differently, the early adult years may amplify the diverging developmental course between rich and poor, and perhaps between the rich and the middle as well.

## THE CHANGING MEANING OF PARENTHOOD

The growing perception that a college degree is necessary to achieve a secure position in the middle class began to take shape in the 1980s, as the realities of deindustrialization and the loss of manufacturing jobs set in. This perception has steadily grown within all social strata, and better-educated parents have begun to believe that even college graduation is insufficient to provide economic security for their children. In fact, economic data over the past several decades have reinforced this impression, creating something of a panic among better-off families that their children could not be assured of a bright future without a graduate degree. Risk of downward mobility, whether real or not, has become a driving force in how the role of parent is presently constructed: managing for success in school has become a dominant concern among the highly educated.

At the top, parenthood has become more protective and more actively concerned with promoting skills, talents, and knowledge. Educated parents, especially, have become far more involved in managing their children's cognitive and cultural development. In the apt description of Annette Lareau (2003), affluent parents have increasingly adopted a style of "concerted cultivation" while working-class families continue to adhere to a style of "natural growth," encouraging autonomy and early independence. Of course, these different orientations to parental responsibilities do not perfectly align with the social status of families, but they suggest a dramatic shift away from the dominant style of parenting in the previous generation when upper-middle-class parents favored a style of "sponsored independence" (Miller and Swanson 1958).

I suspect, too, that at least one driving force changing parents' standards of appropriate behavior has been the return of mothers to the labor force. As mothers moved from full-time domesticity into the workplace, they received a good deal of criticism from those who believed that they were depriving their children of needed nurturance and instruction (Hoffman and Youngblade 1999). Their response was to give more attention to the needs of their children. Arguably, and ironically, full-time mothers in earlier generations may have felt more entitled to supervise their children less tightly if only because they felt they were on-call all the time. It may also be that smaller family size has altered time-honored practices of letting older children supervise infants and toddlers. Finally, whether true or not, the belief that we live in a "winner-take-all" society has become widespread among privileged Americans.

Although historical comparisons are largely lacking, it is hard not to see the rising protectiveness, particularly among the better-off. Halloween, once an occasion where children freely roamed neighborhoods, is now a highly supervised event. We have greatly restricted children's independent mobility over the past several decades. Parents chauffeur their children to after-school and weekend activities, when in earlier times children would be far freer to make their own schedules. Children are more carefully monitored with cell phones, e-mail, and the video camera. This supervision now extends into adolescence and even early adulthood. I have become fond of listening to Penn students on the campus in telephone conversations with their parents, seeking advice, support, and approbation.

By most available measures, parental investment has grown, if only because families are generally smaller now than they were a half-century ago. Contrary to critics who say working parents are spending less time with their children, both mothers and fathers are spending more time directly supervising their children and probably devote more of their resources to doing so (Bianchi 2000; Gauthier, Smeeding, and Furstenberg 2004). In ongoing research, Sabino Kornrich and I are finding a distinct rise in the costs of rearing children, owing to pre-school and after-school expenditures aimed at enhancing children's education. The differences by social class are predictably huge.

Changes in both the structure of parenthood and the styles of parenting across social class have probably widened over time, but we have rather limited evidence on the pattern of parental investment. Nonetheless, it appears that the gap in American society between the advantaged families, middle-income families, and the disadvantaged has increased, reflecting the widening chasm between the top and bottom in earnings and in social and cultural capital. It is a daunting task to invent policies that might reverse this trend if only because the advantaged command so many resources to give their children a large head start in the educational system. Assuming the trends I have just sketched are accurate, it would be revealing to see if they have occurred in other nations that have experienced sharp growth in inequality and compare them to those with less inequality. Can the level of government support for less well educated and less wealthy families mitigate the inherent advantages that well-educated and affluent parents possess?

## LOOKING AHEAD: ANTICIPATING FUTURE CHANGE

One inescapable conclusion can be drawn from this overview of what has happened to the family over the past half-century: the family will not be the same as it is today in another half-century. It will keep changing and adapting in response to economic, demographic, technological, and cultural trends. The traditional family is a social fiction. It is only an illusion about the recent past, a receding cultural horizon between the present and the recent past that is usually distorted by hindsight. Will we ever look back on the family of the present time with the same sort of reverence that many feel for the postwar era of mass domesticity? Perhaps. If we do, it will require editing history just as we have done when we glorify the family of the 1950s, which, although it had its virtues, had its problems as well (Coontz 1992).

New and different tensions are undermining existing family practices just as has occurred throughout our past. In this final section, I want to mention a few obvious sources of change currently percolating in American society that may threaten the status quo.

First, the gender revolution is still under way, but it is taking a paradoxical turn. Males, particularly in the bottom tiers of American society, are finding it difficult to adapt to the new order. A growing number are becoming marginalized owing to their inability to find a place in society, and hence in families. The problem of how to help males make a transition to a society that values physical capital less than it once did is not an easy one. The sorts of gender bargains struck in affluent families cannot be so easily achieved in families with limited means. Will we see men and women striking new deals that are not yet widely visible, such as an increase in men as domestic specialists (Doucet 2006)?

Closely related to the shifts in gender roles are changes in sexual practices between unmarried men and women. The process of sexual liberation for young adults has been an untidy one in the United States. We manage the link between nonmarital sex and fertility poorly in this country. If we were to reduce unplanned parenthood to a minimum, it would have a huge impact on the timing and frequency of nonmarital births. Consider, for example, the potential impact of a widely adopted contraceptive method that would make fertility impossible unless it was intentionally reversed. The technology is presently available, but cultural and political resistance remains high even in light of the obvious costs. Still, it is possible to imagine a different course in the future.

Predicting the future of marriage is notoriously difficult. As we have already seen, it is entirely possible that different parts of the population will experience different futures. Or, will we return to an era of greater family convergence because of social and cultural diffusion from the top to the bottom, or vice versa? Convergence, were it to occur, would probably depend on economic changes and shifts in educational attainment, mitigating or exacerbating inequality. Our efforts to expand access to higher education have been puny compared with those of many other countries. Were we to mount a successful campaign to improve educational attainment, we can reasonably infer that the impact on marriage practices and family formation patterns would be large.

The culture of parenting styles has always been subject to change in American society. I see no reason why the current highly protective approach that parents have adopted could not be relaxed if the next generation of parents were to decide (or be convinced by expert observers) that children need more free time or would benefit from greater autonomy. It is equally plausible that new and more effective means of technology will bring about even greater parental supervision and control. Conceivably, the styles will shift differently in different class and ethnic subgroups.

Shifts in the intergenerational flow of resources, which have been almost uniformly downward (except for the foreign-born) could also change in light of an altered life course and increased longevity. Older parents may find that subsidizing their children and grandchildren is unsustainable in light of changes in Social Security and retirement benefits.

As technology changes the form and locus of schooling and work, it will inevitably shift styles of child care and parental supervision. We are only at the dawn of changes in workplace and home innovations, much as we were when industrialization drastically altered the production of goods outside the home, irrevocably helping to undermine the gender-based division of labor. It is not difficult to envision similar changes resulting from new technologies that reduce the distance between work and home.

Nothing that has happened during the past half-century has undermined the importance of the family, despite our apprehensions to the contrary. Indeed, it could easily be argued that parents and children are more closely bound together than they have ever been. Similarly, grandparents and extended kin are arguably more present and active in the lives of their progeny than they have ever been. While the institution of marriage has weakened in some respects, it has been strengthened in others, particularly for advantaged Americans. Parenthood, because it is more voluntary, also entails greater commitment and responsibility for most Americans. How will family life be organized a half-century from now? It is impossible to say, except for the certainty that it will not be the same.

REFERENCES

Allport, Floyd. 1924. *Social Psychology*. Boston: Houghton Mifflin.
Aries, Philippe. 1962. *Centuries of Childhood: A Social History of Family Life*.
    New York: Vintage Books.
Beck-Gernsheim, Elisabeth. 2002. *Reinventing the Family: In Search of New Lifestyles*. Malden, MA: Blackwell.

Bell, Norman W., and Ezra F. Vogel. 1968. *A Modern Introduction to the Family*. Rev. ed. New York: Free Press.

Berger, Brigitte, and Peter L. Berger. 1983. *The War over the Family: Capturing the Middle Ground*. Garden City, NY: Anchor.

Bianchi, Suzanne. 2000. "Maternal Employment and Time with Children: Dramatic Change or Surprising Continuity?" *Demography* 37(4): 401–14.

Burgess, Ernest W., and Harvey Locke. 1960. *The Family, from Institution to Companionship*. New York: American Book.

Carlson, Marcia J., and Sara S. McLanahan. 2004. "Early Father Involvement in Fragile Families." In *Conceptualizing and Measuring Father Involvement*, edited by Randal Day and Michael lamb. Mahwah, NJ: Lawrence Erlbaum.

Carter, Hugh, and Paul C. Glick. 1976. *Marriage and Divorce: A Social and Economic Study*. Cambridge, MA: Harvard University Press.

Cherlin, Andrew J. 1978. "Remarriage as an Incomplete Institution." *American Journal of Sociology* 84(3): 634–50.

———. 1992. *Marriage, Divorce, Remarriage*. Revised and expanded ed. Cambridge, MA: Harvard University Press.

———. 2004. "The Deinstitutionalization of American Marriage." *Journal of Marriage and Family*, 66: 848–61.

———. 2009. *The Marriage-Go-Round: The State of Marriage and the Family in America Today*. New York: Alfred A. Knopf.

Coontz, Stephanie. 1992. *The Way We Never Were: American Families and the Nostalgia Trap*. New York: Basic Books.

———. 2005. *Marriage, a History: From Obedience to Intimacy, or How Love Conquered Marriage*. New York: Viking.

Coser, Rose L. 1974. *The Family: Its Structure and Functions*. 2nd ed. New York: St. Martin's.

Cutright, Phillip. 1972. "Illegitimacy in the United States, 1920–1968." In *Demographic and Social Aspects of Population Growth*, edited by Charles Westoff and Ross Parke. Washington, DC: U.S. Government Printing Office.

Danziger, Sheldon, and Peter Gottschalk. 1997. *America Unequal*. New York: Russell Sage Foundation.

Davis, Kingsley, ed. 1985. *Contemporary Marriage*. New York: Russell Sage Foundation.

De Tocqueville, A. 1945. *Democracy in America*. New York: Knopf.

Doucet, Andrea. 2006. *Do Men Mother? Fathering, Care, and Domestic Responsibility*. Toronto: University of Toronto Press.

Edin, Kathryn, and Maria Kefalas. 2005. *Promises I Can Keep: Why Poor Women Put Motherhood before Marriage*. Berkeley: University of California Press.

Elder, Glen H., Jr. 1974. *Children of the Great Depression*. Chicago: University of Chicago Press.

England, Paula, and Kathryn Edin, eds. 2007. *Unmarried Couples with Children*. New York: Russell Sage Foundation.

Friedan, Betty. 1963. *The Feminine Mystique*. New York: W. W. Norton.

Furstenberg, Frank F. 1966. "Industrialization and the American Family." *American Sociological Review* 31(3): 326–37.

———. 1976. *Unplanned Parenthood: The Social Consequences of Teenage Childbearing*. New York: Free Press.

———. 1982. "Conjugal Succession: Reentering Marriage after Divorce." In *Life Span Development and Behavior*, Vol. IV, edited by Paul Baltes and Orville Brim. New York: Academic Press.

———. 1995. "Fathering in the Inner-City: Paternal Participation and Public Policy." In *Fatherhood: Contemporary Theory, Research, and Social Policy*, edited by William Marsiglio. Thousand Oaks, CA: Sage.

———. 2002. "How It Takes 30 Years to Do a Study." In *Looking at Lives: American Longitudinal Studies of the Twentieth Century*, edited by Erin Phelps, Frank F. Furstenberg, and Anne Colby, pp. 37–57. New York: Russell Sage Foundation.

———. 2007. "The Making of the Black Family: Race and Class in Qualitative Studies in the 20th Century." *Annual Review of Sociology* 33: 429–48.

———. 2009. "If Moynihan Had Only Known: Race, Class, and Family Change in the Later 20th Century." *Annals* 621: 94–110.

———. 2010. "On a New Schedule: Transitions to Adulthood and Family Change." In *The Future of the Children* (Spring).

Furstenberg, Frank F., and Andrew J. Cherlin. 1991. *Divided Families: What Happens to Children When Parents Part*. Cambridge, MA: Harvard University Press.

Furstenberg, Frank, and Graham Spanier. 1984. *Recycling the Family: Remarriage after Divorce*. Newbury Park, CA: Sage.

Furstenberg, Frank F., Sheela Kennedy, Vonnie McLoyd, Ruben G. Rumbaut, and Richard A. Settersten, Jr. 2004. "Growing Up Is Harder to Do." *Contexts* 3(3): 42–47.

Gans, Herbert. 1962. *The Urban Villagers: Group and Class in the Life of Italian Americans*. New York: Free Press.

Gauthier, Anne H., Timothy M. Smeeding, and Frank F. Furstenberg, Jr. 2004. "Are Parents Investing Less Time in Children? Trends in Selected Industrialized Countries." *Population and Development Review* 30(4): 647–71.

Gerth, Hans H., and C. Wright Mills. 1993. "Partnership and Partisanship." *International Journal of Politics, Culture, and Society* 7(1): 133–54.

Gibson-Davis, Christina M. 2007. "Expectations and the Economic Bar to Marriage among Low Income Couples." In *Unmarried Couples with Children*, edited by Paula England and Kathryn Edin. New York: Russell Sage Foundation.

Glendon, Mary Ann. 1989. *The Transformation of Family Law: State, Law, and Family in the United States and Western Europe*. Chicago: University of Chicago Press.

Goode, William J. 1962. *The Family*. Englewood, NJ: Prentice-Hall.

———. 1963. *World Revolution and Family Patterns*. New York: Free Press.

———. 1980. "Why Men Resist." *Dissent* 27(2): 181–93.

Green, Arnold W. 1941. "The Cult of Personality and Sexual Relations." *Psychiatry* 4 (August): 343–48.

Hawke, David Freeman. 1988. *Everyday Life in Early America*. New York: Harper & Row.

Hill, Reuben. 1971. "Modern Systems Theory and the Family: A Confrontation." *Social Science Information* 10 (7).

Hoffman, Lois, and Lise M. Youngblade. 1999. *Mothers at Work: Effects on Children's Well-being*. New York: Cambridge University Press.

Johnson, Colleen. 1988. *Ex Familia*. New Brunswick, NJ: Rutgers University Press.

Kefalas, Maria, Patrick Carr, Frank F. Furstenberg, and Laura Napolitano. 2011 Forthcoming. "Marriage Is More Than Being Together: The Meaning of Marriage for Young Adults." *Journal of Family Issues*.

Komarovsky, Mirra. 1973. "Cultural Contradictions and Sex Roles: The Masculine Case." *American Journal of Sociology* 78(4): 873–84.

Koropeckyj-Cox, T., and Gretchen Pendell. 2007. "Attitudes about Childlessness in the United States: Correlates of Positive, Neutral, and Negative Responses." *Journal of Family Issues* 28: 1054–82.

Lasch, Christopher. 1977. *Haven in a Heartless World: The Family Besieged*. New York: Basic Books.

Lareau, Annette. 2003. *Unequal Childhoods: Class, Race, and Family Life*. Berkeley: University of California Press.

Laslett, Peter. 1972. *Household and Family in Past Time*. New York: Cambridge University Press.

Lesthaeghe, Ronald. 1995. "The Second Demographic Transition in Western Countries: As Interpretation." In *Gender and Family Change in Industrialized Countries*, edited by Karen Oppenheim Mason and Ann-Magritt Jensen. Oxford: Oxford University Press.

Levy, Frank. 1998. *The New Dollars and Dreams: American Incomes and Economic Change*. New York: Russell Sage Foundation.

Liebow, Elliot. 1967. *Tally's Corner: A Study of Negro Streetcorner Men*. Boston: Little, Brown.

Litwak, Eugene, and Ivan Szelenyi. 1969. "Primary Groups and their Structures and Their Functions." *American Sociological Review* 34: 465–81.

Margolis, Rachel, and Frank F. Furstenberg. 2009. "Social Class Differences in the Timing of First Sex, First Birth and First Marriage." Paper presented at the annual meetings of the American Sociological Association, San Francisco, CA, August 8–12.

May, Elaine Tyler. 1988. *Homeward Bound*. New York: Basic Books.

McLanahan, Sara. 2004. "Diverging Destinies: How Children are Faring under the Second Demographic Transition." *Demography* 41: 607–27.

———. 2009. "Fragile Families and the Reproduction of Poverty." *Annals of the American Academy of Political and Social Science* 621: 111–31.

Miller, Daniel R, and Guy E. Swanson. 1958. *The Changing American Parent: A Study in the Detroit Area*. New York: Wiley.

Mills, C. Wright. 1959. *The Sociological Imagination*. New York: Oxford University Press.

Mintz, Steven. 2004. *Huck's Raft: A History of American Childhood*. Cambridge, MA: Harvard University Press.

Modell, John. 1989. *Into One's Own: From Youth to Adulthood in the United States, 1920–1975*. Berkeley: University of California Press.

Modell, John, Frank F. Furstenberg, Jr., and Douglas Strong. 1978. "The Timing of Marriage in the Transition to Adulthood: Continuity and Change, 1860–1875." *American Journal of Sociology* 84 (Supplement): S120–S150.

Moynihan, Daniel Patrick. 1965. *The Negro Family: The Case for National Action*. Washington, DC: U.S. Department of Labor.

Murdock, George Peter. 1957. "World Ethnographic Sample." *American Anthropologist* 59(4): 664–87.

Nisbet, Robert. 1953. *The Quest for Community*. New York: Oxford University Press.

Ozmet, Steven. 2001. *Ancestors: The Loving Family in Old Europe*. Cambridge, MA: Harvard University Press.

Parsons, Talcott. 1964. *Essays in Sociological Theories*. Rev. ed. New York: Free Press.

Rainwater, Lee, and William L. Yancey. 1967. *The Moynihan Report and the Politics of Controversy*. Cambridge, MA: MIT Press.

Rapoport, Rhona. 1964. "The Transition from Engagement to Marriage." *Acta Sociologica* 8(1/2): 36–55.

Riley, Matilda White. 1968. *Aging and Society*. New York: Russell Sage Foundation.

Rodman, Hyman. 1963. "The Lower-Class Value Stretch." *Social Forces* 42(2): 205–15.

Rosenfeld, Michael J. 2007. *The Age of Independence: Interracial Unions, Same-Sex Unions, and the Changing American Family*. Cambridge, MA: Harvard University Press.

Rothman, Ellen R. 1984. *Hands and Hearts: A History of Courtship in America*. New York: Basic Books.

Rumbaut, Ruben G., and Alejandro Portes. Eds. 2001. *Ethnicities: Children of Immigrants in America*. New York: Russell Sage Foundation.

Shorter, Edward. 1977. *The Making of the Modern Family*. New York; Basic Books.

Silverman, Ira. 1977. "A Survey of Cohabitation on Two College Campuses." *Archives of Sexual Behavior* 6(1): 11–20.

Smith, Daniel Scott. 1972. "The Demographic History of Colonial New England." *Journal of Economic History* 32(1): 165–83.

Stone, Lawrence. 1977. *The Family, Sex, and Marriage in England: 1500–1800*. London: Weidenfeld and Nicolson.

Sussman, Marvin B. 1959. "The Isolated Nuclear Family: Fact or Fiction?" *Social Problems* 6(4): 333–40.

Swidler, Ann. 2001. *Talk of Love: How Culture Matters*. Chicago: University of Chicago Press.

Therborn, Goran. 2004. *Between Sex and Power: Family in the World, 1900–2000*. New York: Routledge.

Thomas, William, and Florian Znaniecki. 1996. *The Polish Peasant in Europe and America: A Classic Work in Immigration History*. Urbana: University of Illinois Press.

Thornton, Arland, and Deborah S. Freedman. 1982. "Changing Attitudes toward Marriage and the Single Life." *Family Planning Perspectives*, 14(6): 297–303.

Vincent, Clark. 1961. *Unmarried Mothers*. New York: Free Press.

Waller, Maureen. 2002. *My Baby's Father*. Ithaca, NY: Cornell University Press.

Watkins, Susan Cott. 1991. *From Provinces into Nations: Demographic Integration in Western Europe, 1870–1960*. Princeton, NJ: Princeton University Press.

Weeks, John R. 1976. *Teenage Marriages: A Demographic Analysis*. Westport, CT: Greenwood Press.

Weston, Kath. 1997. *Families We Choose: Lesbians, Gays, Kinship*. New York: Columbia University Press.

Whiting, Beatrice B., and John W. Whiting. 1975. *Children of Six Cultures: A Psycho-Cultural Analysis*. Cambridge, MA: Harvard University Press.

Wilson, William J. 1987. *The Truly Disadvantaged: The Inner City, the Underclass, and Public Policy*. Chicago: University of Chicago Press.

Winch, Robert F. 1958. *Mate Selection: A Study of Complementary Needs*. New York: Harper.

Young, Michael, and Peter Willmott. 1957. *Family and Kinship in East London*. London: Pelican.

Young, Michael, and Peter Willmott. 1957. *Family and Kinship in East London*. London: Routledge & Kegan Paul.

Zelnik, Melvin, John F. Kantner, and Kathleen Ford. 1981. *Sex and Pregnancy in Adolescence*. Beverly Hills, CA: Sage.

Zimmerman, Carle Clark. 1947. *Family and Civilization*. New York: Harpers.

STUDIES IN SOCIAL INEQUALITY